W9-BVP-381

Download Forms on Nolo.com

You can download the forms in this book at:

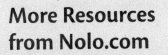

www.nolo.com/back-of-book/FIBA.html

We'll also post updates whenever there's an important change to the law affecting this book—as well as articles and other related materials.

More Resources from Nolo.com

Legal Forms, Books, & Software
Hundreds of do-it-yourself products—all written in plain English, approved, and updated by our in-house legal editors.

Legal Articles
Get informed with thousands of free articles on everyday legal topics. Our articles are accurate, up to date, and reader friendly.

Find a Lawyer
Want to talk to a lawyer? Use Nolo to find a lawyer who can help you with your case.

NOLO
LAW for ALL

☖☖ NOLO **The Trusted Name**

(but don't take our word for it)

"In Nolo you can trust."
THE NEW YORK TIMES

"Nolo is always there in a jam as the nation's premier publisher of do-it-yourself legal books."
NEWSWEEK

"Nolo publications...guide people simply through the how, when, where and why of the law."
THE WASHINGTON POST

"[Nolo's]...material is developed by experienced attorneys who have a knack for making complicated material accessible."
LIBRARY JOURNAL

"When it comes to self-help legal stuff, nobody does a better job than Nolo..."
USA TODAY

"The most prominent U.S. publisher of self-help legal aids."
TIME MAGAZINE

"Nolo is a pioneer in both consumer and business self-help books and software."
LOS ANGELES TIMES

9th Edition

The New Bankruptcy

Will It Work for You?

Attorney Cara O'Neill

NINTH EDITION	JANUARY 2022
Editor	CARA O'NEILL
Cover Design	SUSAN PUTNEY
Book Design	SUSAN PUTNEY
Proofreading	IRENE BARNARD
Index	ACCESS POINTS INDEXING
Printing	SHERIDAN

ISSN: 2326-7089 (print)
ISSN: 2326-6473 (online)

ISBN: 978-1-4133-2905-6 (pbk)
ISBN: 978-1-4133-2906-3 (ebook)

This book covers only United States law, unless it specifically states otherwise.

Copyright © 2005, 2007, 2009, 2011, 2013, 2015, 2018, 2019, and 2021 by Nolo. All rights reserved. The NOLO trademark is registered in the U.S. Patent and Trademark Office. Printed in the U.S.A.

No part of this publication may be reproduced, stored in a retrieval system, or transmitted in any form or by any means, electronic, mechanical, photocopying, recording, or otherwise without prior written permission. Reproduction prohibitions do not apply to the forms contained in this product when reproduced for personal use. For information on bulk purchases or corporate premium sales, please contact tradecs@nolo.com.

Please note

Accurate, plain-English legal information can help you solve many of your own legal problems. But this text is not a substitute for personalized advice from a knowledgeable lawyer. If you want the help of a trained professional—and we'll always point out situations in which we think that's a good idea—consult an attorney licensed to practice in your state.

About the Author

Cara O'Neill is a legal editor and writer at Nolo focusing on bankruptcy and small claims. She authors, coauthors, and edits several Nolo books, including *How to File for Chapter 7 Bankruptcy, Chapter 13 Bankruptcy, Everybody's Guide to Small Claims Court, Solve Your Money Troubles, Credit Repair,* and *The Foreclosure Survival Guide.*

Before joining Nolo, Cara practiced for over 20 years as a civil and criminal trial lawyer. During that time, she also served as an administrative law judge mediating disputes in the automotive industry and taught undergraduate and graduate law courses. She added bankruptcy to her practice after the 2008 economic downturn. Cara earned her law degree in 1994 from the University of the Pacific, McGeorge School of Law, where she served as a law review editor and graduated a member of the Order of the Barristers—an honor society recognizing excellence in courtroom advocacy.

Table of Contents

The Bankruptcy Law: A Work in Progress

On October 18, 2005, a new law took effect that substantially changed the bankruptcy system. Shortly afterward, *The New Bankruptcy* hit the bookshelves. Now, sixteen years later, the fledgling law is no longer new. This ninth edition accounts for the many court interpretations and rules that have put the 2005 law into effect. During that period, we have explained the rights and duties in Chapter 7 and Chapter 13 bankruptcies for many bankruptcy filers. This edition reflects the advice and information we've provided regarding how bankruptcy works and which type of bankruptcy is best for each individual.

More specifically, this book explains how eligibility for Chapter 7 and Chapter 13 bankruptcy is determined, what debts are canceled (discharged), what happens to your home, car, and other property, what complications might occur, the paperwork involved, and where you can find help with your bankruptcy. Taken together, this information will help you decide whether it makes sense to handle your debt problems through bankruptcy and, if so, which type of bankruptcy is the best choice for you.

Although it provides valuable guidance for consumers who are considering bankruptcy, this book isn't intended as an authoritative reference on every detail of bankruptcy law. Nor should it be viewed as a guide on how to handle your bankruptcy. For more detailed information on bankruptcy, see Nolo's *How to File for Chapter 7 Bankruptcy*, and *Chapter 13 Bankruptcy: Keep Your Property & Repay Debts Over Time*.

Despite the years that have passed since the new law took effect, courts throughout the country still weigh in on several key issues, regularly publishing opinions that are contradictory. Because only the U.S. Supreme Court can ultimately resolve these conflicts—which can take years—those of us in the bankruptcy field must live with some degree of uncertainty. Fortunately, for most readers, these contentious issues will never arise should you decide to file for bankruptcy. Still, when you run across language like, "Some courts say this while other courts say that," you'll want to do your best to learn how the courts in your area have ruled, if at all, in the unlikely event that the issue rears its head in your case. You can find out by using the resources described in Chapter 11, or by finding a public-spirited bankruptcy attorney who is willing to share this information without demanding an arm or a leg in return.

Download Worksheets, Get Updates, and More Online

When there are important changes to the information in this book, we'll post updates online, on a page dedicated to this book:

www.nolo.com/back-of-book/FIBA.html

You will find other useful information there, too, including author blogs, and forms.

What Is Bankruptcy?

In the chapters that follow, you'll find more detailed information on the issues you are likely to be interested in, including:

- whether you are eligible to file
- which debts will and will not be canceled
- what will happen to your home, car, and other essential property items
- how your postbankruptcy credit will be affected
- how bankruptcy will affect your personal life, and
- whether you need to be represented by a lawyer or can represent yourself, perhaps with some outside help.

Types of Bankruptcy

Consumers and small business owners can choose from among several types of bankruptcy "chapters," including Chapter 7, Chapter 11, Chapter 12, and Chapter 13. Let's look at each one quickly.

Chapter 7. Chapter 7 bankruptcy is by far the most popular. In Chapter 7 bankruptcy, you fully disclose your property, debts, and financial activities over the past several years. Approximately three months later you receive a discharge (cancellation) of most types of debts and emerge with all or most of the property you owned going in—except luxury items and investment real estate in which you have more equity than you can keep. These are the types of property you might have to give up in Chapter 7.

Chapter 11. Chapter 11 bankruptcy helps a business stay afloat by encouraging negotiation and compromise by all concerned so that the business can keep going and at least pay the creditors something. While individuals can file under Chapter 11, the process is unaffordable for most primarily because attorneys' fees can easily surpass $20,000. Even a business that starts off in Chapter 11 will often end up in Chapter 7, where the business is liquidated. Because this book is intended primarily for individual consumers, we don't discuss Chapter 11 further (except briefly in Ch. 12).

Chapters 12 and 13. Chapter 12 and Chapter 13 are reorganization programs for individuals, except that Chapter 12 is specially designed for owners of family farms, while Chapter 13 can be used by everybody else who qualifies, including farmers if they wish. Here we discuss only Chapter 13. As used in Chapter 13, the term "individual" includes sole proprietors and independent contractors, but not business entities, such as corporations or limited liability companies (LLCs). However, if you own a corporation or an LLC to operate a small business, you are still eligible to file for Chapter 13 as an individual and thereby get rid of your liability for the business debts (but your business will still owe the debts).

In a Chapter 13 bankruptcy, you prepare and file the same basic forms as you do in a Chapter 7 bankruptcy. However, you also propose a three- or five-year plan under which you typically must repay certain types of debt in full (such as back child support) and usually some portion of your unsecured debt (such as credit card balances, medical bills, and personal loans), although some judges will approve of plans that pay 0% of unsecured debt. Chapter 13 provides some remedies that aren't available in Chapter 7—such as the opportunity to pay off missed mortgage payments over the life of the plan so you can keep your house—but usually isn't the bankruptcy of choice because of the extra legal fees it involves and because people would rather get their fresh start in three months instead of three or five years.

Chapter 7 Bankruptcy

As we mentioned above, Chapter 7 is a three- to four-month process that requires the filing of some paperwork and one brief appearance before the bankruptcy trustee, the official appointed to handle the case for the court. You might have to make additional brief appearances before a bankruptcy judge if you seek approval of a reaffirmation agreement you signed in order to keep a car or other property you are making monthly payments on, or if a creditor wants payment for a luxury purchase made shortly before the bankruptcy filing.

(You can learn more about the presumption of fraud in Ch. 2 and about reaffirmation agreements in Ch. 6.)

Prefiling Credit Counseling Requirement

Before you can file your papers, you must have completed a credit counseling session from a nonprofit agency, which typically costs about $50 or less, depending on your income. The agency provides a certificate of completion that you file with your other papers. There are a couple of exceptions to this prefiling counseling requirement, discussed in Ch. 2. The counselor is available online, over the telephone, and through the mail. Take the time to shop around; you might be able to get counseling for much less.

The Automatic Stay

After completing the credit counseling, your next step is to file your case and obtain a bankruptcy filing number. Once you have a filing number, you have a powerful shield—called the automatic stay—against any efforts by most creditors to collect their debts. All you have to do if a creditor calls you after you file is to produce your case number, the date of filing, and the name of the court in which you filed. The creditor will immediately back off. All proceedings to garnish wages, repossess cars, and foreclose homes will also grind to a halt, with a few exceptions.

Collection of child support and alimony can proceed, and the stay might expire sooner than you would want if you have had a bankruptcy case dismissed in the previous year. Still, as a general rule, filing for bankruptcy will give you almost total relief from your creditors while the bankruptcy is pending. For more information about the automatic stay, see "How Bankruptcy Stops Collection Efforts," later in this chapter.

The Skeleton Petition

Sometimes it's important to obtain a filing number fast. For instance, if you're faced with an imminent foreclosure or car repossession, you'll need the automatic stay to keep things as they are so you can figure out a way to keep your house or car. But a complete bankruptcy filing involves a lot of forms and disclosure of information, and you might not have the time to prepare them all. Fortunately, you can file a skeleton petition. You'll file a few forms initially and the remaining paperwork within 14 days. The forms in a skeleton filing include:

- the petition (three pages plus exhibits)
- a mailing list of your creditors
- a form showing your complete Social Security number, and
- the certificate showing you've completed your credit counseling.

Lifting the Stay

In some situations, creditors can successfully request that the court remove (lift) the stay

The Big Choice: Use a Lawyer or Handle Your Own Case?

When you file your bankruptcy, your case will automatically fall within one of two categories:

- You will be represented by a lawyer who will sign your petition as your representative.
- You will be representing yourself (that is, you'll be acting as your own lawyer).

If you are represented by a lawyer, the lawyer's responsibility is to help you select the type of bankruptcy that will best work for you, get the right information in your forms, and make the choices that will be most appropriate for your situation. If, on the other hand, you are acting as your own lawyer, you will be responsible for these same tasks. While print and online resources will give you the information you need to make informed decisions and properly complete the paperwork, you will be solely responsible for the outcome of your case.

The court wants to make sure you understand these duties. It requires you to sign a form that explains:

- the different types of bankruptcies (discussed earlier)
- the services available from credit counseling agencies
- the penalties for knowingly and fraudulently concealing assets or making a false statement under penalty of perjury, and
- the fact that all information you supply is subject to examination by the employees of the U.S. Department of Justice.

in their particular situation. For instance, if the automatic stay derailed a foreclosure action, the mortgage owner can request permission from the bankruptcy judge to proceed with the foreclosure. Other common reasons for lifting the stay are car repossessions and evictions of month-to-month tenants.

A Brief Description of the Chapter 7 Paperwork

Ch. 9 gives you a more detailed look at these and other official forms, and in Appendix A, you'll find a list of the resources you can download from this book's online companion page, including a sample of the paperwork involved in a typical Chapter 7 case. The text that follows is just an overview.

You can expect your Chapter 7 filing to be about 50 pages in length. Along with the paperwork required for a Chapter 7 skeleton petition, you'll prepare forms that:

- describe all your personal property and real estate, including where it is located and its approximate value
- provide information about your debts and creditors
- describe certain economic and financial transactions that occurred within the previous several years, such as property you sold or gave away within the previous two years, or certain payments you may have made to creditors, especially family and other "insiders"
- state how you want to handle debts concerning cars and other property

that is collateral for loans (called secured debts)
- disclose your monthly income and monthly expenses
- state whether you want to keep any leases and contracts you have in effect or cancel them, and
- summarize your assets and liabilities.

Also, you'll demonstrate that you qualify for Chapter 7 by disclosing your average monthly gross income for the full six months before you file on one or more forms. As explained in Ch. 2, that income figure will be your starting point for determining if you're eligible to file a Chapter 7 bankruptcy or whether you'll have to use Chapter 13. These forms are known as the "means test" and must be filed in every Chapter 7 case.

The Creditors' Meeting

About 30 days after you file your bankruptcy papers, you will be required to attend a hearing known as the "creditors' meeting" or the "341 hearing." You and your spouse (if you filed jointly) are required to attend.

You'll each bring photo identification and proof of your Social Security numbers to the meeting, which will be held in a hearing room in the courthouse or federal building, but not in the bankruptcy court itself. A bankruptcy trustee, the official appointed to handle your case for the court, conducts the meeting. Another official known as the U.S. Trustee might attend and ask questions if it seems you might be ineligible for Chapter 7—perhaps because your income or debt totals are too high—but this rarely happens. (See "The Bankruptcy Trustee," later in this chapter.)

The primary purpose of the creditors' meeting is to verify your identity and check that the information contained in your papers is honest, complete, and accurate. You can expect the trustee to ask you— and all other debtors appearing at that time—whether all of the information in your papers is 100% correct and whether you expect to receive any money from any source.

The trustee might ask particular questions about your filing, too. For instance, it isn't uncommon for a trustee to question property values to determine whether equity exists that could be used to pay toward your unsecured debt (debt that isn't secured by collateral). Other areas the trustee might want to discuss include:

- a tax refund you expect to receive
- recent large payments made to creditors or relatives
- the value of big-ticket property items you're claiming you can keep under exemption laws, such as a house or car
- whether you should proceed under Chapter 13 rather than Chapter 7
- your failure to file any required documents, and
- inconsistencies that might indicate you've been less than honest.

If you've done a good job on your paperwork and you qualify for Chapter 7,

your participation in the creditors' meeting will be brief. Most meetings take ten minutes or less because trustees get to the point quickly and creditors rarely show up.

The Role of Lawyers in Creditors' Meetings

Many people hire lawyers to represent them because they don't want to attend creditors' meetings on their own. Having a lawyer by your side can be reassuring, especially if an answer to one of the trustee's questions requires legal analysis. But when the trustee asks you basic questions about your income, debts, assets, and transactions, you—not your lawyer— must answer the questions. You are expected to be knowledgeable about the information you provided in your papers.

Which Debts Are Discharged

Approximately 60 to 90 days after the creditors' meeting, you will receive a discharge order from the court. The discharge order won't refer to your specific debts but instead will indicate that all legally dischargeable debts are discharged (wiped out) in your case. It will also include a list of the most common types of debts wiped out in bankruptcy.

In a Chapter 7 bankruptcy, absent a successful objection by a creditor (which is rare), most credit card, medical, and legal debts are discharged. Court judgments, balances owed after a foreclosure or repossession (called "deficiencies"), and personal loans will also be erased. For many filers, all of their debts are discharged.

But not all debts get wiped out in Chapter 7 bankruptcy. You'll remain responsible for paying some obligations, the most common being:

- debts incurred to pay nondischargeable taxes (see Ch. 3)
- court-imposed fines and restitution
- back child support and alimony
- debts owed to an ex-spouse as a result of a divorce or separation
- loans owed to a retirement plan, such as a 401(k) (because you are the creditor as well as the debtor in this situation, bankruptcy doesn't discharge the debt)
- student loans (unless you can show that repaying the loans would be an undue hardship, which is tougher than you might think and requires a separate trial in the bankruptcy court)
- federal and state taxes that became due less than three years before your bankruptcy filing date (for example, taxes due on April 15, 2021, for the tax year 2020 will not qualify for discharge until April 16, 2024), and
- debts for personal injuries or death resulting from your drunk driving.

Keep in mind that property liens remain after bankruptcy unless you file a motion with the court and the bankruptcy judge agrees to lift the lien. So while a money judgment will be discharged, a lien filed against your property as a result of a money judgment will remain. You'll have to repay the lien amount, plus interest, before transferring the property to someone else.

Some types of debt will survive your bankruptcy, but only when the creditors seek and obtain orders from the bankruptcy court excluding the debts from your bankruptcy. These debts arise from fraudulent actions, recent credit card charges for luxuries, and willful and malicious acts causing personal injury or property damages. (For more on which debts are and are not discharged in a Chapter 7 bankruptcy, see Ch. 3.)

What Happens to Your Property?

With few major exceptions, as of your filing date all the property you own or are entitled to receive becomes part of your bankruptcy estate and is managed by the bankruptcy trustee. Also, property transferred within the previous two years for significantly less than its value (up to ten years for some transfers), and certain types of property acquired during the six-month period after filing, are also considered part of your bankruptcy estate. Marital property in community property states is also part of the bankruptcy estate, even if only one spouse files. There are other categories of property that might belong in your estate, but these are the main ones. (See Ch. 4 for more on what property belongs in your bankruptcy estate.)

What does the bankruptcy trustee do with the bankruptcy estate? The trustee looks for any property that, when sold, will generate a profit that can be used to pay your creditors. In fact, that's how these trustees earn a living—from commissions on the bankruptcy estate property sold to benefit creditors.

Before you worry about losing property, keep in mind this rule: A trustee who sells property must use the sales proceeds to pay off any outstanding loans related to the property before paying other creditors. Property that lacks equity won't produce any proceeds for your creditors, so the trustee has no interest in property that is worth less than what you owe.

For example, if you owe more on your house or car than it's worth, you have no equity and the trustee won't be interested in selling it. The proceeds from the sale would, by law, all go to the lender. On the other hand, if you have equity in your house or car (or any other property, for that matter), the trustee will evaluate the property's worth and consider selling it for the benefit of the creditors (and the trustee).

In many cases, you'll be able to protect some property equity from creditors using bankruptcy exemptions, and, if it's enough, keep the property out of the trustee's reach. We explain how to do this in the next section.

How Exemptions Help You Keep Your Property

Fortunately, all states have exemption laws that allow you to keep property you'll need to work and live when you file for Chapter 7 bankruptcy. The idea is that everyone needs basic items like household furnishings, clothing, and a reasonably-priced car to maintain a home and job. And, because most retirement accounts are protected too, it's truly possible to get a fresh start using bankruptcy exemptions. Here's how it works.

Exemption laws keep certain possessions out of the reach of the trustee and creditors. Each state has a set of exemption laws for its residents and a federal list of exemptions exists, too.

In some instances, an asset will be fully exempt regardless of its value. For instance, under one of the two California exemption systems, you can keep all of your furniture no matter how much it's worth. In the other California exemption system, furniture is only exempt up to $725 per item. The same limit applies to appliances, musical instruments, clothing, books, animals, and crops.

Of course, not all assets are exempt. Finding out what you can protect starts with identifying the exemption list or lists you're entitled to use.

Some states require a bankruptcy filer to use the state exemptions. However, many states allow filers to choose either the state list or the federal exemptions.

To find out whether your state gives you this choice, turn to the exemption chart on the online companion page and look at the entry just below your state's name. It will indicate whether federal exemptions are allowed. If you have a choice, you'll want to compare the state and federal sets to determine which list will protect the property you'd like to keep. You'll find the federal list at the end (it follows the Wyoming exemptions).

Most people can use the exemptions of the state where they file. But if you haven't been residing in that state for at least two years, you might have to use the federal exemptions if they're allowed by the current state or exemptions from the state you resided in previously, and it can make a big difference. For example, filers can keep up to $60,000 worth of equity in a home in New Mexico and up to $500,000 in Massachusetts (other timing rules can drastically limit how much home equity you can protect, too).

Houses and Cars

People often ask whether they can keep their home and car in a Chapter 7 bankruptcy. The answer is yes in the following circumstances:

- You are current on your mortgage or car note.
- You have no significant nonexempt equity in the house or car (you can protect all of your equity with an exemption).

Mortgages

If all of the home equity is exempt, the trustee won't be interested in selling the house, which means you can keep it—unless you are behind on your mortgage payments.

If you're behind, your mortgage lender can initiate foreclosure proceedings and will probably be able to get permission from the bankruptcy judge to proceed.

It works a bit differently if you have significant equity but the state (or federal) exemption isn't large enough to cover all of it. The trustee will sell the home, give you the exemption amount, and use the remaining proceeds to pay creditors.

Car Loans

Cars encumbered by car notes work pretty much the same way as houses. If an exemption protects all of the equity in your car, you can keep it as long as you are current on the note. However, if you're behind on the payment, the lender could ask the bankruptcy judge for permission to proceed with repossession or simply wait to repossess the car after the bankruptcy closes.

Your Car or Home After Bankruptcy

Meeting the requirements for keeping your home or car as described just above doesn't mean that your bankruptcy will end your obligation to the mortgage holder or bank. To understand what happens next, let's back up a little bit.

When you take out a mortgage or car loan, you are actually doing two things:

- signing a promissory note for the amount of the loan, and
- agreeing that if you default on the loan, the lender can foreclose or repossess the property and use the proceeds to pay down the loan.

When the mortgage is recorded at your local land records office, it becomes a lien (a claim) against the house. Similarly, when you take out a car loan, you are signing a promissory note and a "security agreement" that allows the car to be repossessed in case you default. When the seller records the security agreement, it becomes a lien against the car.

When you file for bankruptcy, the promissory note part of a secured debt is canceled. However, the lien securing your payment remains. For example, if you owe $400,000 on your house when you file, the $400,000 promissory note is canceled. The lender cannot come after you and force you to make a payment.

However, that doesn't mean that you can stop paying your mortgage and keep your home. If you don't pay (default), the mortgage lender still has the lien—which

hasn't been affected by your bankruptcy—and can foreclose on the lien, take the home, and sell it at auction. Similarly, for secured debts involving a car, your Chapter 7 bankruptcy will cancel the amount you

---

What Happens If You Have Nonexempt Equity in Property?

If your equity in property is worth more than an exemption allows, the trustee can:

- seize and sell the property at auction, even if you own the property jointly with others
- pay any lender in the picture the amount that's owed on the property, if any
- give you the amount you are entitled to under the exemption system you are using
- distribute what remains to your unsecured creditors, and
- put in for a commission on the sale.

Frequently, before selling property with nonexempt equity, the trustee will give you an opportunity to buy it back at whatever amount you can agree upon. For instance, if you have a motorcycle that could be sold for $8,000 and you only have $3,000 worth of exemption (meaning $5,000 is nonexempt), the trustee might let you buy it back for the amount the trustee would end up with after a sale. Since sales of personal property cost time and money, the trustee might let you buy the motorcycle back for 20% less, or for as little as $4,000.

owe on the promissory note but it won't affect the lien—which means that even though the lender can't force you to pay the debt by garnishing your wages or through some other collection means, the lender can repossess the car if you default. To avoid foreclosure or repossession, you must continue paying the amount that you owe.

Especially in the case of car notes, many lenders don't like the idea of your not being legally liable for the balance after bankruptcy. While many will let you keep the car after a debt discharge as long as you continue making the payment, most lenders would prefer to keep you on the hook for the underlying debt. The lender doesn't want you to trash the car, give it back, and wash your hands of the whole thing. Bankruptcy gives them the option of requiring you to sign an agreement reaffirming the underlying promissory note (called a "reaffirmation agreement"). Once in place, you wouldn't be able to walk away from the debt.

EXAMPLE: Marisol owes $25,000 on her Tesla Model 3 when she files for Chapter 7 bankruptcy. If she doesn't reaffirm the debt, the bankruptcy will cancel the $25,000 debt, which means she'll still have to make her payments under power of the lien but won't owe the actual debt. If, after her bankruptcy, Marisol decides to turn in the car, she won't owe a cent on it. On the other hand, if Marisol reaffirms the debt, she

will continue to be liable for the entire amount of the reaffirmed debt after bankruptcy, even if she turns in the car. Many courts believe that Marisol is better off not owing the money (that is, not reaffirming). By contrast, the lender will be better off having her owe the money to prevent her from escaping liability if the car is repossessed or she gives it back.

See Ch. 6 for more on reaffirmation agreements and how secured debts are treated in Chapter 7 bankruptcy.

As for houses, reaffirmation is rare. Instead, lenders have historically relied on foreclosure as their enforcement remedy and haven't worried about your walking away from the house. Keep in mind that payments won't show up in your credit history, which could impact your future borrowing ability. See Ch. 5 for more about houses in bankruptcy.

 RELATED TOPIC

Later chapters include detailed information on exemptions. Ch. 4 covers exemptions in general, Ch. 5 explains exemptions for a home, and Ch. 6 covers cars and other property that secure a loan.

Costs and Fees

As of this writing, the filing fee for a Chapter 7 bankruptcy is $338. If you can't afford the fee, you can apply for a fee waiver or permission to pay in installments. You'll have to file an Application to Have the Chapter 7 Filing Fee Waived (or an application to pay in installments) when you file your bankruptcy papers. The court clerk will let you know whether you must appear before the judge—who will decide whether you qualify for the waiver—or whether you'll receive a determination in the mail. If your request isn't approved, the judge will set a payment schedule. The form, rules, and eligibility guidelines for getting a fee waiver are available at www.uscourts.gov/forms/bankruptcy-forms.

If you want to be represented by a lawyer, you will likely have to pay an additional $1,200 to $2,000 in attorneys' fees. Not everyone has that kind of money, however, especially when you're facing bankruptcy.

If you decide to handle your own case, you will probably want to get some outside help. This will typically consist of some of the following:

- one or more do-it-yourself books on bankruptcy (roughly $30 a pop)
- telephonic legal advice from a lawyer (roughly $100 an hour, although many lawyers provide one free consultation), and
- clerical assistance with your form preparation from a bankruptcy petition preparer (between $100 and $200 depending on your jurisdiction).

See Ch. 11 for more on resources you can use to file for bankruptcy.

Issues That Must Be Decided by a Judge

Chapter 7 bankruptcy is designed to run smoothly with very few bankruptcies requiring a decision by an actual judge. Instead, the bankruptcy trustee oversees the case for the most part. However, you and your attorney (if you have one) will have to appear before a judge in the following cases:

- Your income appears to make you ineligible for Chapter 7 bankruptcy and you want to argue that an exception should be made in your case.
- A creditor contests your right to file for Chapter 7 bankruptcy or discharge a particular debt (which is rare, but it does happen).
- You want the judge to rule that you are entitled to discharge a particular type of debt (such as student loans—see Ch. 3 for more information on debts that can be discharged in Chapter 7 bankruptcy only with the judge's approval).
- You want to eliminate a lien on your property that will survive bankruptcy (see Ch. 10).
- You are handling your own case, are making payments on a car or other personal property, and want to keep the property and continue the contract after bankruptcy. This is called "reaffirming" the contract.

(See Ch. 6 for more on reaffirmation agreements.)

See Ch. 10 for more on these and other types of issues that require action by a judge.

How a Chapter 7 Case Ends

If you complete all of the necessary requirements, Chapter 7 bankruptcy ends with a discharge of all qualifying debts. (For information on which debts can be discharged in Chapter 7, see Ch. 3.) When a debt is discharged, the creditor is forever barred from trying to collect it from you. However, the debt will still appear on your credit report as "discharged in bankruptcy." Government entities cannot discriminate against you simply because you've received a bankruptcy discharge, but private companies can and do in some circumstances. (See Ch. 9 for more on the consequences of receiving a bankruptcy discharge.)

Mandatory Budget Counseling

In addition to the requirement that you obtain credit counseling before you file for bankruptcy, you must also participate in a course on budget management before you can get your discharge. Most filers use the same agency for budget counseling as they used for prefiling credit counseling. See Ch. 2 for more information about this requirement.

Changing Your Mind

If you file for Chapter 7 bankruptcy and then change your mind, you can ask the court to dismiss your case. As a general rule, the court will not do so if it wouldn't be in the best interests of your creditors. For example, your request to dismiss might be denied if you have significant nonexempt assets that the trustee could sell to raise money to pay your creditors.

> **EXAMPLE:** Jake files for Chapter 7 assuming that all of his property is exempt. Shortly after he files, Jake's mother tells him that he is on the deed for a 20-acre ranchette that he, his sister, and his mother inherited from his father. Under the exemption laws applicable to Jake's bankruptcy, his share of the ranchette is not exempt. The trustee can sell the property and distribute Jake's share to his unsecured creditors. Because Jake wants to keep the property, he files a motion asking the court to dismiss his case. The judge denies his request because it would not be in the best interest of Jake's creditors. The point should be clear: Don't file Chapter 7 unless you know what property you own and what will happen to it in bankruptcy.

If you do dismiss your case, you can file again later, although in some circumstances you might have to wait

180 days and pay a new filing fee. Instead of dismissing your Chapter 7 case, you can always convert it to another type of bankruptcy for which you qualify (typically Chapter 13 for individuals). In Jake's case, for example, he could convert to Chapter 13 to save the ranchette. However, in his plan, Jake would have to pay his unsecured creditors at least as much as they would have received had Jake filed under Chapter 7—essentially, the market value of his share of the ranchette, less sale costs and the trustee's commission. Jake should plan to pay an amount equal to the unprotected equity amount, minus sales costs, throughout his three- or five-year bankruptcy plan. (Learn more about the Chapter 13 repayment plan below.)

Why File a Chapter 13 Bankruptcy?

Most people who have a choice between Chapters 13 and 7 choose Chapter 7. After all, it lasts about three months instead of three to five years, it is cheaper than Chapter 13 if you hire a lawyer, and you don't have to pay down any of your dischargeable debt. So, why would you choose to file a Chapter 13 bankruptcy? You can accomplish some things in Chapter 13 that wouldn't be available to you in Chapter 7. Here are some examples:

- In Chapter 13, you can get rid of a second mortgage lien on your real estate—called a lien strip—if the market value of the house is less than the amount owed on the first mortgage.
- Chapter 13 can provide a way to reduce your secured debts to the value of the collateral so you pay only what the property is worth currently (for instance, reducing a $10,000 car note on a $5,000 car to $5,000).
- Chapter 13 lets you make up for missed payments on a house, car, or other collateral over a three- to five-year period so you can keep the property instead of losing it to foreclosure or repossession.
- Chapter 13 gets rid of certain types of debts that aren't discharged in Chapter 7 (for instance debts owed because of property division in a divorce, but not support).
- Chapter 13 allows you to operate a business while you are in bankruptcy (unlike Chapter 7, which might require that you close the business).
- If you previously received a Chapter 7 discharge, you can't get another Chapter 7 discharge for eight years, but you can get a Chapter 13 discharge after only four years. And you can file for Chapter 13 immediately after a Chapter 7 discharge (but you won't get a discharge). (See Ch. 2 for reasons why this can help.)

See Ch. 7 for an example of a conversation between a bankruptcy lawyer and client in which they discuss whether the client should file a Chapter 7 or Chapter 13 bankruptcy.

Chapter 13 Bankruptcy

Chapter 13 bankruptcy works quite differently from Chapter 7 bankruptcy. In Chapter 13, the trustee does not sell your property and assets to repay your creditors. You use a portion of your income to pay some or all of what you owe to your creditors over time (anywhere from three to five years, depending on your income and how much of your debt you can afford to repay). But, many people are surprised to learn that a significant number of debts, such as some taxes and domestic support arrears, must be paid in full through the plan. The trick to successfully using Chapter 13 to get out of debt is to make sure you have enough income to meet all of your payment obligations under the Chapter 13 laws. Being unable to fund a plan is the most common reason people aren't able to qualify for Chapter 13. (See Ch. 2 to learn about the eligibility requirements for filing under Chapter 13.)

How a Chapter 13 Case Begins

Before filing a Chapter 13 bankruptcy, you must complete a credit counseling course, then fill out and file a packet of forms— mostly the same forms as you would use in a Chapter 7 bankruptcy—and provide the court with:

- a feasible plan to repay some or all of your debts over the plan period (three years if you qualify for Chapter 7 and are electing to file for Chapter 13; five years otherwise)

- proof that you've filed your federal and state income tax returns for the previous four years, and
- a copy (or transcript) of your most recently filed IRS income tax return. (See Ch. 10 for more on Chapter 13 paperwork.)

The Repayment Plan

Under a Chapter 13 repayment plan, you make payments, usually monthly, to the bankruptcy trustee, the official who over-sees your case. The trustee uses that money to pay the creditors covered by your plan and to pay his or her statutory fee (usually 10% or less of the amount distributed under your plan).

Under Chapter 13, you are required to devote all of your "projected disposable income" to your plan (essentially, the amount left over after paying your allowed expenses) or the value of your nonexempt property, whichever is more. Your repayment period could be as short as three years if you qualify for Chapter 7 (your gross average income over the six months before you file is below your state's median income) and five years if your income is above the amount allowed for a Chapter 7 discharge. (See Ch. 2 for more on making this calculation.) In some cases, the filer needs a five-year plan to make all required payments regardless of whether his or her income is above or below the median income.

Postconfirmation Increases in Income

If your repayment plan is based on an income level that increases after the court confirms your plan, the trustee can request the court to order a jump in your monthly payments due to your new ability to pay this extra amount. The basic idea in Chapter 13 is that you have to devote all your disposable income to your plan payments.

In Chapter 13, some creditors are entitled to receive 100% of what you owe them, while others may receive a much smaller percentage or even nothing at all. For example, a Chapter 13 plan must propose that any child support you owe to a spouse or child (as opposed to a government agency) will be paid in full over the life of your plan; otherwise, the judge will not approve it. On the other hand, the judge could approve a plan that doesn't repay any portion of your credit card debts if you won't have any projected disposable income left after paying obligations that must be paid in full under the Chapter 13 laws, such as support arrearages or recent tax debt.

To have your debts fully discharged under Chapter 13, you must usually make all payments required by your plan and:

- remain current on your federal and state income taxes
- remain current on any child support or alimony obligations, and
- annually file a copy of your federal income tax return or transcript of the return with the court.

You also have to provide your creditors with copies of the income tax returns or transcripts you file with the court if they request them.

Which Debts Are Discharged

If your Chapter 13 bankruptcy pays your unsecured debts in full, then you will receive a complete discharge of those debts no matter what type they are. If your plan pays less than 100% of a debt, the balance will be discharged unless it is a type of debt that isn't discharged in Chapter 13 bankruptcy.

As a general rule, most credit card, medical, and legal debts are discharged, as are most court judgments, deficiencies from foreclosures or repossessions, and personal loans. Debts that have to be fully paid in a Chapter 13 bankruptcy are:

- court-imposed fines and restitution
- back child support and alimony owed to an ex-spouse or child
- recent back taxes
- unfiled taxes, and
- debts you owe because of a civil judgment arising out of your willful or malicious acts or for personal injuries or death caused by your drunk driving.

Debts arising from your fraudulent actions or recent credit card charges for luxuries will not be discharged if the creditor gets a court order to that effect.

Ch. 3 explains which debts are discharged in a Chapter 13 bankruptcy.

Not All Disposable Incomes Are Equal

One of the oddities of Chapter 13 law is that your qualifying disposable income could be different than your actual disposable income. It's usually more than what you have remaining after paying your monthly expenses—which is one of the reasons why finishing a plan can be tough. Here's how it works.

Your first step will be determining whether you will have a three- or five- year "commitment period." Your average gross income over the six months before your filing date will determine the plan length. If your gross income falls above the median for your state, you'll pay into a five-year plan. If it falls below, you'll be obligated for three years.

Your disposable income comes into play only if you must pay into a five-year plan, and you'll determine what it is by deducting expenses from your gross income. In some cases, you'll deduct your actual expense. In others, you're limited to the amount allowed by law, which is why after completing the calculations, it would be unusual if your qualifying disposable income mirrored the actual amount of funds remaining after paying your monthly bills. (Ch. 2 explains qualifying disposable income in more detail.)

Chapter 13 Plan Must Pay Unsecured Creditors as Much as They Would Receive in a Chapter 7 Bankruptcy

People sometimes choose to avoid Chapter 7 bankruptcy because they stand to lose certain property that isn't exempt. Chapter 13 bankruptcy initially looks like a good alternative, because in Chapter 13 you don't have to give up any property. Rather, your obligations under your plan are based on your disposable income.

However, even though Chapter 13 won't take your property, it does require that you pay your unsecured creditors the value of what they would have received in Chapter 7. For example, if you have $50,000 equity in your home that isn't protected by an exemption, you wouldn't lose the home in Chapter 13 bankruptcy, but you would have to propose a plan that pays your creditors at least $50,000 less sale costs and the trustee's commission. This rule often makes it difficult to propose a feasible Chapter 13 plan, due to the size of the required payment, although making such large Chapter 13 payments occurs more frequently than you might suspect.

Which Property Is at Risk in Chapter 13 Bankruptcy

As mentioned, you are not required to give up any property you own when you file your Chapter 13 bankruptcy case. In

Chapter 13, your income is used to pay off some portion of your debt. However, the value of your nonexempt property can be the determining factor regarding your ability to propose a valid repayment plan. The amount received by creditors through the plan must equal or exceed the value of your nonexempt property (minus sales costs). If you don't have enough income to comply with this rule, you might be able to lower the payment by selling some property and using the funds to pay down debt.

Houses and Cars

Filing for Chapter 13 bankruptcy lets you keep your house and car as long as you stay current on the payments and can afford to pay for any nonexempt equity. You can also pay off owed arrearages over time—a mechanism that isn't available in Chapter 7 and that allows Chapter 13 filers to catch up on monthly payments to keep homes. For instance, suppose you are $5,000 behind on your mortgage payments. In that case, you can pay an extra amount and catch up on the arrearages over the course of the plan. That's why Chapter 13 is typically the remedy of choice for people facing foreclosure. (See Ch. 5 for more on what happens to your home when you file for either type of bankruptcy.)

Costs and Fees

The filing fee for a Chapter 13 bankruptcy is currently $313. If you want to be represented by a lawyer, you will probably have to pay $2,500 to $4,000 in legal fees, most of which can be paid through your plan.

If you decide to handle your case (as relatively few do), you will likely want to get some outside help. This will typically consist of one or both of the following:

- using one or more self-help law books on Chapter 13 bankruptcy (roughly $40), and
- retaining a lawyer to provide legal answers as needed.

Unlike the situation in Chapter 7, bankruptcy petition preparers are seldom, if ever, willing to prepare Chapter 13 cases. Also, keep in mind that due to the complexity of Chapter 13 cases, bankruptcy courts strongly recommend retaining a bankruptcy attorney. See Ch. 11 for more on resources you can use to file for bankruptcy.

The Meeting of Creditors

When you file your Chapter 13 bankruptcy petition, the court schedules a "meeting of creditors" (usually within about a month) and sends an official notice of the bankruptcy filing and the meeting to you and all of your creditors. You (and your spouse if you have filed jointly) are required to attend. You'll need to bring two forms of identification—a qualifying picture ID and proof of your Social Security number.

A typical creditors' meeting in a Chapter 13 case lasts less than 15 minutes.

The trustee will briefly go over your paperwork with you. No judge will be present. The trustee is likely to be most interested in whether your repayment plan meets all legal requirements and whether you will be able to make the payments you have proposed. (See Ch. 2 for more on Chapter 13 requirements.) The trustee has a vested interest in helping you successfully navigate the Chapter 13 process because the trustee gets paid a percentage of all payments doled out under your plan; however, the trustee's first responsibilities are to the creditors and ensuring that legal requirements get followed.

For instance, the trustee will make sure you have filed your tax returns for all taxable periods during the four prior years. If not, the trustee will continue the creditors' meeting to give you a chance to file these returns or provide proof of filing if you've already done so. You cannot proceed with a Chapter 13 bankruptcy unless and until you bring your tax filings up to date.

When the trustee is finished asking questions, any creditors who show up will have a chance to question you. Secured creditors might come if they have any objections to the plan you have proposed as part of your Chapter 13 filing (but will usually file a motion with the court instead). They might claim for example, that your plan isn't feasible, or that you're not paying sufficient interest on a secured debt. (See Ch. 6 for more information on collateral and other property that secures a loan.)

Challenging the Legality of a Mortgage in Chapter 13 Bankruptcy

When you file Chapter 13 bankruptcy, creditors are supposed to file a proof of claim setting out how much they think you owe. This proof of claim will determine how much they get paid as part of your Chapter 13 plan. If a secured creditor fails to file a proof of claim, you can file one on their behalf.

If the court does not approve the claim, don't expect to get out from under the mortgage entirely. It's much more likely that legal defects in lenders' claims will result in negotiated settlements reducing the amount of your mortgage principal and interest. You'll likely want to retain an attorney to help you navigate this process.

An unsecured creditor who is scheduled to receive very little under your plan might object, too, if that creditor thinks you should cut your living expenses and thereby increase your disposable income (the amount from which unsecured creditors are paid).

Come to the meeting prepared to listen to disgruntled creditors or the objections of the trustee. If you agree to make changes to accommodate objections, you must submit a modified plan and have it served on all of your creditors.

Objections raised by creditors or the trustee won't be ruled on during the creditors' meeting (because the judge won't be there). Instead, if the objections aren't resolved informally, the trustee or creditor will raise any objections by filing a motion with the bankruptcy court, which will be scheduled for a couple of weeks later. You will want to respond in writing to any motion, either by agreeing to make the correction, or by explaining why the party bringing the motion is wrong. In most cases, you'll probably choose the former approach (because let's face it, if you file on your own behalf, the likelihood of making an error is high), but, if you are right, you'll also have an opportunity to argue your point to the judge at a hearing.

The Confirmation Hearing

In both Chapters 7 and 13, you'll attend a meeting of creditors before the bankruptcy trustee (this is the meeting we discussed earlier in the chapter). Unlike Chapter 7, you'll have a second appearance in Chapter 13 bankruptcy in court before a judge. At this appearance, called the confirmation hearing, the judge either confirms (approves of) your proposed plan or sends you back to the drawing board for various reasons—usually because your plan doesn't meet Chapter 13 requirements in one or more particulars. For example, a judge might reject your plan because you don't have enough projected disposable income to at least pay your priority creditors in full and stay current on your secured debts—such as a car note or mortgage. For more information on Chapter 13 confirmation hearings, see Ch. 10.

You are entitled to amend your proposed plan until you get it right or until the judge decides that it's hopeless. Each amendment requires a new confirmation hearing and appropriate written notice to your creditors.

You'll pay the proposed monthly payment while you go through this process. You don't wait until the plan confirmation to start paying. Because it's not unusual for it to take upwards of six months to confirm a plan, paying the proposed payment amount from the beginning helps ensure that you complete your plan no later than five years after the initial filing date.

Other Common Reasons to Go to Court

In addition to attending the confirmation hearing, you might need to go to court to:

- modify your plan after it has been confirmed
- value an asset (if your plan proposes to pay less for a car or other property than the creditor thinks it's worth)
- respond to requests by a creditor or the trustee to dismiss your case
- respond to a creditor who opposes your right to discharge a particular debt (perhaps because of an allegation that you engaged in fraud when incurring the debt)
- discharge a type of debt that must be allowed by a judge (such as discharging a student loan because of hardship)

- eliminate a lien on your property that will survive your Chapter 13 bankruptcy unless the judge removes it, or
- oppose a secured or unsecured claim filed by a creditor.

These procedures are described in Ch. 10.

How a Chapter 13 Case Ends

If you do the following, the remaining unpaid balance on any debts qualifying for discharge will be wiped out:

- complete your three- or five-year repayment plan
- stay current on your income tax returns and your child support or alimony payments, and
- complete a budget management course approved by the U.S. Trustee.

If any balance remains on a long-term debt that doesn't qualify for discharge, such as a student loan or your home mortgage, you will continue to owe the unpaid amount. (The debts that qualify for discharge in a Chapter 13 bankruptcy are explained in Ch. 3.)

Modifying the Plan and Alternatives to Full Discharge

If you can't complete your Chapter 13 plan as written, you can ask the court to modify it. As long as it's clear that you're acting in good faith, the court is likely to approve your request. If it isn't feasible to modify the plan, you might still be able to get what's called a "hardship" discharge if both of the following apply:

- You failed to complete your plan due to circumstances "for which you should not justly be held accountable" (like a job loss).
- Your unsecured creditors have received at least what they would have gotten if you had filed for Chapter 7 bankruptcy (that is, at least the value of your nonexempt property minus sale costs and the trustee's commission).

If the bankruptcy court doesn't let you modify your plan or won't give you a hardship discharge, you can:

- convert your Chapter 13 bankruptcy to a Chapter 7 bankruptcy, unless you received a Chapter 7 discharge in a case filed within the previous eight years (this is explained in Ch. 10), or
- dismiss your Chapter 13 case. In this case, you'll owe your creditors the balances on your debts from before you filed your Chapter 13 case, less the payments you made, plus the interest that accrued while your Chapter 13 case was open.

As you can imagine, Chapter 13 bankruptcy requires discipline. For the entire length of your case, you will have to live strictly within the Chapter 13 plan budget. The Chapter 13 trustee will not allow you to spend money on anything deemed nonessential. In past years, only about half of Chapter 13 plans were completed. Some Chapter 13 filers drop out early in the process, without ever submitting a feasible repayment plan to the court. However, recently, the number of people finishing Chapter 13 plans appears to be on the rise. And, keep in mind that even if you fail to complete your plan, filing Chapter 13 bankruptcy could provide you with valuable time to get your finances under control or make other adjustments.

How Bankruptcy Stops Collection Efforts

One of the most powerful features of bankruptcy is that it stops most debt collectors dead in their tracks and keeps them at bay for the rest of your case. Once you file, all collection activity (with a few exceptions, explained below) must go through the bankruptcy court—and most creditors cannot take any further action against you directly.

> **TIP**
>
> **You don't need bankruptcy to stop your creditors from harassing you.** Many people begin thinking about bankruptcy when their creditors start phoning their homes and places of employment. Federal law prohibits this activity by third-party debt collectors once you tell the collector, in writing, that you don't want to be called. (See Ch. 12 for a sample letter.)

The downside to this strategy is that you leave the creditor with no choice other than to forget about the debt or sue you.

Credit Card Debts, Medical Debts, and Attorneys' Fees

Anyone trying to collect credit card debts, medical debts, attorneys' fees, debts arising from breach of contract, or legal judgments against you (other than child support and alimony) must cease all collection activities after you file your bankruptcy. They cannot:

- file a lawsuit or proceed with a pending lawsuit against you without court permission
- record liens against your property
- report the debt to a credit reporting bureau, or
- seize your property or income, such as money in a bank account or your paycheck.

Public Benefits

Government entities that are seeking to collect overpayments of public benefits, such as unemployment, SSI, Medicaid, or welfare benefits, cannot do so by reducing or terminating your benefits while your bankruptcy is pending. If, however, you become ineligible for benefits, including Medicare benefits, bankruptcy doesn't prevent denial or termination of the benefits on that ground.

Domestic Relations Proceedings

Almost all proceedings related to a divorce or paternity action continue as before—they are not affected by the automatic stay. These include:

- the setting and collection of current child support and alimony
- the collection of back child support and alimony from property that is not in the bankruptcy estate (see Ch. 4 for more on what's in the bankruptcy estate)
- the determination of child custody and visitation
- a lawsuit to establish paternity
- an action to modify child support and alimony
- proceedings to protect a spouse or child from domestic violence
- withholding of income to collect child support
- reporting of overdue support to credit bureaus
- the interception of tax refunds to pay back child support, and
- withholding, suspension, or restriction of drivers' and professional licenses as leverage to collect child support.

Criminal Proceedings

If you have a case filed against you, the criminal component will be allowed to continue. For example, if you were convicted of a minor vandalism offense and have been sentenced to community service,

your obligation to do community service will not be stopped by the automatic stay.

Landlord-Tenant Proceedings

With a few exceptions (check your state law), the automatic stay does not stop the eviction of a tenant if:

- the landlord obtained a judgment of possession before the bankruptcy filing, or
- the tenant is endangering the property or using controlled substances on it.

Ch. 5 explains when evictions on these grounds may occur. It also covers the law in a few states allowing a tenant to remain after paying back rent.

Tax Proceedings

The IRS can continue certain actions, such as a tax audit, issuing a tax deficiency notice, demanding a tax return, issuing a tax assessment, or demanding payment of a post-petition assessment. The automatic stay does, however, stop the IRS from issuing a lien or seizing (levying against) any of your property or income.

Pension Loans

The stay doesn't prevent withholding from a debtor's income to repay a loan from an ERISA-qualified pension (this includes most job-related pensions and individual retirement plans). See Ch. 4 for more on how pensions are treated under bankruptcy.

Foreclosures

Foreclosure is the way a mortgage holder obtains title to the property that secures the mortgage. It is the main (and sometimes only) remedy available to a mortgage holder when the homeowner defaults by failing to make a payment or by breaching another contractual requirement. Foreclosure procedures differ from state to state. In about half the states, foreclosures are carried out in court just like any other civil proceeding (these are called judicial foreclosures). In the other states, foreclosures occur outside of court (called nonjudicial foreclosures) and typically involve complex state rules regarding notices, reinstatement periods, and redemption periods.

When you file for bankruptcy, pending foreclosure proceedings are stopped dead in their tracks and won't resume until your bankruptcy is completed or the bankruptcy judge lifts the stay upon request by the mortgage holder. Importantly, one thing that bankruptcy doesn't stop is the passage of time required by a particular foreclosure notice. For instance, in California, a foreclosing party must provide the homeowner with a three-month notice of default before setting a date for the actual foreclosure sale. While a bankruptcy filing would delay the issuance of the three-month notice in the first place, it won't prevent the passage of time under the three-month period once the notice is filed. So, a Chapter 7 filing would substantially delay the foreclosure process if it were filed before the three-month notice but would have little or no effect on the foreclosure if

it were filed during the three-month notice period. See *The Foreclosure Survival Guide* by Amy Loftsgordon (Nolo) for a more detailed look at how bankruptcy works to delay or prevent foreclosures.

Although foreclosure activities initially are stayed by your bankruptcy filing, the stay won't apply if you filed for bankruptcy within the previous two years and the court, in that proceeding, lifted the stay and allowed the lender to proceed with the foreclosure, or if you filed two bankruptcies within the past year. In other words, the law doesn't allow you to prevent a foreclosure by filing serial bankruptcies.

Utilities

Companies providing you with utilities (such as gas, heating oil, electricity, phone service, and water) cannot discontinue service because you file for bankruptcy. However, they can shut off your service 20 days after you file if you don't provide them with a deposit or another means to assure future payment. They can also cut you off if you don't pay for services you receive after you file for bankruptcy.

Special Rules for Multiple Filers

If you had one bankruptcy case pending during the previous year, then the stay will terminate 30 days after you file unless you, the trustee, the U.S. Trustee, or the creditor asks for the stay to continue as to certain creditors and proves that the current case was filed in good faith.

This rule doesn't apply to any case that was dismissed because you should have filed under Chapter 13 instead of Chapter 7 (see Ch. 2 for more on when a case could be dismissed on that ground).

If a creditor had a motion to lift the stay pending during a previously dismissed case, the court will presume that you acted in bad faith in your current case. You will have to overcome this presumption in order to obtain continuing stay relief. If you had two or more cases pending during the previous year, then there will be no automatic stay. You'll have to seek a court order to obtain any stay relief.

CAUTION
It is particularly important to be aware of these rules if you are dealing with a foreclosure.

The Bankruptcy Trustee

Until your bankruptcy case ends, your financial assets and problems are in the hands of the bankruptcy trustee, who acts under the supervision of another type of trustee called the U.S. Trustee.

The Bankruptcy Trustee's General Duties

With few exceptions, the bankruptcy trustee assumes control of your case.

The bankruptcy trustee's primary duties are:

- in a Chapter 7 bankruptcy, to see that your nonexempt property is seized and sold for the benefit of your unsecured creditors
- to make sure that the paperwork submitted in your bankruptcy is accurate and complete
- to schedule and operate the creditors' meeting (the 341 hearing), and
- to administer the case for the court.

The bankruptcy trustee could be a local bankruptcy attorney or a nonlawyer who is knowledgeable about Chapter 7 or Chapter 13 bankruptcy generally and the local court's rules and procedures in particular.

Just a few days after you file your bankruptcy papers, you'll get a Notice of Filing from the court, giving the name, business address, and business phone number of the bankruptcy trustee. The trustee might follow up with a list of any financial documents the trustee wants to see, such as bank statements, property appraisals, or insurance documents. In addition, you will send the trustee paycheck stubs and a copy of your most recently filed federal tax return (or file them with your court, depending on your court's local rules). You'll provide all documents at least seven days before the creditors' meeting.

As used in this book, the term "trustee" means the bankruptcy trustee who will actually be handling your case on behalf of the bankruptcy court, unless otherwise stated.

The U.S. Trustee's Office

In addition to the bankruptcy trustee assigned to your case, another type of trustee—a U.S. Trustee—will be involved, usually behind the scenes. The Office of the U.S. Trustee is a part of the United States Department of Justice. Its role is to supervise the bankruptcy trustees who actually handle cases in the bankruptcy court, to make sure that the bankruptcy laws are being followed and that cases of fraud and other crimes are appropriately handled. There are 21 regional U.S. Trustee offices and 92 field offices throughout the country.

If a U.S. Trustee decides to take an active part in your case, the parties to the case—including you—will be sent a notice about the proposed action, and you will be given an opportunity to oppose whatever action the U.S. Trustee proposes. Later chapters in this book suggest some ways to respond to various actions the U.S. Trustee might propose.

Happily, most filers never have to deal with the U.S. Trustee unless they:

- have a "current monthly income" that is more than the median income for their state (see Ch. 2)
- earn enough actual income to support a Chapter 13 plan (see Ch. 2)
- report an expense high enough to trigger review, or
- have apparently engaged in illegal actions that warrant investigative follow-up (such as perjury).

Also, some cases are selected for random audits. The number of bankruptcy cases audited varies depending on current budget funding.

If You Owe Back Child Support

If you owe back support, the trustee is required to provide notices to the holder of the support claim and the state child support agency to keep them apprised of your bankruptcy and help them find you after your bankruptcy discharge. Specifically, the trustee is required to provide:

- the payee with information about the state child support enforcement agency and his or her rights under the bankruptcy law
- the state child support enforcement agency with information about the back support and the payee, and
- the state child support agency and payee with information about the discharge, your last known address, the last known name and address of your employer, and the name of any creditor who holds a nondischargeable claim or a claim that has been reaffirmed.

Both the payee and the child support enforcement agency can ask these creditors to provide your last known address. The laws specifically authorize these creditors to release such information without any penalty.

Chapter 7 Bankruptcy Trustee

In a Chapter 7 bankruptcy, the trustee is tasked with ensuring the accuracy of your filing, checking your identity, and finding assets that can be liquidated to repay your debt. Largely, the trustee is interested primarily in what you own and what property you claim as exempt—and with good reason. The court pays the trustee a commission on property that is sold for the benefit of the unsecured creditors. The trustee may receive up to 25% of the first $5,000, 10% of any amount between $5,000 and $50,000, and 5% of any additional money up to $1,000,000.

If your papers indicate that all of your property is exempt (which means you get to keep it), your case initially is considered a "no-asset" case and your creditors are told not to file claims because you don't have any property that will be sold to pay them. The trustee also won't show much interest in a no-asset case unless the facts of your case suggest that you could be hiding or mischaracterizing assets. After all, if there is no property for the trustee to seize and sell to pay your unsecured creditors, then there is no commission for the trustee.

The first time you will personally encounter the trustee in a Chapter 7 case is when you appear at your creditors' meeting, which you must attend if you don't want your bankruptcy dismissed. Typically, if all of your assets are exempt, you will hear nothing further from the trustee. However, if there are (or it appears that there might be) nonexempt assets in your bankruptcy estate, the trustee might continue your creditors' meeting to another date and ask you to submit appropriate documentation in the meantime. More rarely, the trustee might hire an attorney to pursue nonexempt assets you appear to own or to recover money or assets that you transferred before bankruptcy. The trustee might even refer your case to the U.S. Trustee's office for further action if it looks like you have engaged in dishonest activity or that you should be in a Chapter 13 case instead of Chapter 7.

If there are nonexempt assets for the trustee to seize and sell, you will be expected to cooperate in getting them to the trustee for disposition. You will also be given the opportunity to "buy the assets back" from the trustee at a negotiated price or substitute exempt assets for the nonexempt assets.

If you have nonexempt property that isn't worth very much or would be cumbersome for the trustee to sell, the trustee can abandon the property and you'll get to keep it. For example, no matter how much your used furniture may be worth in theory, many trustees won't bother selling it. Arranging to sell used furniture is expensive and rarely produces much, if any, proceeds for the creditors.

Many people wonder whether a trustee can inventory their homes to determine whether they are hiding property. While unusual, part of your duty to cooperate with the trustee could consist of opening up your home upon the trustee's request. And if you don't voluntarily cooperate, the trustee can obtain an order from the court to force the issue.

The trustee is also required, under the supervision of the U.S. Trustee, to assess your bankruptcy papers for accuracy and for signs of possible fraud or abuse of the bankruptcy system.

Chapter 13 Bankruptcy Trustee

In a Chapter 13 bankruptcy, the trustee's role is to:

- examine your proposed plan and make sure it complies with all legal requirements
- object to the approval of your plan if the trustee feels you have not met all legal requirements
- receive the payments you make under the plan and distribute them to your creditors in the manner required by law
- monitor your duty to file tax returns with the appropriate federal and state taxing authorities for the four years previous to your filing date and annually while your Chapter 13 case is pending, and
- if you owe back child support, provide the payee and your state's child support enforcement agency with information described in "If You Owe Back Child Support," above.

Chapter 13 trustees pay themselves by keeping up to 10% of the payments they disburse to creditors.

Many Chapter 13 trustees play a fairly active role in cases they administer. This is especially true in small suburban or rural judicial districts, or in districts with a lot of Chapter 13 bankruptcy cases. For example, a trustee might:

- help you create a realistic budget (the trustee cannot, however, give you legal advice)
- explain how to modify your plan, if necessary, or
- give you a temporary reprieve or take other steps to help you get back on track if you miss a payment or two.

Despite the trustee's great interest in your success, your financial relationship with the trustee is not as stifling as it may sound. In most situations, you control your money and the property you acquire after filing—as long as you make the payments called for under your repayment plan and you make all regular payments on your secured debts. However, if your income or property increases during the life of your plan (for instance, you receive a substantial promotion or you win the lottery), the trustee can seek to amend your plan to pay your creditors a greater percentage of what you owe them rather than the lesser percentage originally called for in your plan.

It's important to remember that the trustee is an important person in your life for the duration of your case. Your cooperation with the trustee will probably speed the process of gaining court approval for your plan.

Business Bankruptcies

If you own your own business as a sole proprietor or an independent contractor, you and your business are considered the same when it comes to filing for bankruptcy. All debts owed and all assets owned by your business are also considered to be yours. While you might have to provide some additional paperwork for your bankruptcy, such as a profit and loss or income and expense statement, the procedures are the same as if you weren't in business—with one important exception. If your business has assets that frequently change, such as inventory, and you file under Chapter 7, the bankruptcy trustee might require you to shut the business down while your bankruptcy is pending, which is usually about three months. If the business assets are valuable and can't be protected with exemptions, you'll risk losing the inventory or equipment. If, however, you have a service business that doesn't carry valuable inventory, such as an

---

Nolo Resources on Bankruptcy, Debt, and Credit

Nolo publishes a number of books on bankruptcy, dealing with debt, and credit repair. Look for the latest editions of these books:

- *How to File for Chapter 7 Bankruptcy*, by Cara O'Neill and Albin Renauer. This do-it-yourself bankruptcy book takes you step-by-step through the filing process for a liquidation bankruptcy.
- *Chapter 13 Bankruptcy: Keep Your Property & Repay Debts Over Time*, by Cara O'Neill. This book explains the Chapter 13 bankruptcy process in detail.
- *Solve Your Money Troubles: Strategies to Get Out of Debt and Stay That Way*, by Amy Loftsgordon and Cara O'Neill. A practical book to help you prioritize debts, negotiate with creditors, stop collector harassment, challenge wage attachments, contend with repossession, respond to creditor lawsuits, and rebuild your credit.
- *Credit Repair*, by Amy Loftsgordon and Cara O'Neill. This book shows how to fix your credit report, rebuild credit, and avoid credit problems in the future.
- *Divorce & Money: How to Make the Best Financial Decisions During Divorce*, by Violet Woodhouse and Lina Guillen. This book can help you with the overwhelming financial decisions of divorce: selling the house, dividing debts, discovering assets, setting alimony and child support, handling retirement benefits and taxes, and negotiating a fair settlement.

Nolo also provides free bankruptcy information online at www.nolo.com. You'll find hundreds of articles and FAQs on bankruptcy topics, including information particular to each state.

accounting or consulting firm, you might be allowed to continue business operations during the pendency of the bankruptcy and can provide proof of liability insurance.

If you own an interest in a corporation or limited liability company, it works differently. You and your corporation (or LLC) are separate entities and cannot file together.

If you decide to take a corporation or limited liability company into bankruptcy, you cannot use Chapter 13—only Chapter 7 and Chapter 11 are available to business entities.

In Chapter 7, you must liquidate (close) the business. In Chapter 11, the business can continue operations, but you'll have to pay an attorney to represent the business in bankruptcy. Although Chapter 11 used to be too cost prohibitive for small businesses, a new bankruptcy type— Chapter 11 subchapter V—works much like Chapter 13 and provides small businesses with a simpler, cheaper way to reorganize and stay open.

If you file a personal bankruptcy under Chapter 7 or Chapter 13, corporate-owned assets and liabilities are not part of the bankruptcy, although you can discharge any personal liability you have for corporate debt.

Keep in mind that you must disclose the value of your interest in the company as an asset, and as with all assets, keeping it will require you to protect it with an exemption. If you own 100% of nonexempt corporate stock as part of a Chapter 7 personal bankruptcy, the trustee can liquidate the corporation and treat the assets as the debtor's personal assets—which means they can be sold for the benefit of your creditors. By contrast, if you own less than 100%, the trustee is limited to selling your shares and distributing the proceeds to the creditors.

CAUTION

If you owe debts jointly with your corporation or LLC, and you file a personal bankruptcy, your bankruptcy discharge will protect you personally but it does not protect your business. Business creditors won't be able to collect against your personal assets but will still be able to collect against the business assets and income. If you are in this situation, it might make sense to dissolve your corporation or LLC before you file a personal bankruptcy case. However, be aware that if you open a similar business shortly after the bankruptcy, a discharged creditor might accuse you of fraudulently doing so in an attempt to avoid paying your debt. Be sure to talk to a bankruptcy attorney before you file.

Who Can File for Bankruptcy

Bankruptcy might be a good solution to your debt problems—but only if you are eligible to file. For example, you won't be allowed to file for Chapter 7 or Chapter 13 bankruptcy if you don't first seek credit counseling. Before reading the rest of this book to find out what effect bankruptcy will have on your life, you should figure out whether you'll be eligible to file for bankruptcy in the first place.

Unlike Chapter 7 bankruptcy, Chapter 13 eligibility is intended, in large part, to require people to pay back at least a portion of their debts if they can. And if you do file under Chapter 13, your repayment plan will have to repay certain types of debts in full. This chapter explains these and other eligibility rules for Chapter 7 and Chapter 13. You'll also find a hypothetical discussion between a bankruptcy lawyer and a would-be filer regarding which type of bankruptcy would be more appropriate given that person's circumstances.

Getting Help With Eligibility Issues

As you'll see from this chapter, eligibility rules for Chapter 7 and Chapter 13 bankruptcy are not always simple. Thanks to the bankruptcy means test and Chapter 13 repayment plan requirements, among other things, figuring out if you can file for Chapter 7 or Chapter 13 bankruptcy can be tricky. And even if you qualify to file for bankruptcy, rules about presumed fraudulent transactions and prebankruptcy payments to certain creditors might mean you should

think carefully about *when* you file. Things can get even more confusing when timing factors conflict, making it difficult to know whether you should file soon or wait.

If you want to file for Chapter 7 bankruptcy but something in this chapter raises a red flag, be sure to consult with an experienced bankruptcy attorney. A bankruptcy specialist can often help you overcome eligibility problems, timing concerns, and other tricky issues.

Credit Counseling

Before you can file for Chapter 7 or Chapter 13 bankruptcy, you must consult a nonprofit credit counseling agency. The purpose of this consultation is to see whether there is a feasible way to handle your debt load outside of bankruptcy, without adding to what you owe.

Counseling Requirements

To qualify for bankruptcy relief, you must show that you received credit counseling from an agency approved by the U.S Trustee's office within the 180-day period before you file your bankruptcy. Once you complete the counseling, the agency will give you a certificate of completion to file with your petition. It will also give you a copy of any repayment plan you worked out with the agency. You can find out which agencies have been approved for your judicial district by visiting the Office of the U.S. Trustee's website at www.justice.gov/ust;

click "Credit Counseling & Debtor Education" to see the list.

The purpose of credit counseling is to give you an idea of whether you really need to file for bankruptcy or whether an informal repayment plan would get you back on your economic feet. Counseling is required even if it's obvious that a repayment plan isn't feasible—that is, your debts are too high and your income is too low—or you are facing debts that you find unfair and don't want to pay. For instance, credit card balances inflated by high interest rates and penalties are particularly unpopular with many filers, as are emergency room bills, debts you cosigned, and deficiency judgments based on auctions of repossessed cars.

Bankruptcy law requires only that you participate in the counseling—not that you go along with whatever the agency proposes. Even if a repayment plan is feasible, you aren't required to agree to it. However, if the agency does come up with a plan, you must file it along with the other bankruptcy documents described in Ch. 10.

> **CAUTION**
>
> **The court might agree with the agency's plan.** If it's clear from the documents you file that you could complete the repayment plan proposed by the agency, the court could use this as a reason to question your Chapter 7 filing and try to push you into a Chapter 13 repayment plan (see Ch. 10). If that happens, you'll have an opportunity to argue about whether you should have to pay into a repayment plan.

Rules Counseling Agencies Must Follow

In addition to providing services without regard to the debtor's ability to pay, counseling agencies have to meet a number of other requirements. They must:

- disclose to you their funding sources, their counselor qualifications, the possible impact of their proposed plan on your credit report, the costs of the program, if any, and how much of the costs will be borne by you
- provide counseling that includes an analysis of your current financial condition, factors that caused the condition, and how you can develop a plan to respond to the problems without adding to your debt
- use trained counselors who don't receive any commissions or bonuses based on the outcome of the counseling services (kickbacks to individual counselors are not allowed), and
- maintain a funding level that will allow the agency to service your case over the plan period.

Counseling Costs

Credit counseling agencies can charge a reasonable fee for their services. However, if a debtor cannot afford the fee, the counseling agency must provide services free or at reduced rates. Ask about a sliding fee scale or fee waiver if your income falls below 150% of the poverty level for a family of equal size. The Office of the U.S. Trustee, the law enforcement agency that oversees credit counseling agencies, has indicated that a "reasonable" fee might range from free to $50, depending on the circumstances.

Exceptions to the Counseling Requirement

You don't have to get counseling if the U.S. Trustee certifies that there is no appropriate agency available to you in the district where you will be filing. However, counseling can be provided by telephone or (usually) online, so it is unlikely that approved debt counseling will ever be "unavailable."

You can also avoid this requirement if you certify to the court's satisfaction that:

- You had to file for bankruptcy immediately, such as to stop a wage garnishment or foreclosure.
- You were unable to obtain counseling within seven days after requesting it.

If you can prove that you didn't receive credit counseling for these reasons, you must certify that to the court and complete the counseling within 30 days after filing. Although you can ask the court to extend this deadline by 15 days, doing so would probably take more time than simply completing the course online.

Incentive for Creditors to Settle?

If a credit counseling agency proposes a settlement that would repay at least 60% of your debt to a creditor, and that creditor refuses to go along with the plan, the creditor might be penalized when and if your property is distributed in bankruptcy. The creditor will be allowed to collect a maximum of 80% of the total claim if you can show, by clear and convincing evidence, that the creditor was offered the deal at least 60 days before you filed and the creditor unreasonably refused the offer.

Although this 20% penalty is billed as an incentive for creditors to accept settlement prior to bankruptcy, the creditor stands to lose only 20 cents on the dollar for turning down an offer to lose 40 cents on the dollar. It's not clear why a creditor would agree to take a large hit early to avoid the possibility of a smaller hit down the road. Also, it will generally cost you more to prove that the creditor's refusal was unreasonable than the penalty is worth. And finally, this will be a factor only in Chapter 13 cases; creditors of Chapter 7 debtors rarely recoup 60% of their debt, let alone 80%.

You might escape the credit counseling requirement if, after notice and hearing, the bankruptcy court determines that you couldn't participate because of:

- a physical disability that prevents you from attending counseling (this exception probably won't apply if the counseling is available online or over the phone)
- mental incapacity (you are unable to understand and benefit from the counseling), or
- your active duty in a military combat zone.

But keep in mind that most judges won't believe that counseling was not available. Most counseling agencies can provide immediate service if you request it and some even provide 24-hour service, so it's best to figure out a way to get the counseling before you file.

Calculating Your Income Status

In 2005, Congress decided that higher-income people with primarily consumer debts should file Chapter 13 bankruptcy if possible, given their income and expenses. To learn whether you fit within the Chapter 7 or Chapter 13 group, take the following steps:

1. Calculate your current monthly income (CMI).
2. Compare your CMI multiplied by 12 to the appropriate median income figure.

Calculate Your Current Monthly Income

The bankruptcy law defines your CMI as your average monthly income received during the six-month period that ends on the last day of the month preceding your filing date—whether or not the income is taxable. When including wages or other sources of income, you must include the gross amount, not the net income you actually receive after deductions from taxes and other withholdings are made.

In Chapter 7, your CMI includes income from all sources except:

- payments you receive under the Social Security Act (including Social Security Retirement, SSI, SSDI, and TANF)
- payments to victims of war crimes or crimes against humanity based on their status as victims of such crimes, or
- payments to victims of international or domestic terrorism.

In Chapter 13, CMI includes income from all sources, with the same exclusions as for Chapter 7.

Use Worksheet A: Current Monthly and Yearly Income shown below and located on the online companion page. You'll take the following steps to calculate your CMI:

1. Add up all of the income you received during that six-month period.
2. Divide by six to come up with your current monthly average.

You can download the form (and all other forms in this book) from Nolo.com; for details, see Appendix A.

Worksheet A: Current Monthly and Yearly Income

Use this worksheet to calculate your current monthly and yearly income for your household. You'll use both amounts when taking the means test. Include amounts for all people who contribute to the household.

Line 1. Calculate your total income over the last six months before any deductions from wages, salary, tips, bonuses, overtime, and so on.

    A. Month 1 $ _____

    B. Month 2   _____

    C. Month 3   _____

    D. Month 4   _____

    E. Month 5   _____

    F. Month 6   _____

    G. TOTAL WAGES (add Lines 1A–1F) $ _____

Line 2. Add up all other income for the last six months.

    A. Net business, profession, or farm income   _____

    B. Interest, dividends, and royalties   _____

    C. Net income from rents and real property   _____

    D. Pension and retirement income   _____

    E. Alimony or family support   _____

    F. Spousal contributions (if separated and not filing jointly)   _____

    G. Unemployment compensation   _____

    H. Workers' compensation   _____

    I. State disability insurance   _____

    J. Annuity payments   _____

    K. Other   _____

    L. TOTAL OTHER INCOME (add Lines 2A–2K) $ _____

Line 3. Calculate total income over the six months prior to filing.

    A. Enter total wages (Line 1G).   _____

    B. Enter total other income (Line 2L).   _____

    C. TOTAL INCOME OVER THE SIX MONTHS PRIOR TO FILING. Add Lines 3A and 3B together. $ _____

Line 4. Divide your total income by six. This is your "current monthly income" for purposes of the means test. $ _____

Line 5. To find the yearly income you'll use to compare to your state's median income, multiply your "current monthly income" by 12. $ _____

EXAMPLE: John and Samantha are married and have two young children. They fell quickly into debt after John was forced out of his job because of a work-related injury on April 1, 20xx. Three months later, on July 1, 20xx, John and Samantha decide to file for bankruptcy.

To calculate their CMI, Samantha reviews the family's income for the period between January 1 and June 30, 20xx (the six-month period ending in the calendar month prior to their bankruptcy filing date). This includes John's gross salary for the first three months (he made $8,000 a month as a software engineer), plus $1,800 in workers' compensation benefits for each of the last three months. Samantha made $1,000 a month during the first three months and had no income for the last three months. The total family income for the six-month period is $32,400. Divided by six, the family's CMI is $5,400 (the six-month average), even though the monthly amount they actually took in during each of the

How to Determine Your Household Size

Determining your household size is very important—the more members you have in your household, the less likely it is that your income will exceed the median for a similar size household. For example, assume that your CMI is $6,000, the median income for a household of three is $5,800, and the median income for a household of four is $6,500. It will be to your benefit to have four people in your household instead of three.

Unfortunately, neither Congress nor the courts have given clear guidance on how to calculate your household size. Most courts adopt the census test for a household, which includes all of the people, related and unrelated, who occupy a house, an apartment, a group of rooms, or a single room that is intended for occupancy as separate living quarters. Under this test, you can count your children or stepchildren even if they are not dependents for tax purposes, called "heads on beds." However, some courts count only dependents as part of the household and require that you list in your bankruptcy papers any money donated to the household by any other person or entity.

Domestic partners count as one house-hold. But mere roommates are not a single household when they have separate rooms within a house but don't act as one economic unit by commingling their incomes and jointly paying expenses. One vexing issue yet to be decided is whether children can be counted as part of a household in situations where they are only living with the parent part-time under a custody and visitation agreement. For clarification, call your local trustee's office and speak with one of the attorneys.

three months before filing was only $1,800. The following types of income should be included in the form:

- wages, salary, tips, bonuses, overtime, and commissions
- net income from the operation of a business, profession, or farm (the amount you report as taxable income, after subtracting reasonable and necessary business expenses on IRS Schedule C)
- interest, dividends, and royalties
- net income from rents and other real property income
- pension and retirement income, including any one-time withdrawals
- regular contributions to the household expenses of the debtor or the debtor's dependents, including child or spousal support
- regular contributions by the debtor's spouse if he or she isn't part of the household either because of a separation or a joint debtor in the bankruptcy
- unemployment compensation
- workers' compensation insurance
- state disability insurance, and
- annuity payments.

Compare Your Yearly Income to Your State's Family Median Income

The census bureau periodically publishes family median income figures for all 50 states. To compare your yearly income to the family median income for your state, you'll need to multiply your CMI by 12 (remember that for this calculation, your CMI, or "current monthly income," is the average monthly amount received during the full six months immediately preceding your bankruptcy). In John and Marcia's case, the family's CMI ($5,400) multiplied by 12 would be $64,800.

Once you've computed your CMI and located the same size household (for your state), compare the two figures to see whether your yearly income is more or less than the median income for the same size household for your state. You can download the state median figures (as of the publication date of this book) in the Median Family Income chart on the online companion page. You can also find up-to-date figures at www. justice.gov/ust by clicking "Means Testing Information" (the figures change regularly).

You can see from the online chart that John and Samantha's yearly income would be more than the family median income in many states.

If Your Yearly Income Is Less Than or Equal to Your State's Family Median Income

If your yearly income is less than or equal to your state's family median income, you'll qualify for Chapter 7 and won't need to take the second part of the Chapter 7 bankruptcy means test. If you decide to file for Chapter 13, you can propose a plan that is based on your actual expenses and lasts for three years instead of five years.

For Larger Families

Although the U.S. Census Bureau generates median figures for families that have up to seven members, Congress does not want you to use these figures if you have a larger family. The Census figures are to be used for families that have up to four members. If there are more than four members of your family, you must add $9,000 per additional person to the four-member family median income figure for your state. This figure increases periodically, so check the means testing numbers on the U.S. Trustee's website.

If Your Yearly Income Is More Than Your State's Family Median Income

If your yearly income, as calculated above, exceeds your state's family median income, the consequences depend on whether you are filing for Chapter 7 or Chapter 13 bankruptcy.

Chapter 7: If the majority of your debt is consumer debt (meaning it doesn't come from operating a business, tax debts, or debts for personal injury or property damage you caused to someone else), you'll take the second part of the means test. It allows you to figure in expenses when determining if you have enough money to repay something to creditors. If you pass, you'll be eligible to file for Chapter 7. If you don't pass the means test but file anyway, your Chapter 7 case will be dismissed on the basis of "abusing" the bankruptcy law.

The means test starts with your current monthly income (explained earlier in this chapter). You then subtract a combination of real and hypothetical living expenses (these are called "allowable expense deductions" and are explained later in this chapter). The final figure will show whether you have enough projected disposable income to pay some of your debts.

The presumption of abuse is automatic for debtors with above-median income if they have enough projected disposable income to pay general unsecured creditors:

- at least $13,650 or more over a period of 60 months, or
- at least 25% of general unsecured debts if the projected disposable income totals between $8,175 and $13,650 over a period of 60 months.

If your remaining income would be less than $8,175 when projected over the next five years, you will pass the means test and can file for Chapter 7 if you meet the other eligibility requirements explained in this chapter. (The figures will adjust on April 1, 2022. The means test is explained in more detail in "Chapter 7 Eligibility Requirements," below.)

> **EXAMPLE:** Jonas makes $4,500 a month as a section manager in a large general-purpose store. His current monthly income is more than the median income for his state, so he has to pass the means test to file for Chapter 7 bankruptcy. He deducts allowable expenses from his income and comes up with $300 a

month extra. Because his excess income comes to $18,000 when projected over the next five years ($300 x 60 months), Jonas fails the means test.

If Jonas had only $130 a month extra ($7,800 over a five-year period), he would have to figure out whether this amount would pay at least 25% of his unsecured, nonpriority debt in that five-year period. For instance, if Jonas owed $36,000 in credit card debt, he would be barred from Chapter 7 if he could pay $9,000 (25% of the debt) over a five-year period. Because Jonas only has $7,800 extra, however, he would pass the means test and be eligible for Chapter 7 as long as he meets the other eligibility factors.

No matter how high your income is, you don't have to take the means test if you fit into either of the following situations:

- **You are a disabled veteran.** You don't have to take the means test if you are a disabled veteran with a disability rating of at least 30% and your debts were primarily incurred while on active duty or performing a homeland defense activity.
- **Your debts are not consumer debts.** You can skip the means test if your debt is not primarily consumer debt—that is, if more than 50% of your debt load comes from business debts, taxes, or debts for personal injury or property damage you caused to someone else (called "tort debts"). However, a personal mortgage not used for

business purposes is considered a consumer debt and is often high enough to swing your overall debt into the consumer category.

Chapter 13: If your yearly income is more than the median for your state and you file for Chapter 13, you must propose a five-year repayment plan to which you commit all of your disposable income. You will also have to use the IRS expense standards—and other allowable deductions—to calculate your projected disposable income (the amount of income you'll have to pay into the plan every month for the benefit of your nonpriority, unsecured creditors). These rules are explained in "Chapter 13 Eligibility Requirements," below.

> **TIP**
>
> **Choose your filing date to lower your CMI.** If your income has been uneven during the six months prior to your projected filing date, you might want to delay or speed up your filing if either strategy would move your CMI from the high income to the low income category. For instance, if you received a large bonus or had a high paying job during the first three months and a low paying job during the second three months, each month you wait before filing reduces your CMI. On the other hand, if you've recently landed a high paying job after having a low income job, the sooner you file, the lower your CMI will be. However, in order to remain in Chapter 7, you will still have to show that your ongoing income is completely used up by reasonable and necessary regular living expenses.

If your income and expense forms (Schedules I and J) show that you have extra money each month, the trustee might recommend converting to a Chapter 13 bankruptcy, even if you passed the means test.

Chapter 7 Eligibility Requirements

There are several basic eligibility requirements you must meet to file a "consumer" Chapter 7 bankruptcy. In addition, if your current monthly income is more than your state's family median income for a family of your size, and your debts are primarily consumer debts, you will have to pass the means test, explained below. To figure out whether you can meet these requirements, you'll first need to know how various debts are classified.

The Means Test

By now you know that if your CMI multiplied by 12 (yearly income) exceeds your state's median income for a similar size household, you are required to take the second part of the means test. The means test measures certain expenses and deductions against your CMI to see whether you have any income you can spare to propose a Chapter 13 bankruptcy plan. In the words of the law, the means test determines whether a "presumption of abuse" arises—that is, whether filing a Chapter 7 bankruptcy would be presumed to be an abuse of the bankruptcy laws in the absence of facts proving the contrary.

 SKIP AHEAD

If your CMI multiplied by 12 is below the median income, no need to take the means test. But see the discussion below regarding "abuse under all the circumstances."

When a presumption of abuse arises, it's up to the filer to rebut the presumption, which means the filer has to convince the court that special circumstances entitle him or her to file under Chapter 7, even though the means test indicates a different result. On the other hand, if no presumption of abuse arises, then the way is clear to file under Chapter 7 (with some exceptions discussed below).

Take the Means Test

The means test itself is contained in Official Forms 122A-1, 122A-1Supp, and 122A-2. You'll find filled-out samples on this book's online companion page. To complete the test, you must use certain predetermined expenses formulated by the IRS that vary according to state and region. These expense figures are available online at www.justice.gov/ust. The following is a rough guide to help you organize the information you'll need to actually take the test.

Use Worksheet B: Allowable Monthly Expenses, available online, to help you with the actual figures as you work through the following steps.

You Cannot Use the Car Ownership Deduction If You Don't Have Car Payments

In the past, some courts allowed you to deduct the standard predetermined transportation ownership expense for purposes of the means test, even if you weren't making payments on your car. Other courts ruled that you couldn't take this deduction if you weren't making car loan or lease payments.

However, in 2011, in *Ransom v. FIA Card Services, MBNA, America Bank*, 131 S. Ct. 716 (2011), the United States Supreme Court held that in a Chapter 13 bankruptcy, a debtor cannot use the car ownership deduction if the debtor does not make car loan or lease payments. In a Chapter 13 bankruptcy, the car ownership deduction is one of the deductions used to determine the amount of debtor's disposable income, and thus the amount that the debtor must repay creditors.

Although the *Ransom* case deals with Chapter 13 bankruptcies, some courts have applied the same reasoning to the car ownership deduction in Chapter 7 bankruptcies for means test calculations. Others (but not all), have gone even further by applying the *Ransom* case to house payments. In such courts, a debtor can't factor a mortgage payment into the Chapter 7 means test calculation if the debtor intends to surrender the home.

Enter Actual Expenses

In addition to your CMI, which is the starting point for the means test, and the predetermined expenses, you'll also have to provide the following information about your actual expenses computed on a monthly basis:

- all federal, state, and local taxes, such as income taxes, self-employment taxes, Social Security taxes, and Medicare taxes (but not excess tax withholding that will result in a tax refund). Do not include property taxes or sales taxes.
- total payroll deductions that are required for your employment, such as retirement contributions, union dues, and uniform costs. Do not include discretionary amounts, such as voluntary 401(k) contributions.
- term life insurance premiums for yourself. Do not include premiums for insurance on your dependents, for whole life, or for any other form of insurance.
- payments you are required to pay under a court or administrative agency order, such as spousal or child support payments. Do not include payments on arrearages.
- payments expended for education that is a condition of employment and for education that is required for a physically or mentally challenged dependent child for whom no public education providing similar services is available

- payments for child care, such as baby-sitting, day care, nursery, and preschool (this includes money you pay to a family member to care for your children). Do not include other educational payments.
- payments for health care not required for the health and welfare of yourself or your dependents and not reimbursed by insurance or a health savings account and that exceeds the standard health care expense entered on Form 122A-2, Line 7g. Do not include payments for health insurance or health savings accounts listed in Form 122A-2, Line 25.
- payments for telecommunication services other than your basic home telephone and cellphone service—such as pagers, call waiting, caller ID, special long distance, or Internet service—to the extent necessary for your health and welfare or that of your dependents. Do not include any amount previously deducted.
- payments to care for a member of your household or immediate family because of the member's age, illness, or disability
- payments for security systems and any other method of protecting your family
- actual payments for home energy costs that exceed the IRS expense

- payments for your children's education. (The maximum you can deduct is $170.83; the amount will adjust on April 1, 2022.)
- payments for food and clothing that exceed the predetermined expense, but no more than 5% of the predetermined expense, and
- charitable contributions (tithing), but only if you have a history of making them.

Mortgage Obligation Payments When Surrendering Your Home

It's not uncommon for people filing for bankruptcy to be in some stage of foreclosure and months behind on their payments. Some courts refuse to allow a deduction for mortgage payments when it's clear that the filer doesn't intend to keep the house. Other courts let you deduct them as long as you are still liable for them, regardless of what your intent might be for the future. The best approach is to first run the means test without counting the mortgage. If you pass without this deduction, then don't make it. If you need the deduction, however, then you'll need to be prepared to argue in a hearing that your court should follow the courts that allow it. This issue has not yet been decided by the U.S. Supreme Court.

You might want to contact the local U.S. Trustee's office and ask about the approach in your area. Otherwise, speak with a local bankruptcy attorney.

Understanding How Debts Are Classified

When you take the means test, different types of debts are handled differently in the calculations. This section includes definitions that will help you figure out which numbers to use.

Secured Debts

A debt is "secured" if you stand to lose specific property when you don't make your payments to the creditor. Most secured debts are created when you sign loan papers giving a creditor a security interest in your property—such as a home loan or car loan. But a debt might also be secured if a creditor has filed a lien (a legal claim against your property that must be paid before the property can be sold). Here is a list of common secured debts and liens:

- **Mortgages.** Called deeds of trust in some states, these are loans to buy or refinance a house or other real estate. If you fail to pay, the lender can foreclose on your house.

- **Home equity loans (second mortgages).** If you fail to pay, the lender (typically a bank or finance company) can foreclose on your house.

- **Loans for cars, boats, tractors, motorcycles, or RVs.** If you fail to pay, the lender can repossess the vehicle.

- **Store charges with a security agreement.** Almost all store purchases on credit cards are unsecured. Some stores, notably Best Buy and Home Depot, however, claim to retain a security interest in all hard goods (durable goods) purchased, or they make customers sign security agreements when they use their store charge card.

- **Personal loans from banks, credit unions, or finance companies.** Often, you must pledge valuable personal property, such as a paid-off motor vehicle, as collateral for these loans. The property can be repossessed if you don't make the payments.

- **Judicial liens.** A judicial lien can be imposed on your property only after somebody sues you and wins a money judgment against you. In most states, the judgment creditor then must record (file) the judgment with the county or state. The recorded judgment creates a lien on your real estate and, in some states, on some of your personal property as well.

- **Statutory liens.** Some liens are automatic, by law. For example, in most states, when you hire someone to work on your house, the worker and the supplier of materials can assert a mechanic's lien (sometimes called a materialman's or contractor's lien) on the house if you don't pay.

- **Tax liens.** If you owe money to the IRS or other taxing authority, the debt is secured if the agency has recorded a lien against your property.

Unsecured Debts

Unsecured debt is any debt for which you haven't pledged collateral and for which the creditor has not filed a lien against you. If the debt is unsecured, the creditor is not entitled to repossess or seize any of your property if you don't pay.

Most debts are unsecured. Some of the common ones are:

- credit and charge card purchases and cash advances
- department store credit card purchases for clothing and other apparel
- gasoline company credit card purchases
- back rent
- medical bills
- alimony and child support
- student loans
- utility bills
- loans from friends or relatives, unless you signed a promissory note secured by some property you own
- health club dues
- lawyers' and accountants' bills
- church or synagogue dues, and
- union dues.

Priority Debts

Priority debts are unsecured debts that are considered sufficiently important to jump to the head of the bankruptcy repayment line. This means they are paid first if a Chapter 7 trustee disburses property in the course of the case. This can be very helpful when the priority debt can't be discharged in your bankruptcy (which is usually the case).

For example, liability for a recent income tax is both a priority debt and a debt that can't be discharged in bankruptcy. Having your property pay off the tax debt—which you will have to pay anyway—is a lot better than having your property go to pay off debts that would otherwise be discharged in your bankruptcy.

Priority debts that might come up in consumer bankruptcies include:

- wages, salaries, and commissions owed by an employer
- contributions to employee benefit plans
- debts of up to $6,725 (each) owed to certain farmers and fishermen
- up to $3,025 in deposits made for the purchase, lease, or rental of property or services for personal, family, or household use that were not delivered or provided
- alimony, maintenance, or support, and
- income taxes that became due within the three-year period before the bankruptcy filing date and taxes that were collected or withheld from an employee (trust fund taxes); also, customs, duties, and penalties owing to federal, state, and local governmental units.

Enter Monthly Contractual Payments or Secured Debts

You are entitled to deduct the contractual monthly payments you owe on your mortgage, car, and other collateral you are making payments on. The deduction will be based on the total payments due over the next five years, divided by 60. However, if your monthly payments are due to end prior to the end of the five-year period, you still divide the total due by 60 and use the resulting number as your deduction.

EXAMPLE: You are paying $1,500 a month on a mortgage that has ten years left on it. You also pay $300 a month on a home equity loan that has three years left on it. And you have a car note for $200 a month that has two years left. The monthly deduction for the mortgage will be $1,500, since the mortgage is due to last beyond the next five years. To calculate the deduction for the home equity loan, you first multiply $300 by 36 (the number of months left on the loan) and then divide that amount by 60 (the amount left amortized over a five-year period). The resulting deduction will be $180 a month. Finally, multiply $200 by 24 to obtain the amount you have left to pay on the car note ($4,800) and divide by 60, for a monthly deduction of $80. In this example, the total deduction for the mortgage, home equity loan, and car note is $1,760 a month.

Use Worksheet C (located on this book's online companion page at www.nolo.com/back-of-book/FIBA.html) to help you calculate the actual figures.

Enter One-Sixtieth of Arrearages

You are entitled to deduct a monthly amount equal to one-sixtieth of the arrearage you owe on a secured debt, such as a mortgage or car note. Incidentally, the one-sixtieth fraction represents a monthly payment over a five-year period. For example, if you owe three missed payments on your mortgage totaling $4,500, the deduction would be $75 a month (one-sixtieth of $4,500). Before using this deduction, however, see "Mortgage Obligation Payments When Surrendering Your Home," above.

Enter One-Sixtieth of Your Priority Debts

You are entitled to deduct a monthly amount equal to one-sixtieth of your priority debts. The reason for this is that priority debts must be paid in full over the life of a Chapter 13 plan, and this deduction represents the amount you'll have to pay. For instance, recent taxes (taxes that first became due within the three years immediately preceding your bankruptcy filing date) are priority debts. If you owe $5,000 in recent taxes, you'll deduct one-sixtieth of that amount, or about $83 a month.

The Trustee Fee

You are entitled to deduct the commission the trustee would earn in a Chapter 13 case if you filed one, which is roughly 10% of all payments that would be made under the plan (but it could be less—check with the trustee's office). This is a difficult figure to come up with without more information about which payments you must make under the plan and which payments you can make directly, so you should wrestle with it only if you can't pass the means test by some other way.

A sample completed means test (Forms 122A-1, 122A-1Supp, and 122A-2) can be found on this book's companion page at www.nolo.com/back-of-book/FIBA.html.

Special Circumstances

If the U.S. Trustee seeks to dismiss or convert your Chapter 7 bankruptcy to a Chapter 13 case on the ground of presumed abuse, you can defend against that motion by showing that special circumstances apply in your case. These special circumstances must increase your expenses or decrease your income to bring your net monthly income down to a level that passes the means test. While the bankruptcy law does not define the term "special circumstances," Congress cited as examples "a serious medical condition" or "a call or order to active duty in the Armed Forces."

And the U.S. Trustee's office has noted that common special circumstances might include:

- job loss or reduction in income for which there is no reasonable alternative

- a one-time "bump" in prepetition income that is not likely to happen again, such as a one-time pension withdrawal or taking cash out of an IRA
- debtors who have separate households due to pending divorce or job relocation, and have filed a joint bankruptcy petition, and
- a postpetition household size increase due to pregnancy or a reasonable need to support an additional person.

For instance, assume you were activated from the reserves and faced a sharp drop in income as well as the costs of moving your family. If the judge agrees that these are special circumstances, and your changed economic picture gives you a net monthly income that passes the means test, you will be able to file a Chapter 7 bankruptcy.

This is the time to be creative, although keep in mind that your argument will have to be strong enough to persuade the judge. See Ch. 10 for more on using special circumstances to get you past the means test.

When Your Leftover Is Between $136.25 and $227.50

If you have some income left over after all the deductions, and the monthly income is less than $136.25, you are home free. On the other hand, if the monthly income is over $227.50, abuse is presumed (unless you can show special circumstances). What happens if your income is right in the middle? You'll need to determine whether the amount of leftover income will pay at least 25% of your unsecured, nonpriority debt. If it will, a Chapter 7 case will be considered presumptively abusive, and you'll have to file for Chapter 13 bankruptcy. If not, you qualify for Chapter 7 bankruptcy.

Abuse Under All the Circumstances

Even if you pass the means test, you aren't out of the woods. As you know, the means test is based on your CMI, a figure that could have no relationship to your actual income at the time you file bankruptcy. For instance, it's possible to be unemployed during the six-month look-back period, but then land a good job shortly before filing. Or, even if you pass the means test with flying colors, your actual monthly income, when compared to your actual expenses, could leave you with a few hundred extra dollars that could be used to pay down debts. Bankruptcy law allows the trustee to challenge your Chapter 7 bankruptcy on the basis that this extra actual income would fund a Chapter 13 program. The trustee will ask the court to dismiss or convert a case upon a finding of "abuse under all the circumstances." Most courts agree with this approach (using your actual income and expenses to determine abuse rather than your CMI).

Cases are sometimes ordered dismissed or converted with your consent to Chapter 13 under the "abuse under all the circumstances" test when the filer's mortgage and car payments are unreasonably high for someone filing bankruptcy and the judge decides that lesser obligations would free up some money for a Chapter 13 plan. For example, if Alejandro's monthly mortgage payments are $5,000 on a $750,000 note in an area where the median home price is $400,000, or Brianna is paying $900 a month on a note secured by a new model Mercedes, the court might disallow a portion of these expenses and rule that Alejandro and Brianna could now afford Chapter 13 plans. Of course this means that Alejandro would have to give up his house and Brianna her car, if they wanted to proceed in the bankruptcy court, rather than having their cases dismissed.

Bad Faith

Another doctrine that could affect your eligibility for a consumer Chapter 7 bankruptcy is what's commonly called "bad faith." Under this doctrine, a judge can dismiss your bankruptcy if he or she believes you filed for reasons other than to get a fresh start, or you engaged in prebankruptcy behavior that is inconsistent with the need for a bankruptcy discharge. For example, in one case, the court dismissed a case because the debtor purchased an expensive motorcycle shortly before filing and could have easily paid off his debts in a Chapter 13 bankruptcy had he not had to make the high monthly payments on his motorcycle.

Individuals and Businesses Can File for Chapter 7 Bankruptcy

Individuals and businesses can file for Chapter 7 bankruptcy. When individuals file, they get rid of their debts and go on with their lives. When business entities file, the business is liquidated, the assets are sold, and the proceeds go to the unsecured creditors. In between these extremes are individuals who are also in business as sole proprietors or independent contractors.

Sole Proprietors

If you run your business as a sole proprietor, you and your business are considered to be one and the same. If there are business assets, they are subject to being sold for the benefit of your creditors—unless they qualify for an exemption (see Ch. 4). If, on the other hand, your business is service or profession-oriented—such as contractors, lawyers, accountants, electricians, real estate agents, and the like—there are usually no assets worth selling and your business can continue without interruption. Retail businesses that have inventories or other assets that might generate income for creditors will likely have to cease operations upon filing bankruptcy. This gives the trustee time to inventory and value the assets as of the date of the bankruptcy filing and decide whether they are covered by any exemption you claim or whether they can be seized and sold for the benefit of your creditors. Also, in some circumstances, a trustee might close a business in order to avoid potential liability in the event that a customer is injured.

Owners of Small Business Entities

The owner of a small business that has incorporated or formed as a limited liability company (LLC) often has a choice to make, because there are two potential bankruptcy debtors: the owner personally and the business entity. You can:

- file as an individual and leave the business intact
- file as an individual and also have the business entity file separately
- have the business entity file and not file as an individual, or
- dissolve the business and file as an individual.

These decisions will depend on the following factors:

- the degree to which you have followed the necessary formalities in maintaining the business as a separate entity. For instance, did you maintain corporate minutes, issue stock or memberships, hold corporate meetings and pass resolutions as appropriate? Did you title business assets in the name of the business and keep your individual and business financial transactions separate (by using separate checkbooks, maintaining separate books, and observing basic rules of accounting regarding the use of the business assets, income, and expenses)?

- the degree to which the business entity has its own debts and property separate and apart from the owner's, and
- the degree to which the owner has personally signed off on loans and other debt.

One large downside to taking a business entity through Chapter 7 is that you have to use a lawyer. Even if you own all the interest in the entity, you can't represent it in bankruptcy court. Lawyers don't come cheap, and this fact alone could affect your decision to have the entity file or just let it lapse and deal with your personal liability for any corporate debt in personal bankruptcy.

But that's not the only downside. We don't discuss all of the potential problems here because business bankruptcies are outside of the scope of this book. However, you'll find a brief overview and suggested reading in the "Resource" section, below.

TIP

If you are filing a business-related bankruptcy, make sure you have good records. Although all bankruptcy debtors are required to produce records of certain financial transactions as part of their bankruptcy cases, this requirement is especially common when a debtor is in business (or has recently been in business). The records that trustees most commonly request of businesses are profit and loss statements, bank statements, and canceled checks for the previous 12 months. If the bankruptcy trustee moves to dismiss a case on the ground that the absence of financial records makes the case impossible to administer, the court might not accept the excuse that you're a sloppy bookkeeper, especially if you are a professional or in a type of business that requires some degree of sophistication. Lack of records can also be grounds to deny a discharge.

TIP

Find business bankruptcy information online. When a business fails and closes, most owners don't choose to put the company through bankruptcy. Instead, many owners opt to unwind the company outside of bankruptcy before wiping out the owner's business-related obligations, such as personal guarantees, in an individual Chapter 7 or 13. If you'd like to learn why, start by reading "Chapter 7 for Small Business Owners: An Overview" (nolo.com/legal-encyclopedia/chapter-7-bankruptcy-small-businesses.html). Learning about the benefits and limitations of Chapter 13 might be helpful, too (nolo.com/legal-encyclopedia/chapter-13-bankruptcy-small-businesses.html). It can be a good option if you want to keep property you'd lose in Chapter 7. And sometimes it even eases a business owner's personal debt burden enough to allow the business to stay open.

For more business-related options—including information about the new small business reorganization Chapter 11 subchapter V—check out Nolo's Small Business Bankruptcy section (nolo.com/legal-encyclopedia/small-business-bankruptcy).

Partnerships

Similarly, if you are a member of a business partnership with people other than your spouse, you can file for Chapter 7 bankruptcy as a consumer and include all business debts on which you are personally liable. Your partners will remain fully liable for the debts you wipe out, however.

SEE AN EXPERT

If you are a member of a business partnership, consider consulting a small business lawyer before you file for bankruptcy. Your obligation to your partners may be governed by a buy-sell agreement that requires you to terminate your partnership interest before filing for bankruptcy. If you don't follow that agreement or any other understanding you and your partners have, you probably will be putting the partnership's property at risk. And your partners (or ex-partners) might ask the bankruptcy court to lift the automatic stay so they can file a lawsuit against you. A lawyer can help you assess your obligations and options.

You Haven't Had a Previous Bankruptcy Discharge

You can't get a Chapter 7 discharge if you previously had your debts discharged in:

- a Chapter 7 bankruptcy *filed* within the previous *eight* years, or
- a Chapter 13 bankruptcy *filed* within the previous *six* years.

EXAMPLE: On June 14, 2021, you filed for Chapter 7 bankruptcy. You received your discharge on November 2, 2021. You've fallen on hard times again and are considering filing another Chapter 7 case. You cannot file before June 15, 2029.

You Aren't Barred by a Previous Bankruptcy Dismissal

You can't file for Chapter 7 bankruptcy if your previous bankruptcy case was dismissed within the past 180 days for any of the following reasons:

- You violated a court order.
- The court ruled that your filing was fraudulent or an abuse of the bankruptcy system.
- You requested the dismissal after a creditor asked the court to lift the automatic stay.

EXAMPLE: You filed for Chapter 7 bankruptcy on February 12, 2022, after your landlord started eviction proceedings. A week after you filed, your landlord filed a motion with the bankruptcy court to have the automatic stay lifted to continue the eviction proceedings. You dismissed your case. You've found a new place to live, but your debt problems haven't gone away and you want to refile. You must wait at least 180 days before filing again—that is, until August 12, 2022.

You Can Produce a Tax Return, Wage Stubs, and a Credit Counseling Certificate

To file a Chapter 7 case, you must produce your most recently filed tax return. You'll also need a certificate showing that you completed a credit counseling course, as well as wage stubs for the previous 60 days. (See Ch. 10 for more on these requirements.)

You Have Taken an Approved Personal Financial Management Course

You are required to take an approved personal finance course before the court will discharge your debts in a Chapter 7 bankruptcy. The agencies providing this service must be approved by the Office of the U.S. Trustee and must offer approximately two hours of required curriculum. Unlike the credit counseling agencies, personal financial management agencies don't have to be nonprofits, but they must offer in-person services on a sliding fee scale. For more information about the requirements for these agencies and how to find one in your area, visit the U.S. Trustee's website at www.justice.gov/ust; click "Credit Counseling & Debtor Education."

Before you can receive your Chapter 7 discharge, you must file an official form (Form 423) with the bankruptcy court, showing that you have completed this counseling. This must be accompanied by a certificate of completion from the counseling agency. You must file these forms no later than 45 days after the date on which your creditors' meeting was first scheduled. If you miss this deadline, the court could close your case without discharging your debts. This means you'll have to pay another filing fee to reopen your case so you can file the form and request a discharge.

Chapter 13 Eligibility Requirements

Like Chapter 7 bankruptcy, Chapter 13 bankruptcy has several important eligibility requirements.

Prior Bankruptcy Discharges

You can't get a Chapter 13 discharge if you received a discharge in a previous Chapter 13 case in the last two years, or a discharge in a Chapter 7 case filed within the last four years. You aren't barred from filing a Chapter 13 in these circumstances, but you can't get a discharge. For instance, you can file a Chapter 13 bankruptcy the instant you receive a Chapter 7 discharge (to handle liens that survived your Chapter 7 case or pay debts that weren't discharged in that case), and you can operate under a plan confirmed by the court for a three- to five-year period. But you can't get the Chapter 13 discharge, which means you'll still owe any debt that you don't pay off in the course of your Chapter 13 case. (Filing for Chapter 13 after receiving a Chapter 7 discharge is informally known as a "Chapter 20 bankruptcy.")

You might be wondering what good it would do you to file a Chapter 13 case when you don't qualify for the discharge. Doing so could provide a structured way for you to handle your debt load under the protection of the stay. For instance, suppose that you owe a substantial debt, and the creditor is threatening to garnish your wages or take your property. You can stop these actions by paying off the debt in Chapter 13 bankruptcy.

However, keep in mind that you might not be able to take advantage of every Chapter 13 tool. For example, many courts have ruled that a Chapter 13 debtor who is not eligible for discharge cannot "strip off" a junior mortgage. (See Ch. 5 for more about lien stripping.)

Business Entities Can't File for Chapter 13 Bankruptcy

To file a Chapter 13 bankruptcy case, you must be an individual (or a husband and wife filing jointly). If you own your own business as a sole proprietor or partner, you can include all business debts on which you have personal liability. You have to file your case in your name, however, and not in the name of your business, because a business cannot file for Chapter 13 bankruptcy. On your bankruptcy papers, you will need to list all fictitious business names or DBAs ("doing business as" names) that you've used as a sole proprietor or partnership.

EXAMPLE: Shelby Ferra operates a graphic design business under the name "Shelby Designs," and also has a seasonal tax preparation business called "AAA Tax Preparation Services." Shelby's bankruptcy petition would read as follows: Shelby Ferra AKA Shelby Designs AKA AAA Tax Preparation Services. There is no limit to the number of "AKAs" in a bankruptcy petition, provided that they aren't separate business entities requiring their own bankruptcy filings.

As with Chapter 7 bankruptcy, if you operate your business as a sole proprietorship or in a partnership with your spouse or another party, you or you and your partner are personally liable for the debts of the business. For bankruptcy purposes, you and your business (or your share of a partnership) are one and the same. There is one exception: Stockbrokers and commodity brokers cannot file Chapter 13 bankruptcy cases, even for personal (not business) debts.

You cannot file a Chapter 13 bankruptcy on behalf of a corporation, limited liability company (LLC), or partnership as such. If you want to file a reorganization bankruptcy in that situation, you must file a business Chapter 11 bankruptcy, which is beyond the scope of this book.

Your Debts Must Not Be Too High

You do not qualify for Chapter 13 bankruptcy if your secured debts exceed

$1,257,850 or your unsecured debts are more than $419,275. If you need help figuring out which of your debts are secured and which are unsecured, see "Understanding How Debts Are Classified," above.

Chapter 11 Alternative for Business Entities

Although business entities don't qualify to file Chapter 13 bankruptcy, they certainly can file under Chapter 11. Unfortunately, Chapter 11 bankruptcy is very expensive because of attorneys' fees and the need for both intensive and endless negotiations with secured creditors and creditor committees. Still, if you have a going business and the ability to raise cash in the range of $20,000 to $100,000 or more, Chapter 11 might be workable.

You Must Be Current on Your Income Tax Filings

You will have to offer evidence that you have filed your federal and state income tax returns for the four tax years prior to your bankruptcy filing date. This evidence can be provided by the returns themselves or by transcripts of the returns obtained from the IRS. You have to provide this evidence no later than the date set for your first meeting of creditors (about a month after you file). The trustee can keep the creditors' meeting open for up to 120 days

to give you time to file the returns, and the court can give you an additional 120 days. Ultimately, if you don't produce your returns or transcripts of the returns or transcripts for those four preceding years, your Chapter 13 will be dismissed. Keep in mind that filing the returns is different from owing taxes; you can owe taxes and file for bankruptcy, but you must still file the returns.

Your Proposed Repayment Plan Must Satisfy Legal Requirements

Your eligibility for Chapter 13 bankruptcy depends on your ability to propose a plan that the court will approve of (confirm).

To determine whether a judge will confirm your plan, follow these steps:

Step 1: Compute your current monthly income (CMI) and compare it to the median income figure for your state located on this book's online companion page at www.nolo.com/back-of-book/FIBA.html.

If you are married (not separated), you must count the income of both spouses when computing your disposable income on Forms 122C-1 and 122C-2, even if only one spouse is filing. However, you can exclude certain kinds of income, like Social Security benefits, received by either spouse when making that computation.

Step 2A: If your CMI exceeds the median income figure, use Worksheet C located on the online companion page to compute your disposable income (income available to pay your unsecured nonpriority debt after all

When Your CMI Is Different From Your Actual Monthly Income

Because your CMI is based on the six-month average prior to your filing date, your actual income might be much less or much more.

Since the bankruptcy laws changed in 2005, courts have differed on what to do when a debtor's "current monthly income" figure is different from the debtor's actual monthly income. Some judges have based Chapter 13 plan payments on projected disposable income that was calculated using the CMI, even if the CMI was different from the debtors' actual monthly incomes. Other judges have been more flexible and permitted plans based on the debtors' actual incomes going forward. Similarly, in some cases, judges considered phantom expenses (such as mortgage payments even though the debtor's intention was to walk away) while others did not.

Fortunately, in 2010, the U.S. Supreme Court provided some guidance on this issue in *Hamilton v. Lanning*, 130 S. Ct. 2464 (2010).

The Court ruled that, when deciding whether to confirm a Chapter 13 plan, bankruptcy courts can take into consideration changes in income or expenses that have occurred, or are known or virtually certain to occur, at the time of confirmation (confirmation usually occurs about two to three months after a petition is filed). In other words, when called on to confirm a Chapter 13 plan, a court can base its decision on the reality of the debtor's income going forward rather than on the formula created by Congress, which looks backward six months. However, the keyword here is change. If there has been no significant change from the time the current monthly income and allowable expenses were computed, those figures will determine the amount to be repaid to unsecured creditors under the plan.

required payments have been taken care of under your plan). A copy of Worksheet C is located on this book's online companion page at www.nolo.com/back-of-book/FIBA.html.

Step 2B: If your CMI is less than the median income for your state, compute your disposable income by subtracting your actual living expenses from your net income (see sample Forms I and J on this book's online companion page at www. nolo.com/back-of-book/FIBA.html).

Step 3A: If you have enough disposable income to pay the percentage of your unsecured nonpriority debt that is required by your court (after paying all required debt under the plan), you qualify for Chapter 13.

Step 3B: If you have negative disposable income, forget about Chapter 13, unless you can reduce your living expenses or sell some property to create a positive disposable income.

CAUTION

Your plan might not be confirmed if your actual expenses look too low. If your current monthly income is less than your state's family median income, you can use your actual expenses to calculate how much you could devote to a Chapter 13 plan, provided those expenses are reasonable. Some people are tempted to decrease their stated expenses in order to increase their disposable income so they can qualify for Chapter 13. If it appears that your expenses are unreasonably low, however, the court might reject your plan. And even if the court approves your plan, remember that you still need enough money to live on. So, be realistic.

In Step 2A, you calculated your mandatory debts and deducted them from the income you had left after deducting IRS-allowed amounts or actual expenses. If you have any remaining income after paying your mandatory debts, you will have to commit that income to paying your unsecured, nonpriority debts.

If your current monthly income is more than your state's median, you have to commit all of your projected disposable income to your plan for a five-year period. If your current monthly income is less than your state's median, you have to commit all of your disposable income to your plan for at least three years. Depending on which category you fit into, your plan will have to show what your projected disposable income can accomplish during the period in question.

For instance, if you are in the five-year category, will your projected disposable income cover all mandatory debts and necessary payments when spread out over 60 monthly payments? If there is anything left, does your plan apply that money to your unsecured, nonpriority debts? If so, then your plan should be confirmed by the court.

Similarly, if your current monthly income is less than the state's median, you need only commit to a three-year plan. So if you can make all required payments within 36 monthly payments, your plan will be confirmed provided that anything left over goes to your unsecured, nonpriority creditors.

If you need a longer repayment period to pay all required debts, you can propose a 60-month plan.

In fact, many debtors who qualify for a 36-month plan instead opt for a 60-month plan so that their plan payment is lower. For example, suppose you are trying to save your home from foreclosure and you owe $36,000 in back mortgage payments. If you are eligible for and propose a 36-month plan, you will have to pay at least $1,000 per month to catch up in 36 months ($1,000 x 36 months = $36,000). However, if you propose a 60-month plan, your plan payment might be as low as $600 per month ($600 x 60 months = $36,000). This can be critical to your bankruptcy's success if you have a tight budget.

By now, you should understand that it's possible to propose a confirmable Chapter 13 plan without paying anything to your unsecured, nonpriority creditors—including credit card companies and hospital bills—assuming you have no nonexempt property (see below).

RESOURCE

Get help calculating expenses in Chapter 13. If your disposable income falls short, it might be because you've deducted too many expenses or misinterpreted the meaning of a particular expense. There are many twists and turns to accurately computing the appropriate expenses in a Chapter 13 case, whether you are using the IRS expenses or actual expenses. A bankruptcy lawyer versed in the new law can be very helpful in this situation. You'll find additional guidance in *Chapter 13 Bankruptcy: Keep Your Property & Repay Debts Over Time,* by Cara O'Neill (Nolo).

Child Support and Alimony Owed to the Government

The general rule is that a Chapter 13 plan may be confirmed only if it provides for all priority debts to be paid in full over the life of the plan. However, if all of your disposable income is dedicated to repayment of debts over a five-year period, the plan may be confirmed even if you won't be able to fully repay back child support and alimony you owe to a governmental unit (such as a child support enforcement agency) during the five-year period. But, you will still be liable for the remaining back support after your Chapter 13 discharge.

Your Proposed Payments Must Equal the Value of Your Nonexempt Assets

The total amount of payments to your unsecured creditors under your proposed plan must equal at least what those creditors would have received had you filed for Chapter 7 bankruptcy—that is, the value of your nonexempt property less what it would cost to sell the property and the amount of the trustee's commission. (Exempt property is the property you are allowed to keep if you file a Chapter 7 case. The important topic of exempt property is discussed in Ch. 1 and explained in more detail in Chs. 4 and 5.)

As emphasized throughout this book, many bankruptcy filers have little or no nonexempt property, and thus, probably need not be concerned with this particular eligibility requirement.

However, if you do have nonexempt property, you will have to perform what's called a "liquidation analysis" to determine how much your unsecured creditors would actually receive if you used Chapter 7 (and, therefore, how much they are entitled to receive under your Chapter 13 plan).

Start with the value of your equity in the property. If a portion of the property is exempt, subtract the exempt amount. For example, many states exempt up to a certain amount of equity in a car. If you own a car outright that's worth $10,000, and the exemptions you are using allow you to exempt $4,000 of equity in a car, your total nonexempt amount is $6,000.

Next, subtract the trustee's commission. This amount represents what the trustee would get to keep if your property were taken and sold in a Chapter 7 case. Because this amount would not be distributed to your creditors, you can subtract it from the amount you have to pay them in a Chapter 13 case.

For each item of property sold, the trustee gets 25% of the first $5,000, 10% of the next $50,000, and 5% of the rest up to $1 million. So, if you have a nonexempt bank account containing $25,000, the trustee gets to keep $1,250 (25% of $5,000) plus $2,000 (10% of the remaining $20,000) for a total of $3,250. Put another way, your creditors would receive $21,750 instead of $25,000.

In addition to the trustee's commission, you can also subtract the costs of taking the property and selling it. For certain types of property, there are few (if any) costs of sale. Cash on hand, bank accounts, and investments that can easily be converted to cash fit within this category of property. However, other types of property—such as a home, a car, or furniture—have significant resale costs. Because your unsecured creditors wouldn't get any of this money in a Chapter 7 case, they also aren't entitled to it in your Chapter 13 case. And, because personal property (a piano or furnishings, for example) often sells at auction for significantly less than its replacement value, you might be able to argue for an even lower total.

You Have Taken an Approved Personal Financial Management Course

As in Chapter 7, you (and your spouse, if you're filing jointly) are required to take a course on personal financial management before you can obtain a Chapter 13 discharge. This course is known by several names, including predischarge counseling and budget counseling. It's important to distinguish this mandatory counseling from the credit counseling you were required to take before you filed your bankruptcy. This course takes about two hours and can be taken online or by phone, the same as with credit counseling. As with the credit counseling, you are entitled to pay on a sliding scale if you can't afford the full price. As a general rule, you can save some money if you sign up with the same company for both counseling sessions—the one before you file and the one after you file.

You must provide evidence that you've completed the counseling on or before the date of your last plan payment. Otherwise, the court will not issue your Chapter 13 discharge. For more information about these counseling agencies, visit the U.S. Trustee website at www.justice.gov/ust. Click on "Credit Counseling & Debtor Education."

Avoidable Transfers Don't Require a Guilty Mind

The concept of avoidable transfers is actually a simple one. When you file bankruptcy, all your property is part of your bankruptcy estate. This property consists of the property you own on the date you file (if there is sufficient equity) and, in some circumstances, the property you had before you filed. Whether you sold the property for less than its market value—for instance, a $3,000 car to a friend for $1,000—or just gave it away, it doesn't matter. It also doesn't matter whether your method of sale was direct—cash in exchange for the property—or a retitling that resulted in your interest being transferred to the other party. The property belongs to your bankruptcy estate and it's the trustee's job to avoid the transfer (collect it for the benefit of your creditors).

If your mindset was innocent—you had no idea you were going to file for bankruptcy when you transferred the property—the trustee will simply collect it from the transferee and distribute it to your creditors according to bankruptcy priority rules. Your bankruptcy won't be affected. However, if it appears that you deliberately got rid of it because you were planning your bankruptcy, the trustee can take your case to the bankruptcy judge and ask that your bankruptcy discharge be denied. Whether the judge denies your discharge will depend on the individual facts of your case.

Other Issues That Might Affect Your Decision to File

Sometimes you find yourself in a situation that does not prohibit you from filing for bankruptcy, but might produce consequences you don't want—such as the dismissal of your case, your inability to discharge a debt, or the trustee's taking back money that you recently paid to a relative or business associate. Understanding the rules for prefiling transfers of property and presumptions of fraud will help you decide if you should wait before filing for bankruptcy.

Prefiling Transfers of Real and Personal Property

Certain types of prefiling activities have such serious consequences that, as a practical matter, they render you ineligible to file bankruptcy for a period of time. Transactions involving the gift or sale of any type of personal property or real estate during the two-year period immediately preceding your filing date are heavily scrutinized in bankruptcy.

The basic problem here is that some filers are tempted to unload various assets so that the bankruptcy trustee won't find and seize the property and sell it for the benefit of the creditors. These transactions often take the form of selling the property to a friend or relative for a nominal amount, such as $1.00 with the understanding that the friend will cough up the property after the bankruptcy is completed. Other common examples are taking one's name off of a joint account, deed, or vehicle title (which is really a gift of half of the property to the other owner).

EXAMPLE: You want to file for Chapter 7 bankruptcy but you realize that you are listed on a deed as the co-owner of property where a friend is living—which was necessary to buy the property because your friend had bad credit. After learning that the trustee could take that property and sell it for the benefit of your unsecured creditors, you have yourself taken off the deed before filing. In your bankruptcy papers, you would have to list that transaction, and then the bankruptcy trustee might sell the property and recover your share of the proceeds.

Whatever form it takes, a prebankruptcy gift or sale for substantially less than the property is worth is frequently judged to be a fraudulent transfer, which can result in the transferred property being seized and sold for the benefit of the creditors, and the bankruptcy being dismissed. And even if you convince the bankruptcy trustee that you had an honest intent, the trustee can still demand that the person to whom you transferred the property give it back to be sold for the benefit of the creditors. And in these situations, it usually is not possible to claim the transferred property as exempt, which means you won't get any of the sale proceeds.

Lawyers are often asked, how will the trustee find out about a particular transfer? If title is involved (as with cars, boats, and real estate), the transfer will show up in the trustee's routine search of the various state and local databases (such as the DMV) that would document the transfer. Also, when you go to your creditors' meeting, you must affirm under oath that you've truthfully answered the questions in the Statement of Intention for Individuals Filing Under Chapter 7, the form where you are asked about prebankruptcy transfers. Trustees are skilled in picking up any discrepancy on this point. If they suspect something is wrong, they can follow up the meeting by questioning you under oath in a deposition-like proceeding. The bottom line: Don't ever assume that the trustee won't find out about your transfers. And, more importantly, it's a bad idea to commit perjury. The punishment could involve going to jail.

When all is said and done, some property that is transferred prior to bankruptcy could easily have been retained and claimed as exempt. As for any remaining property, it's better to let it go, or, if you don't want to lose (or pay for) it, not to file at all.

Preference Payments

A basic principle of bankruptcy law is that all creditors deserve to be treated fairly in comparison to each other. In many cases, fair treatment means that no one gets anything. In some cases, your unsecured creditors share in the proceeds if the trustee takes your nonexempt property and sells it.

This principle is undermined if you make a payment to some creditors and not others before you file for bankruptcy. Payments like these might be considered "preferences" because you are favoring some creditors over others. When payments qualify as preferences, the trustee can demand that the creditor return the money to your bankruptcy estate, where it will be divided equally among all of your creditors (subject to any exemptions you can claim).

For consumer debtors (those whose debts are primarily for personal debt rather than business debt), any payment of more than $600 might be considered a preference if it was made within a year to insider creditors (business associates or close relatives), or within three months to others (see below). If, however, you are a business debtor—that is, a majority of your debt arises from your business activities—the court will look only at transactions that exceed $6,825. (How to determine whether you are a business debtor for purposes of this rule is explained above.)

Payments to Insiders

The time period during which payments will be considered a preference depends on whether the creditor is an insider (a business associate, friend, or relative). If you pay more than $600 (or $6,825 if you are primarily a business debtor) to any creditor who's an insider during the year before you file for bankruptcy, that payment is a preference. For example, if you use your tax refund to pay back an emergency loan from your sister, brother,

or mother, you have preferred that creditor over your other unsecured creditors. Bluntly put, when in bankruptcy, you are required to treat your mother and Visa equally.

EXAMPLE: In October, Robyn borrows $2,000 from her mother to pay off a supplier. In March of the following year, Robyn receives a tax refund of $3,000. She pays her mother back and uses the remaining $1,000 to catch up on other bills. Even though no one could blame Robyn for paying back her mom, this would likely be considered a preference payment if she files for bankruptcy within the year. She'll have to disclose it in her bankruptcy paperwork, and her mom might have to come up with the money.

There is one important exception to this rule: A payment to an insider won't be considered a preference if you made the payment more than 90 days prior to filing for bankruptcy and you weren't insolvent at the time. For example, if you repaid a $3,000 loan from your mother more than three months before you file, and you can show that the value of your assets was greater than your liabilities at the time you repaid her, the payment won't be considered a preference. This insolvency rule also applies to preferences to noninsiders.

Insolvency is presumed during the 90-day period before you file for bankruptcy, so if you made a preference payment within the past 90 days, you should expect it to be undone if you file for bankruptcy.

Payments to Others

If the creditor is not an insider, but instead is a regular "arms-length" creditor like most of your business creditors, such as a vendor or credit card company, the rules are different. The court will look at your transactions with that creditor for only three months before you file for bankruptcy. During this time period, any payment of more than $600, or $6,825 if you are primarily a business debtor, will be considered a preference.

Payment of criminal restitution, like other debts, can be considered a preference if it is made within the three-month period prior to your bankruptcy filing and is over the $600 threshold.

Antecedent Debt Rule

To qualify as a preference, the payments must be made on an "antecedent" debt. In other words, the debt must already be past due and owing. Even if you are current on an account, it might still qualify as an antecedent debt. For example, you might be current on a large credit card debt because you have been making the minimum monthly payments. As long as interest is being charged on the underlying debt, however, it will be considered an antecedent debt, and paying off the debt would be considered a preference.

Payments Made in the Ordinary Course of Business or Financial Affairs

A payment is not a preference if it is made in the ordinary course of business or the debtor's financial affairs.

EXAMPLE: Avery, a masonry contractor, owes Tom's Tile $3,500 from a past job. Although it's always been Avery's practice to immediately pay for supplies as soon as he's paid for the job, he hasn't paid Tom's Tile because of a dispute over the quality of materials provided. Avery lands another job, for which he secures $10,000 worth of tile on credit from ABC Masonry Supplies. Two months later, when he is paid for the job, he pays ABC $10,000, which brings his ABC account current. This transaction would most likely qualify as one made in the ordinary course of Avery's business, because it meets his normal practice of immediately paying his suppliers.

Regular payments for personal expenses—such as utilities or services—typically also qualify as payments made in the ordinary course of business or financial affairs, rather than preferences. And regular monthly payments on long-term debt (for example, making a usual monthly payment on a mortgage, credit card bill, or student loan) also fall within this exception.

Even if a payment to a creditor was not made in the ordinary course of business or financial affairs, it still might escape the trustee's clutches if the debtor receives "new value" as a result of making the payment. This means the debtor is receiving some current benefit for making the payment, not just paying off an old debt. For instance, let's say Avery, from the example above, paid off Tom's Tile so he could order more materials on credit from that company. This extension of credit might be considered new value received for paying off the old debt, which means the payment wouldn't be a preference.

TIP

Transferring balances may be a preference. At least one court has found that transferring a balance from one credit card to another might be considered a preference. In this case, the debtor used her credit on one credit card to pay off her debt on another credit card. Because she made the transfer within three months of filing for bankruptcy, and she could have used the money for any purpose (in other words, she didn't have to use it to pay off her other card), the court ruled that the transfer was a preference. (*In re Dilworth*, 560 F.3d 562 (8th Cir. 2009).)

If You've Made Preference Payments

The consequences of violating the preference rules can be harsh for the person who received the payment. The bankruptcy trustee is authorized to take back the money and distribute it among your creditors. If you paid back a family member, this might cause some tension. Even if you paid back a creditor that isn't an insider, it could cause problems. For example, if you paid back a credit card issuer so you could keep your card, the issuer will probably revoke your credit card if it has to cough up the money to the trustee. The same problem could come up if you paid a debt to a core vendor or a commercial landlord or an equipment leasing company.

The trustee doesn't have to go after every preference payment. For example, the trustee might decide not to go after a preference if the cost of suing to collect it would outweigh the amount to be gained.

If you can claim an exemption that covers an involuntary preference, the trustee has even less incentive to pursue it. (An example of an involuntary preference is when a creditor takes your money through wage garnishment or a bank levy.) However, you cannot claim an exemption to cover voluntary preference payments.

Even though you can't pay a favorite creditor before you file, nothing prevents you from doing so after you file, as long as you do it with income earned after you file for bankruptcy or with property that isn't in your bankruptcy estate.

Presumptions of Fraud

If you charge a credit card for an amount exceeding $725 for luxuries within three months of filing, or take out a cash advance from any single creditor exceeding $1,000 within 70 days before filing, the charge or advance will be presumed to be fraudulent if the creditor challenges it in court.

You can also get into trouble if you:

- run up large debts for luxury items when you clearly are broke and have no way to pay the debts, or
- conceal property or money from your spouse during a divorce proceeding.

These activities cast suspicion of fraud over your entire bankruptcy case. (These debts are discussed further in Ch. 3.)

How Bankruptcy Affects Your Debts

Most people consider bankruptcy because they want to get rid of debts quickly in Chapter 7 bankruptcy or over time using a Chapter 13 repayment plan. Many debts get wiped out regardless of the chapter chosen. However, some do not—debtors are responsible for paying "nondischargeable" debts during the Chapter 13 case or after the Chapter 7 concludes.

If you successfully complete bankruptcy, you will receive a court notice discharging all qualifying debts. Although the notice will list the types of debts discharged, it won't tell you the particular debts eliminated in your case. This chapter explains what you can expect to be discharged in Chapters 7 and 13 and which obligations you might still owe at the end of your bankruptcy case.

Debts That Will Be Discharged in Bankruptcy

Whether you file for Chapter 7 or Chapter 13 bankruptcy, certain types of debts will be discharged and you'll no longer be responsible for repaying them. In a Chapter 7 bankruptcy, you won't have to repay any portion of these debts directly: The bankruptcy trustee will divide your nonexempt assets (if you have any) among your creditors, then the court will discharge any amount that remains unpaid. In a Chapter 13 bankruptcy, your repayment plan will most likely provide for some portion of these debts to be paid back but not necessarily in full. If you complete your plan successfully, the remaining unpaid amount will be discharged.

Credit Card Debts

Without a doubt, the vast majority of those who file for bankruptcy are trying to get rid of credit card debts. Happily for these filers, the vast majority of bankruptcies succeed in this mission. With a few rare exceptions for cases involving fraud or luxury purchases made immediately before your bankruptcy (outlined in "Debts That Survive Chapter 7 Bankruptcy," below), you can expect to get rid of your credit card debt in a Chapter 7 or Chapter 13 bankruptcy.

Medical Bills

Many people who file for bankruptcy are in financial trouble because of medical bills. Millions of people are inadequately insured or have high-deductible plans that require them to pay thousands of dollars out of pocket.

Luckily, bankruptcy provides an out: Your medical bills will be discharged at the end of your bankruptcy case.

Lawsuit Judgments

Most civil court cases are about money. If someone wins one of these lawsuits against you, the court issues a judgment ordering you to pay. If you don't come up with the money voluntarily, the judgment holder is entitled to collect on it by, for example, withdrawing the funds in your bank account, levying your wages, or placing a lien on your home.

Money judgments and the debts that underlie them are almost always discharge able in bankruptcy, regardless of the facts that led to the lawsuits in the first place. There are a couple of exceptions (discussed in "Debts That Survive Chapter 7 Bankruptcy," below), but in the vast majority of cases, money judgments are discharged. Even liens on your home arising from a court judgment can be canceled if they interfere with your homestead exemption. (See "Voluntary Secured Debts Are Dischargeable, But the Lien Remains the Same," below.)

Obligations Under Leases and Contracts

Increasingly in our society, things are leased rather than owned, be it a lease of real property (such as an apartment) or personal property (such as a car). If you enter into a lease contract and then become unable to make the monthly payment or otherwise perform your obligations under the lease, there will be consequences. The other party might want to hold you to the deal, and failing that, expect you to pay damages as a result of your breach (the damages are typically a reasonable, predetermined amount, or the actual financial hit the other

party takes when you don't come through). If you don't pay what you owe, the other party can go after you in a lawsuit.

Some debtors also have ongoing contractual obligations, such as a contract to sell or buy real estate, buy a business, deliver merchandise, or perform in a play. The other party might want to force you to hold up your end of the deal and could sue you for breach of contract damages if you fail to perform.

Obligations and liabilities under these types of agreements can also be canceled in bankruptcy. Almost always, filing for bankruptcy will wipe out your lease or contractual obligation if you want to get out of it.

If you wish, you can choose to keep the contract or lease in effect by "assuming" it. For example, you might have a time-share contract that you have been paying on for years and are close to paying off. Rather than canceling the contract, you might want to keep it in effect. Or, you might be leasing your car and want to "assume" the lease. You indicate your choice—whether to assume or reject a lease or contract—in a document called a Statement of Intention for Individuals Filing Under Chapter 7.

Personal Loans and Promissory Notes

Money you borrow in exchange for a promissory note (or even a handshake and an oral promise to pay the money back) is almost always dischargeable in bankruptcy.

As with any debt, however, the court might refuse to discharge a loan debt if the creditor can prove that you obtained the loan fraudulently. But that rarely happens, and it's unlikely to take you by surprise. Most people know when someone might accuse them of engaging in fraud.

Debts Owed to Coborrowers Who Paid the Original Debt

If you have jointly incurred a debt with another person, and that person pays off the debt in full, the debt you owe to the cosigner for your share of the debt (that was paid off) is dischargeable in Chapter 7 bankruptcy. However, this rule doesn't necessarily apply if the coborrower is your spouse and you have taken responsibility for payment of the debt in a divorce or separation agreement. You should always list coborrowers as creditors in your bankruptcy.

Other Obligations

The sections above outline the most common debts that are discharged in bankruptcy, but this isn't an exhaustive list.

Voluntary Secured Debts Are Dischargeable, But the Lien Remains the Same

Secured debts are typically contractually linked to specific items of property, called collateral. If you don't pay the debt, the creditor can take the collateral. The most common voluntary secured debts include loans for cars and homes.

If you have a voluntary debt secured by collateral, bankruptcy eliminates your personal liability for the underlying debt—that is, the creditor can't sue you to collect the debt itself. But bankruptcy doesn't eliminate the creditor's hold, or "lien," on the property that served as collateral under the contract.

Other types of secured debts arise involuntarily, often as a result of a lawsuit judgment or an enforcement action by the IRS on taxes that are old enough to be discharged. In these cases too, bankruptcy gets rid of the underlying debt, but might not eliminate a lien placed on your property by the IRS or a judgment creditor. However, you might be able to get rid of involuntary judgment liens that are attached to property you can exempt. (See "Avoiding Judicial Liens" in Ch. 6 for more on this.)

Chapter 7 bankruptcy offers several options for dealing with secured debts, ranging from buying certain types of property from the creditor for its replacement value, reaffirming the debt, surrendering the property, or (in some cases) getting rid of the debt while keeping the property and continuing to make payments as before. Secured debts and options for dealing with them in Chapter 7 bankruptcy are discussed in Ch. 6.

Actually, you can pretty much count on discharging any obligation or debt unless it fits within one of the exceptions discussed below.

Debts That Survive Chapter 7 Bankruptcy

Under bankruptcy law, there are several categories of debt that are "not dischargeable" in Chapter 7 (that is, you will still owe them after your bankruptcy is final):

- Some of these debts can't be discharged under any circumstances.
- Some will not be discharged unless you convince the court that the debt fits within a narrow exception to the rule.
- Some might survive your bankruptcy, but only if the creditor files a formal objection and convinces the court that they should.

Debts Not Dischargeable Under Any Circumstances

There are certain debts that bankruptcy doesn't affect at all: You will continue to owe them just as if you had never filed.

Domestic Support Obligations

Obligations defined as "domestic support obligations" are not dischargeable. Domestic support obligations are child support, alimony, and any other debt that is

in the nature of alimony, maintenance, or support.

To be nondischargeable under this section, a domestic support obligation must have been established—or must be capable of becoming established—in:

- a separation agreement, divorce decree, or property settlement agreement
- an order of a court that the law authorizes to impose support obligations, or
- a determination by a child support enforcement agency (or another government unit) that is legally authorized to impose support obligations.

Other Debts Owed to a Spouse, Former Spouse, or Child

You can't discharge any debt you owe to a spouse, former spouse, or child that was incurred:

- in the course of a divorce or separation, or
- in connection with a separation agreement, divorce decree, or other court order.

Simply put, debts you owe to a child or former spouse because of a divorce are not dischargeable in Chapter 7. However, they can be discharged in Chapter 13—see "Debts Discharged in Chapter 13 (But Not in Chapter 7)," below.

Importantly, while your Chapter 7 bankruptcy will get rid of your obligation to pay the creditor, you are still liable to your exspouse for your share if the creditor goes after him or her for payment. Assume, for example, that Leah and Paul agree in their marital settlement agreement that Paul will be responsible for the couple's credit card debt of roughly $50,000, while Leah will assume responsibility for the family car, a 2019 BMW on which they owe $50,000. If Paul files for bankruptcy, he will no longer owe anything to the credit card creditors, but if the creditors try to collect from Leah as a joint debtor, Leah can hold Paul responsible. Similarly, if Leah defaults on the BMW and files bankruptcy after a deficiency judgment of $20,000 is obtained, Paul can sue Leah for the $20,000 if he is forced to pay it. Of course, if both Leah and Paul file bankruptcy, then they are both freed of obligations to the creditors. In this situation, filing for Chapter 13 could wipe out a spouse's ability to recover against the other because Chapter 13 will wipe out a responsibility to pay under a property division agreement.

Fines, Penalties, and Restitution

You can't discharge fines, penalties, or restitution that a federal, state, or local government has imposed to punish you for violating a law. Examples include:

- fines or penalties imposed under federal election law (these might be dischargeable in Chapter 13)
- fines for infractions, misdemeanors, or felonies
- fines imposed by a judge for contempt of court
- fines imposed by a government agency for violating agency regulations
- surcharges imposed by a court or an agency for enforcement of a law, and
- restitution you are ordered to pay to victims in federal criminal cases.

Certain Tax Debts

Regular income tax debts are dischargeable if they are old enough and meet the other requirements (discussed below). Other types of taxes might not be dischargeable at all. The specific rules depend on the type of tax, as well as the unique rules of your state. For instance, in California, you can't discharge income tax debt if you filed your return late.

Fraudulent income taxes. You cannot discharge debts for income taxes if you didn't file a return or you were intentionally avoiding your tax obligations.

Property taxes. Property taxes aren't dischargeable unless they became due more than a year before you file for bankruptcy. However, even if your personal liability to pay the property tax is discharged, the tax lien on your property will remain. From a practical standpoint, this discharge is not meaningful because you'll have to pay off the lien before you can transfer the property with clear title. In fact, you might even face a foreclosure action by the property tax creditor if you take too long to come up with the money.

Other taxes. Other types of taxes that aren't dischargeable are business related: payroll taxes, excise taxes, and customs duties. Sales, use, and poll taxes are also probably not dischargeable.

Debt Incurred to Pay Nondischargeable Taxes

In a Chapter 7 bankruptcy, you can't discharge debts that you incurred to pay taxes owed to a government entity. For example, if Jose uses his Visa card to pay his income taxes of $2,000, Visa can bill Jose for the $2,000 after the bankruptcy is over. Similarly, if Valentina borrows $5,000 from her credit union to pay her property tax, the debt will survive her bankruptcy.

This type of debt is dischargeable in a Chapter 13 bankruptcy, however. For instance, if Jasmine owes $25,000 in back taxes after an audit, and uses a credit card to pay it off, she would be on the hook for $25,000 after a Chapter 7 bankruptcy. However, if she files for Chapter 13, she can get rid of the balance of the debt when her plan ends after three or five years (the length of her plan will depend on her income), even though her plan had been paying pennies on the dollar toward the debt.

 SEE AN EXPERT

Get help for business tax debts. If you owe any of these nondischargeable tax debts, see a bankruptcy attorney before you file.

Court Fees

If you are a prisoner, you can't discharge a fee imposed by a court for filing a case, motion, complaint, or appeal, or for other costs and expenses assessed for that court filing, even if you claimed that you were unable to afford the fees. (You can discharge these types of fees in Chapter 13 —see "Debts Discharged in Chapter 13 (But Not in Chapter 7)," below.)

Intoxicated Driving Debts

If you kill or injure someone while you are driving and are illegally intoxicated by alcohol or drugs, any debts resulting from the incident aren't dischargeable. Even if a judge or jury finds you liable but doesn't specifically find that you were intoxicated, the debt might still be nondischargeable if you were impaired during the accident. The judgment against you won't be discharged if the bankruptcy court (or a state court in a judgment collection action) makes an independent determination that you were, in fact, intoxicated.

Note that this rule applies only to personal injuries: Debts for property damage resulting from your intoxicated driving are dischargeable. And these types of debts might be dischargeable in

Chapter 13 bankruptcy if a judgment has not yet been entered.

Condominium, Cooperative, and Homeowners' Association Fees

You cannot discharge fees assessed after your bankruptcy filing date by a membership association for a condominium, housing cooperative, or lot in a homeownership association if you or the trustee have an ownership interest in the condominium, cooperative, or lot. As a practical matter, any fees that become due after you file for Chapter 7 bankruptcy will survive the bankruptcy, but fees you owed before filing will be discharged. Like property taxes, you'll continue to be assessed homeowner fees until you're no longer the legal owner of the property. (You might be able to discharge postfiling fees in Chapter 13 —see "Debts Discharged in Chapter 13 (But Not in Chapter 7)," below.)

Debts for Loans From a Retirement Plan

If you've borrowed from your 401(k) or another retirement plan that qualifies under IRS rules for tax-deferred status, you'll be stuck with that debt. You can, however, discharge a loan from a retirement plan in Chapter 13—see "Debts Discharged in Chapter 13 (But Not in Chapter 7)," below. But you might owe income taxes on the discharged amount.

Debts You Couldn't Discharge in a Previous Bankruptcy

If a bankruptcy court dismissed a previous bankruptcy case because of your fraud or other bad acts (misfeasance), you cannot discharge any debts that you tried to discharge in that earlier bankruptcy. (This rule doesn't affect debts incurred since the date you filed the earlier bankruptcy case.)

Debts Not Dischargeable Unless You Can Prove That an Exception Applies

Some debts cannot be discharged in Chapter 7 unless you show the bankruptcy court that the debt falls within an exception. The two most common examples of this type of debt are student loans and certain taxes.

Student Loans

Student loans are very difficult to discharge. The law excludes student loans from the discharge, whether they are issued or insured by the government or a nonprofit institution, or by a private commercial lender (provided that the loan is a qualified education loan incurred by an individual). To qualify as an education loan, the loan must contain certain payback provisions that give the borrower a tax deduction and some slack in times of economic difficulty or when attending an educational institution. The only way out of an educational loan in bankruptcy is to establish undue hardship, which is harder to do than you might think.

To discharge your student loan on the basis of "undue hardship," you must file a separate action in the bankruptcy court and obtain a court ruling in your favor on this issue. To succeed, an action to discharge a student loan debt typically requires the services of an attorney, although it's possible to do it yourself if you're willing to put in the time. (See Ch. 10 for general information about going to bankruptcy court.)

In determining undue hardship, most bankruptcy courts look at three factors (listed below). If you can show that all three factors are present, the court is likely to grant you an undue hardship discharge of your student loan. These factors are:

- **Poverty.** Based on your current income, you cannot maintain a minimal living standard and repay the loan.
- **Persistence of hardship.** Your current financial condition is likely to continue indefinitely—that is, your situation is hopeless or virtually hopeless. This factor is most likely to be present if you are elderly or you or a spouse has a disability that restricts your opportunities to earn a decent living.
- **Good faith.** You've made a good-faith effort to repay your debt. (You're not likely to be granted a hardship discharge if you file for bankruptcy immediately after getting out of school or if you haven't looked extensively for employment and made efforts to maximize your income.)

> ### Rules for PLUS Loans
>
> Parents can get Parental Loans for Students (PLUS Loans) to finance a child's education. Even though the parent does not receive the education, the loan is treated like any other student loan if the parent files for bankruptcy. The parents must meet the undue hardship test to discharge the loan.

Although it's changed somewhat in recent years, many courts are reluctant to discharge student loans. They take the position that Congress wants student loans to be repaid, absent exceptional circumstances. They also recognize that federal student loan regulations require a lot of flexibility on the creditor's part, including moratoriums on payments, temporary reductions in payments, and extensions of the repayment period that lower the monthly payments to an affordable amount. These options give debtors other ways (short of filing for bankruptcy) to seek relief from student loan debt.

In some cases, however, courts have found that it would be an undue hardship to repay the entire loan and relieved the debtor of a portion of the debt. Other courts take the position that it's an all-or-nothing proposition—either the entire loan is discharged or none of it is discharged. Ask a local bankruptcy attorney how courts in your area handle student loans.

Regular Income Taxes

People who are considering bankruptcy because of tax problems are almost always concerned about income taxes they owe to the IRS or the state equivalent. There is a myth afoot that income tax debts are not discharged in bankruptcy. This is not true if you are able to meet certain conditions. Here are the specifics.

In most jurisdictions, you can discharge federal or state income tax debt in Chapter 7 bankruptcy if all of the following are true:

- You filed a tax return for the tax year or years in question (some jurisdictions require a timely filing).
- The return was filed at least two years before your bankruptcy filing date.
- The tax return was due at least three years before you file for bankruptcy (usually that is either April 15th of the following year or October 15th if you requested an extension).
- The taxing authority has not assessed your liability for the taxes within the 240 days before your bankruptcy filing date (this time period can be extended if the IRS has suspended collection activities because of an offer in compromise or a previous bankruptcy filing).
- You did not willfully attempt to evade the tax.
- You meet all other jurisdictional requirements. For instance, some jurisdictions won't discharge taxes if you filed a late return.

EXAMPLE: Dimitri filed a tax return in August 2016 for the 2015 tax year. In March 2017, the IRS audited Dimitri's 2015 return and assessed a tax due of $8,000. In May 2019, Dimitri files for bankruptcy. The taxes that Dimitri wishes to discharge were for tax year 2015. The return for those taxes was due on April 15, 2016, more than three years prior to Dimitri's filing date in May 2019. The tax return filed in August 2016 was at least two years prior to Dimitri's bankruptcy filing date. Finally, the assessment date of March 2017 was well prior to 240 days of the filing date. There is no evidence that Dimitri schemed to not pay his tax (in other words, that he illegally tried to avoid paying). Because Dimitri met all five conditions for discharging an income tax liability, and his jurisdiction doesn't have other requirements he must meet, Dimitri can discharge those taxes.

Even if you meet each of the five requirements for discharging tax liability, any lien placed on your property by the taxing authority will remain after your bankruptcy. The result is that the taxing authority can't go after your bank account or wages, but you'll have to pay off the lien before you can sell your real estate with a clear title.

However, if your property is essentially worthless or has no equity after your bankruptcy discharge, ask for an "abatement" of the lien; the taxing authority might release the lien.

Taxes Due Under Late-Filed Returns

According to most bankruptcy courts, a late-filed return does not constitute a "return" for purposes of the second prong in the above criteria for discharging tax debt. Your return is "late" if all of your filing extensions have expired and the IRS has filed a substitute return without your assistance. (These courts make an exception if the IRS files a substitute return with your assistance under Internal Revenue Code Section 6020(a)—something the IRS might, but is not obligated, to do.) However, some courts (notably the Eighth Circuit Court of Appeals as well as various lower courts in other jurisdictions) don't follow this reasoning. Instead, they might allow you to discharge income taxes even if you file a late return, as long as you meet the other criteria. If you have filed a late tax return, talk to a bankruptcy lawyer.

CAUTION

Debts incurred to pay nondischargeable taxes will also be nondischargeable in Chapter 7 bankruptcy. If you borrowed money or used your credit card to pay taxes that would otherwise not be discharged, you can't eliminate that loan or credit card debt in Chapter 7 bankruptcy. In other words, you can't turn a nondischargeable tax debt into a dischargeable tax debt by paying it on your credit card. (Note: These debts can be discharged in Chapter 13 bankruptcy, however, as explained below.)

Debts Not Dischargeable in Bankruptcy If the Creditor Successfully Objects

Four types of debts might survive Chapter 7 bankruptcy, but only if both:

- the creditor files a formal objection —called a complaint to determine dischargeability—during the bankruptcy proceedings, and
- the creditor proves that the debt fits into one of the categories discussed below.

Debts From Fraud

In order for a creditor to prove that one of your debts should survive bankruptcy because you incurred it through fraud, the debt must fit one of the categories below.

Debts from intentionally fraudulent behavior. If a creditor can show that a debt arose because of your dishonesty, the court probably will not let you discharge the debt. Here are some common examples:

- You wrote a check for something and stopped payment on it, even though you kept the item.
- You wrote a check against insufficient funds but assured the merchant that the check was good.
- You rented or borrowed an expensive item and claimed it was yours in order to use it as collateral to get a loan.
- You got a loan by telling the lender you'd pay it back, when you had no intention of doing so.

- You received payments from unemployment insurance or another benefit program because of your fraud or misrepresentation.

For this type of debt to be nondischargeable, your deceit must be intentional, and the creditor must have relied on your deceit in extending credit or awarding benefits. Again, these are facts that the creditor has to prove before the debt will be ruled nondischargeable by the court. Keep in mind, however, that a creditor will likely have a seemingly valid case—and you'll have to defend against it. Given the seriousness (and potential criminal ramifications) of fraud charges and the complexity of defending yourself in a lawsuit, it's likely that you'll want to bring in an attorney. Therefore, it's not advisable to file a bankruptcy case without first consulting with a bankruptcy professional if you suspect that a creditor might accuse you of fraud.

Debts from a false written statement about your financial condition. If a creditor proves that you incurred a debt by making a false written statement, the debt isn't dischargeable. Here are the rules:

- The false statement must be written—for instance, made in a credit application, rental application, or resume.
- The false statement must have been "material"—that is, it was a potentially significant factor in the creditor's decision to extend you credit. The two most common materially false

statements are omitting debts and overstating income.

- The false statement must relate to your financial condition or the financial condition of an "insider"—a person close to you or a business entity with which you're associated.
- The creditor must have relied on the false statement, and the reliance must have been reasonable.
- You must have intended to deceive the creditor. This is extremely hard for the creditor to prove based simply on your behavior. The creditor would have to show outrageous behavior on your part, such as adding a "0" to your income (claiming you make $180,000 rather than $18,000) on a credit application.

Again, if you suspect that a creditor might accuse you of providing a false written statement, consult with an attorney about the potential risks you'll face if you choose to move forward with bankruptcy.

Recent debts for luxuries presumed fraudulent. If you run up more than $725 in debt to any one creditor for luxury goods or services within the 90 days before you file for bankruptcy, the law presumes that your intent was fraudulent regarding those charges. The charges will survive your bankruptcy unless you prove that your intent wasn't fraudulent. The term "luxury goods and services" does not include things that are reasonably necessary for the support and maintenance of you and your dependents (what that means will be decided on a case-by-case basis).

If Your Debts Will Be Discharged Unless a Creditor Objects

Even though creditors have the right to object to the discharge of certain debts, many creditors—and their attorneys—don't fully understand this right. And a creditor might decide to write off the debt rather than contesting it. It can cost a lot to bring a "dischargeability action" (as this type of case is called). If your debt isn't huge, a creditor might find it cheaper to forgo collecting the debt rather than to fight about it in court.

Finally, if a creditor or the trustee does object in either of these situations, you may be able to settle the debt for much less than it would have taken to pay it off.

For these reasons, you'll want to consider your total debt burden, as well as the cost and stress involved in defending a dischargeability action (a type of lawsuit). If you are filing primarily to get rid of a debt that won't be discharged if a creditor objects, you might end up with a bankruptcy on your record for nothing. If, on the other hand, you have other debts that will certainly be discharged (such as credit card debts), those debts will be gone after you file for bankruptcy, even if a creditor successfully objects to the discharge of one debt.

If you suspect that a creditor might challenge the dischargeability of a particular debt on fraud grounds, you should discuss your concern with an attorney before moving forward. Such matters can come with penalties, including criminal fines and incarceration.

Recent cash advances presumed fraudulent. If you get cash advances from any single creditor totaling more than $1,000 under an open-ended consumer credit plan within the 70 days before you file for bankruptcy, the debt is presumed to be nondischargeable. "Open-ended" means there's no date when the debt must be repaid, but rather, as with most credit cards, you could take forever to repay the debt as long as you pay a minimum amount each month. Again, the presumption means that if someone objects, you have to prove your intention was not fraudulent.

 RELATED TOPIC

Additional information on credit card issuers' attempts to have credit card debt declared nondischargeable because of fraud is provided in Ch. 9.

Debts Arising From Debtor's Willful and Malicious Acts

If the act that caused the debt was both willful *and* malicious (that is, you intended to inflict an injury to person or property), the debt isn't dischargeable if the creditor successfully mounts an objection in the bankruptcy court.

Generally, crimes involving the intentional injury to people or damage to property are considered willful and malicious acts. Examples are assaults, battery, rape, arson, or vandalism.

Other acts that would typically be considered to be willful and malicious include:

- kidnapping
- deliberately causing extreme anxiety, fear, or shock
- libel or slander
- illegal acts by a landlord to evict a tenant, such as removing a door or changing the locks, and
- trademark and copyright infringement.

If you were simply careless (you should have taken more care, as is true in most automobile accidents), or even reckless (for example, you caused an injury by driving far too fast), the debt will still be discharged.

Willful and Malicious Acts Are Different in Chapter 13

In Chapter 7 bankruptcy, these debts are nondischargeable only if the underlying act is found by the court to be both willful *and* malicious. Under Chapter 13 bankruptcy, however, the underlying act need only be willful *or* malicious. On the other hand, debts for property damage, which can survive Chapter 7 under the willful and malicious rule, can be discharged in a Chapter 13 bankruptcy.

Debts From Embezzlement, Larceny, or Breach of Fiduciary Duty

A debt incurred as a result of embezzlement, larceny, or breach of fiduciary duty is not dischargeable if the creditor successfully objects to its discharge.

"Embezzlement" means taking property entrusted to you for another and using it for yourself. "Larceny" is another word for theft. "Breach of fiduciary duty" is the failure to live up to a duty of trust you owe someone, based on a relationship where you're required to manage property or money for another, or where your relationship is a close and confidential one. Common fiduciary relationships include those between:

- business partners
- attorney and client
- estate executor and beneficiary
- guardian and ward, and
- husband and wife.

And even a debt resulting from mere negligence committed by a fiduciary could be nondischargeable.

Debts or Creditors You Don't List

Bankruptcy requires you to list all of your known creditors on your bankruptcy papers and provide their most current addresses. This gives the court some assurance that everyone who needs to know about your bankruptcy will receive notice. As long as you do your part, the debt will be discharged (as long as it's otherwise dischargeable under the rules), even if the official notice fails to reach the creditor for some reason beyond your control—for example, because the post office errs or the creditor moves without leaving a forwarding address.

Suppose, however, that you forgot to list a creditor on your bankruptcy papers or carelessly misstated a creditor's identity or address. In that situation, the court's notice might not reach the creditor and the debt could survive your bankruptcy. Here are the rules:

- If the creditor knew or should have known of your bankruptcy through other means, such as a letter or phone call from you, the debt will be discharged even though the creditor wasn't listed. In this situation, the creditor should have taken steps to protect its interests, even though it didn't receive formal notice from the court.

- If all of your assets are exempt—that is, you have a "no-asset" case—the debt will likely be discharged (unless the debt is otherwise nondischargeable). In this situation, the creditor wouldn't have benefited from receiving notice anyway, because there is no property to distribute. However, if the lack of notice deprives a creditor of the opportunity to successfully object to the discharge by filing a complaint in the bankruptcy court (such as for a fraudulent debt), the debt could survive your bankruptcy.

If an Unknown Creditor Pops Up After Bankruptcy

If a creditor comes out of the woodwork after your bankruptcy case is closed, you can always reopen your case, name the creditor, and then seek an amended discharge. If it's the kind of debt that will be discharged anyway, many courts won't let you reopen because there is no need to. The debt is discharged by law and most creditors know this. However, if the creditor continues to try to collect the debt, you can haul the creditor into the bankruptcy court on a contempt charge (for violating the court's discharge order).

Debts That Survive Chapter 13 Bankruptcy

The typical Chapter 13 plan pays 100% of back child support, back taxes, and other debts classified as priority debts, and some percentage of other nonpriority unsecured debts, depending on the debtor's disposable income, the amount of priority debts, and the value of the debtor's nonexempt property. (See Ch. 2 for more on Chapter 13 plans.) This section explains what happens to any remaining nonpriority, unsecured debt when your Chapter 13 plan is complete.

As in Chapter 7, several categories of debt might not be discharged in Chapter 13 bankruptcy:

- Some debts can't be discharged under any circumstance and you'll be stuck with them after your case is over.
- Student loans won't be discharged unless you convince the court that it would be an undue hardship to pay off the loan.
- Fraudulent debts won't be discharged, but only if the creditor convinces the court that they shouldn't be.

Debts Not Dischargeable Under Any Circumstances

Certain types of debts survive Chapter 13 bankruptcy, regardless of your income or circumstances.

Domestic Support Obligations

In both Chapter 7 and Chapter 13, child support and alimony debts you owe directly to an ex-spouse or child are nondischargeable. (See "Debts That Survive Chapter 7 Bankruptcy," above, for more on these obligations.) Your Chapter 13 repayment plan must provide for 100% repayment of these debts. In some instances, you might be able to pay less than 100% of these debts through your plan if you commit all of your disposable income to a plan that lasts five years. However, the unpaid portion will not be discharged in your bankruptcy. The same goes for support owed to a governmental child support collection agency—you might not have to pay 100% through your

plan, but you will remain on the hook for the remaining unpaid portion after your bankruptcy.

EXAMPLE: In the final decree issued in his divorce, Dimitri was ordered to pay his ex-wife $500 a month for child support. Shortly after the divorce, Dimitri's ex-wife applied for welfare and assigned her child support rights to the county providing the welfare. Over time, Dimitri fell behind on his child support to the tune of $25,000 principal and interest. When Dimitri files for bankruptcy under Chapter 13, his plan—later confirmed by the court—requires him to pay $15,000 of the $25,000 arrearage. When Dimitri receives his Chapter 13 discharge, he will still owe the $10,000 that won't be paid through his plan.

Criminal Penalties

Debts you owe on fines or restitution orders contained in the sentence for conviction of any crime (yes, even traffic tickets) won't be discharged in Chapter 13.

Fines or Penalties Owed to a Government Agency

If you have been fined by a government agency for some reason, or subjected to a penalty or a forfeiture of property, this debt will not be discharged. However, if the government agency assesses the fine because you were overpaid benefits due to your failure to report income or for some other faulty behavior, only the fine itself is not dischargeable. The amount you were overpaid is dischargeable like any other unsecured debt. However, if the agency files an action in court alleging that you obtained the overpayment through fraud, the court can rule that the overpayment is not dischargeable.

> **EXAMPLE:** Maya was receiving unemployment insurance benefits, and then found a job. While she originally intended to report the job to the unemployment insurance agency—which would result in a termination of the benefits—she found that her wages were insufficient for her needs and decided to continue receiving the unemployment benefits. When she was caught about six months later, she had received over $10,000 in overpayments. She signed an agreement to repay the $10,000 overpayment as well as a $5,000 fine because of her intentionally fraudulent behavior. In bankruptcy, the $5000 fine is not dischargeable as matter of law. However, the $10,000 would be discharged unless the government agency filed an affirmative action in bankruptcy court, asking the judge to except the overpayment from discharge because of fraud.

Certain Taxes

Recent income tax debts—those that first became due within the three-year period prior to your filing date—are priority debts and have to be paid in full in any Chapter 13 plan. If your Chapter 13 ends prematurely for any reason, the tax debts you have not yet repaid will remain; you will either have to pay them outside of bankruptcy or convert your Chapter 13 to a Chapter 7 bankruptcy. (See "Debts That Survive Chapter 7 Bankruptcy," above, for information on which taxes are dischargeable.) If there is evidence in the tax records that you tried to avoid your duty to file an honest return or pay your taxes, the taxes will survive bankruptcy without exception. If you operated a business, you can't discharge taxes related to the business. A trust tax is an amount that you hold on behalf of the taxing agency, such as employee withholdings and sales tax.

Intoxicated Driving Debts

If you operate a vehicle while illegally intoxicated by alcohol or drugs, and you kill or injure someone, any debt arising out of the injury is not dischargeable if the claimant obtained a court judgment prior to your bankruptcy filing. But what if you are sued and the judge or jury finds you liable but doesn't specifically find that you were intoxicated? This might not help you: The judgment against you won't be discharged if the bankruptcy court (or a state court in a judgment collection action) determines that you were, in fact, intoxicated.

Note that this rule applies only to personal injuries: Debts for property damage resulting from your intoxicated driving will be dischargeable.

Debts Arising From Your Willful or Malicious Actions

To prevent a debt resulting from a willful or malicious action from getting wiped out, a creditor will likely need to bring an action in bankruptcy court and ask the court to determine whether the act involved in the underlying judgment meets the willful or malicious injury standard. It isn't always clear. If the court finds that a creditor's civil court judgment against you was due to your willful or malicious act, the judgment will be nondischargeable.

You can expect the bankruptcy court to give the underlying state court judgment great deference, so unless you can prove that your actions weren't willful or malicious, don't count on prevailing.

For example, O.J. Simpson was acquitted of criminal charges but found liable, in a civil suit, for wrongful death—which fits the definition of a "willful or malicious act." Under this rule, O.J. would likely not be able to discharge the debt in Chapter 13 bankruptcy.

Note that the act which gives rise to the debt need only be willful *or* malicious to be nondischargeable in Chapter 13, which greatly expands the types of debt that will survive discharge. For instance, a judgment for injury caused by your reckless driving would most likely survive Chapter 13 bankruptcy on the ground of "maliciousness," whereas it might be discharged in Chapter 7 because reckless driving, though malicious, is seldom considered willful.

Finally, unlike Chapter 7, which includes damage to property, this exception to a Chapter 13 discharge applies only to debts arising from personal injury or death.

Debts or Creditors You Don't List

Bankruptcy requires you to list all your creditors on your bankruptcy papers and provide their most current addresses. That way, the court can mail out notice of your bankruptcy with the best chance of reaching them. If you do your part and the official notice fails to reach a creditor for some reason beyond your control— for example, because the post office errs, or the creditor moves without leaving a forwarding address—the debt will still be discharged (as long as it is otherwise dischargeable). Also, if the creditor knew or should have known of your bankruptcy through other means, such as a letter or phone call from you, the debt will be discharged.

Suppose, however, that you forget to list a creditor on your bankruptcy papers or carelessly misstate a creditor's identity or address. In that situation, the court won't notify the creditor and the debt almost always will survive your bankruptcy (unless the creditor wouldn't have received any payments under your plan, a very rare occurrence). The general rule is that debts not listed in a Chapter 13 case survive the bankruptcy. This means, of course, that you should be extra careful to list all of your creditors in a Chapter 13 case. Also, if a creditor fails to file a proof of claim, you would be well advised to file one for it, especially if the claim is for secured debt.

Student Loans

As in Chapter 7, a student loan cannot be discharged in Chapter 13 unless you show the bankruptcy court that paying the loan back would be a substantial hardship. See "Debts That Survive Chapter 7 Bankruptcy," above, for more on the rules for discharging student loans.

Fraudulent Debts

Debts based on fraud, theft, or breach of fiduciary duty are not dischargeable in Chapter 13. (See "Debts That Survive Chapter 7 Bankruptcy," above, for a description of these types of debts.) However, the discharge is not automatic. Bankruptcy courts in Chapter 13 cases use the same procedure for determining the dischargeability of

these debts as they use in Chapter 7 cases—that is, the debt will be discharged if the creditor fails to come forward and establish fraud in the bankruptcy court.

Student Loan Interest Might Be Discharged in a Chapter 13 Plan

In *United Student Aid Funds, Inc. v. Espinosa*, 559 U.S. 260 (2010), the Chapter 13 debtor submitted a plan, which the bankruptcy court confirmed, that provided for payment of the student loan principal but discharge of the accrued interest. The lender did not object and the interest was discharged upon completion of the plan. The lender then attempted to collect the interest it considered due, arguing that discharge of a student loan, and accompanying interest, could only be accomplished if the debtor sues the lender in an adversary action to determine the loan's dischargeability, and the court finds repayment of the loan would constitute an undue hardship. The U.S Supreme Court refused to set aside the discharge order, ruling that the lender had actual notice of the bankruptcy (and the plan that provided for the discharge of the interest), and could have appeared in the bankruptcy to protect its rights. However, the Supreme Court made clear that discharging student loans (rather than interest) through plan confirmation violates the bankruptcy code and it's uncertain how courts will treat this situation in the future.

If You Convert From One Chapter to Another

In most cases, bankruptcy filers can convert their cases from one chapter to another. If, for example, a court finds that a Chapter 7 filing is an abuse of the bankruptcy system under the means test, the filer can convert to Chapter 13 rather than dismissing the case altogether. Or, you may decide to convert because a particular debt will only be discharged in Chapter 13, for example, or because you won't be able to complete a Chapter 13 repayment plan. In order to convert your case, however, the court must be convinced that your conversion was made in good faith. Once you make the switch, you are subject to the dischargeability rules of the chapter to which you converted, not the chapter you started out using.

EXAMPLE: Connie files for Chapter 13 bankruptcy because she owes a lot of debt from a divorce and has been told that those debts can be discharged in Chapter 13 but not in Chapter 7. Connie proposes a feasible Chapter 13 plan that pays only 25% of her divorce-related debt. Halfway through the plan, Connie loses her job and can't continue her payments. She converts to Chapter 7. Her Chapter 7 discharge won't include the divorce-related debts. However, Connie will receive a credit for the amounts she paid on those debts during her Chapter 13 case.

Debts Discharged in Chapter 13 (But Not in Chapter 7)

Certain debts that cannot be discharged in Chapter 7 (see "Debts That Survive Chapter 7 Bankruptcy," above) can be discharged in Chapter 13. They are:

- marital debts created in a divorce or settlement agreement
- debts incurred to pay a nondischargeable tax debt
- court fees
- condominium, cooperative, and homeowners' association fees incurred after the bankruptcy filing date on property you have given up (in most courts)
- debts for loans from a retirement plan
- debts that couldn't be discharged in a previous bankruptcy, and
- fines or penalties imposed under federal election law.

How Joint Debts Are Handled

Debts for which you have a joint debtor— another person who owes the debt along with you—raise some tricky issues. Let's look at the different kinds of joint debtors and how your bankruptcy filing might affect them.

Cosigners and Guarantors

A cosigner or guarantor is someone who signs onto your debt in order to back up or guarantee your payment. If you don't

Bankruptcy, Joint Debtors, and Preferences

If you file for Chapter 7 bankruptcy and have a joint debtor who is a relative, close friend, or business associate, the joint debtor might have to pay the bankruptcy trustee any amount that you owe the creditor on the loan. Here's how this works.

As mentioned in Ch. 2, when you file for bankruptcy, the bankruptcy trustee will look to see whether you made any payments to creditors within the 90 days before you filed—or within one year of filing, if those payments were made to, or for the benefit of, a relative or close business associate. These payments are called "preferences" and they're not permitted if they exceed certain limits. The idea is that you shouldn't be allowed to single out certain creditors for special treatment just before you file for bankruptcy.

If you make a preferential payment to a creditor, the bankruptcy trustee can demand that the creditor turn over the amount of payment to the trustee, so that it can be divided equally among your unsecured creditors. If the creditor pays up and the debt is then discharged in bankruptcy, you won't owe anything, but your joint debtor will be on the hook for whatever remains of the original debt.

If the creditor can't or won't cough up the preference money you paid, the trustee could sue the creditor. But an easier route for the trustee might be to go after your joint debtor—who benefited from the preference because your payment wiped out or reduced his or her liability for the debt. In this scenario, believe it or not, the joint debtor would have to pay the trustee the amount of the preference. The joint debtor then continues to be liable for the debt, less the amount of the preference kept by the creditor.

Fraudulent transfers are closely related to preferences. If, in the applicable statute of limitations period before filing for bankruptcy, you transfer property to a friend, a relative, or another insider without an exchange of equal value, the transfer might be considered fraudulent. (The applicable statute of limitations period is always two years or more, depending on state laws applied by the trustee.) Fraudulent transfers give the trustee the right to seize the transferred property for the benefit of your creditors. Fraudulent transfers could also result in the denial of your bankruptcy discharge.

pay, the cosigner or guarantor is legally responsible for payment. If you discharge a debt for which you have a cosigner or guarantor in Chapter 7, your joint debtor will still owe the entire thing, even though you are no longer on the hook to repay it.

If you want to file for Chapter 7 bankruptcy but don't want to stick your cosigner or guarantor with the debt, you can try to make an agreement with the creditor to reaffirm the debt—that is, to continue to owe it after your bankruptcy ends.

> **TIP**
>
> **It's usually better to reimburse the cosigner than to reaffirm the debt.** For a variety of reasons, it's almost always a good idea to discharge the debt and agree to owe your cosigner for any potential liability, rather than to reaffirm it and continue to owe your original creditor. This approach gives you more flexibility regarding repayment than you'd have if you defaulted on your payments to the regular creditor under a reaffirmation agreement. Also, the creditor could decide not to try to collect from the cosigner, which means neither one of you would have to repay the debt. And finally, it's possible that the cosigner will also decide to file bankruptcy.

If you file for Chapter 13 bankruptcy, assuming the cosigned or guaranteed debt is a consumer and not a business debt, you can include it as part of your repayment plan, and your joint debtor will not be pursued during your bankruptcy case— typically, at least three years. If you can, you should pay the debt in full during your case. If you don't, you will be entitled to discharge whatever balance remains when your case is over (assuming the debt is otherwise dischargeable in a Chapter 13 bankruptcy). But in that situation, the creditor can still go after the joint debtor for the balance.

Spousal Responsibility for Debts

Married people can file for bankruptcy jointly or separately. If they file jointly, all of their debt is subject to the rules explained above. If only one spouse files, state marital property rules determine which debts qualify for discharge.

Community Property Rules

Some states use what's called a "community property" system to determine who owns the marital property, including debts. These states are Arizona, California, Idaho, Louisiana, Nevada, New Mexico, Texas, Washington, and Wisconsin. (Spouses in Alaska can elect to have their property treated as community property, if they make a written agreement to that effect.)

In community property states, both spouses owe debts incurred by either spouse during the marriage even if one spouse incurs a debt without the other spouse's knowledge. These are termed "community" debts. Debts incurred by a spouse prior to the marriage are considered separate debts, as are debts incurred after separation and divorce.

For example, when Justine and Paul marry in California, each has about $10,000 in credit card debt. In addition, Paul owes taxes to the IRS and Justine owes her uncle $3,000 on a loan she used to buy a car. After they marry, Justine and Paul buy a home and take out a second mortgage a few years later. They also obtain an unsecured loan of $15,000 from a bank to buy a car. When hard times hit in 2020, they separate. Shortly after the separation, Justine starts using the credit cards that are in her name only and adds an additional $20,000 to her personal debt. Under these facts, all the credit card debt is separate debt because Paul and Justine incurred it either before marriage or after separation. So, too, is Justine's debt to her uncle and Paul's debt to the IRS. However, the home mortgages and the bank loan are community debts.

In bankruptcies filed in community property states, community debts are discharged as to community property, even if only one spouse files—which means the nonfiling spouse will benefit from the filing spouse's discharge. This is often called a "phantom discharge" and it protects all community property, even property that the couple acquires in the future. This discharge of community debts, however, does not protect the nonfiling spouse's separate property. The discharge also does nothing to get rid of the nonfiling spouse's separate debts; these will survive the bankruptcy.

Using the facts in the previous example, if Justine files for bankruptcy in a community property state, she will discharge her credit card debt and her debt to her uncle. The debt owed on the house, although a community debt, will be handled differently because it is secured debt. (See Ch. 7 for more on how secured debts are treated in bankruptcy.) The bank loan is also community debt and will likely be discharged as to Justine's separate property and as to the couple's community property, even though Paul doesn't file. Justine's bankruptcy will not affect Paul's separate credit card debt or his separate debt to the IRS.

However, if Justine had used joint credit cards after separating from Paul, those creditors could still collect from Paul, just as they would be able to collect from any other cosigner. The lesson learned: If you separate from your spouse, consider removing your spouse's name from all your accounts.

Common Law Property Rules

All states that don't use the community property system for dealing with marital debts are termed common law states. The rules for those states are a bit simpler. All debts either spouse incurs before the marriage are that spouse's separate debts.

Debts incurred during the marriage might be either separate or joint: If the debt is jointly undertaken (for example, it was incurred from a joint account or the creditor considered the credit information of both spouses in deciding to extend the loan) or the debt benefits the marriage (for example, the debt was for necessary items, such as food, clothing, or child care), it is jointly owed by both spouses. Otherwise, a debt that one spouse incurs separately remains that spouse's separate debt.

When one spouse files for bankruptcy in a common law state, the only debts that come into play are that spouse's separate debts and any debts that can be classified as joint. The other spouse's separate debts continue unaffected by the bankruptcy filing.

Business Partners

As a general rule, all partners are responsible for partnership debts unless the partnership has special provisions limiting the liability of certain classes of partners (as in a limited partnership). If you are in a partnership and file for bankruptcy, you can get rid of your personal liability for partnership debts. However, the remaining partnership and individual partners (if there are any—often partnerships are dissolved if one partner leaves or declares bankruptcy) will still be on the hook. ●

Your Property and Bankruptcy

This chapter explains what happens to the property you own when you file for bankruptcy. It also covers exemptions—the rules that determine which property you can keep, which property you'll have to give up in Chapter 7 bankruptcy, and, in some cases, how much you have to pay out in Chapter 13 bankruptcy.

In Chapter 7, if property is "exempt," you will be able to keep it; you have to forfeit nonexempt property or property that is worth more than the applicable exemption, to the bankruptcy trustee to pay off your creditors.

In Chapter 13, if property is not exempt, your plan will have to provide that your unsecured creditors will be paid at least as much as the value of the nonexempt property minus sales costs. The rule is that Chapter 13 creditors are entitled to receive the same amount that they would receive from nonexempt assets in a Chapter 7 bankruptcy. In essence, this would amount to the value of the property, less any exemption you would be entitled to, less costs of sale, and less the trustee's commission.

In this chapter, we focus only on what happens to personal property (any type of property other than real estate) you own outright. Ch. 5 discusses what happens to real estate, including how bankruptcy can be used to deal with foreclosures. Ch. 6 explains what happens to personal property that is collateral for a debt you are making payments on.

CAUTION

Exempt property can be taken to pay child support, alimony, and taxes. This chapter explains the rules that protect certain types of property from being seized by creditors or the bankruptcy trustee to pay your debts. However, your exempt property is not protected if you owe money to a former spouse for child support or alimony: These obligations must be met, even if it means that you lose property that would otherwise be exempt. The same goes for overdue taxes: The taxing authority or the bankruptcy trustee might be able to take otherwise exempt property.

Many Chapter 7 filers emerge from bankruptcy with their property intact because most of what they own is exempt and the benefit to the creditors of seizing and selling what is not exempt is often not worth the cost. But that is not always the case. Also, in Chapter 13, you are entitled to keep your property regardless of its value, but your plan must pay your unsecured creditors at least as much as they would have received had you filed a Chapter 7 bankruptcy. (See Ch. 2 for more on this.)

Your Bankruptcy Estate

The assets you own on the day you file for bankruptcy is called your "bankruptcy estate." With a few important exceptions (discussed below), property and income you acquire after you file for Chapter 7 bankruptcy aren't included in your bank-ruptcy estate. When you file for bankruptcy, the forms you have to fill out require you to list all of your assets.

What's in Your Bankruptcy Estate

The broad categories of property that make up your bankruptcy estate are described below.

Property you own and possess when you file. Everything in your possession that you own, whether or not you owe money on it—for example, a car, real estate, clothing, books, television, stereo system, furniture, tools, boat, artworks, or stock certificates—is included in your bankruptcy estate. Property that you have in your possession but belongs to someone else, such as the car your friend stores in your garage or the television you borrowed from your sister, is not part of your bankruptcy estate because you don't have the right to sell it or give it away.

Property you own but don't possess when you file. You can own something even if you don't have physical possession of it. For instance, you might own a car that someone else is using. Other examples include a deposit held by a stockbroker, a security deposit held by your landlord or a utility company, or a business in which you've invested money.

Property you are entitled to receive. Property that you have a legal right to receive but haven't gotten yet when you file for bankruptcy is included in your bankruptcy estate. Common examples include:

- wages, royalties, or commissions you have earned but have not yet been paid
- a tax refund legally due you
- vacation or termination pay you've earned
- property you've inherited but not yet received from someone who has died
- proceeds of an insurance policy, if the death, injury, or other event that gives rise to payment has already occurred, and
- money owed you for goods or services you've provided, often called "accounts receivable."

Community property. If you live in a community property state, all property either spouse acquires during the marriage is ordinarily considered "community property," owned jointly by both spouses. The community property states are Arizona, California, Idaho, Louisiana, Nevada, New Mexico, Texas, Washington, and Wisconsin, and—if you have a written community property agreement or trust—Alaska.

Gifts and inheritances to only one spouse are the most common exceptions—these are the separate property of the spouse who receives them. If you're married and file jointly for bankruptcy, all the community property you and your spouse own, as well as all of both of your separate property, is considered part of your bankruptcy estate. If your spouse doesn't file, then your bankruptcy estate consists of all of the community property and all of your separate property—your spouse's separate property isn't included.

Marital property in common law property states. If you are married and filing jointly in a common law state, your bankruptcy estate includes all the property you and your spouse own, together and separately. If you are filing alone for bankruptcy in a common law property state—which includes all states other than the community property states listed above—your bankruptcy estate includes:

- your separate property (property that has only your name on a title certificate or that was purchased, received as a gift, or inherited by you alone), and
- half of the property that is jointly owned by you and your spouse, unless you own the property as tenants by the entirety.

CAUTION

"Tenancy by the entirety" property often is handled differently in bankruptcy. Property you and your spouse jointly own as "tenants by the entirety" usually receives special protection in bankruptcy if (1) it is located in Delaware, the District of Columbia, Florida, Hawaii, Illinois, Indiana, Maryland, Massachusetts, Michigan, Missouri, North Carolina, Pennsylvania, Tennessee, Vermont, Virginia, or Wyoming and (2) only one spouse files for bankruptcy. In that event, the filing spouse's creditors (and therefore the bankruptcy court) typically cannot take property that both spouses own as tenants by the entirety. If both spouses file, however, this protection doesn't apply. If you and your spouse own "tenancy by the entirety" property, consult a local bankruptcy lawyer before you file.

Certain property you acquire within 180 days after filing for bankruptcy. Most property you acquire or become entitled to after you file for bankruptcy isn't included in your bankruptcy estate. But there are a few exceptions. If you acquire or become entitled to the following items within 180 days after you file, you must notify the trustee:

- an inheritance through a will or by operation of law or through a living trust, a beneficiary designation, or through any other transfer device that occurs upon a person's death where the death occurs within the 180-day period
- property you receive or have a right to receive from a marital settlement agreement or divorce decree, and
- death benefits or life insurance policy proceeds.

Unless an exemption applies, the trustee can take this property and distribute it to your creditors.

Revenue generated by estate property. This type of property typically consists of the proceeds of contracts—such as those providing for rent, royalties, and commissions—that were in effect at the time of the bankruptcy filing, but which produced earnings after that date. For example, if you are a composer or an author and receive royalties each year for work that was written before you filed for bankruptcy, the trustee could collect those royalties as property of your estate. Proceeds from work you do after your filing date belong to you.

Property that appreciates in value after you file. If you own property that has appreciated in value after you file for bankruptcy, the amount of the appreciation is also part of your bankruptcy estate and, absent an available exemption, can be taken by the trustee right up until the time your bankruptcy case is closed. For example, assume your home has equity worth $100,000 when you file and you live in a market where the real estate prices are appreciating. The trustee decides to keep your case open. A few years later, while your case is still open, the equity in your home appreciates to $150,000 and your exemption protects only $100,000. At this point the trustee can decide to sell your home, give you the $100,000 exemption, and use the $50,000 to pay your unsecured creditors.

Property you transferred prior to your bankruptcy. The rules discussed in Ch. 2 regarding preferences and fraudulent transfers create a type of property—

property illegally transferred or paid out in a preference—that is considered part of your bankruptcy estate. However, since by definition you no longer own or have possession of the property, the bankruptcy trustee is authorized to "avoid" the transfer or preference—this means the trustee can sue the party who has received the property to have it returned to the bankruptcy estate, and then sell the property for the benefit of your creditors.

Consignment goods. Under the bankruptcy code, property your business stocks on a consignment basis, such as folk art in a crafts shop or jewelry in a consignment store, is generally considered to be an asset of your business and can be liquidated without payment to the people who have placed the property with you on consignment.

Property That's Not Part of Your Bankruptcy Estate

Property that is not in your bankruptcy estate is not subject to the bankruptcy court's jurisdiction, which means that the bankruptcy trustee can't take it to pay your creditors under any circumstances.

The most common examples of property that doesn't fall within your bankruptcy estate are:

- Social Security payments, whether they be past, present, or future (Section 407 of the Social Security Act)
- property you buy or receive after your filing date (with the few exceptions described above)

- property in your possession that belongs to someone else (for instance, property you are storing for someone), and
- wages that are withheld, and employer contributions that are made, for employee benefit and health insurance plans.

CAUTION

Even if they are technically part of your bankruptcy estate, most retirement plans are exempt, which means you'll get to keep them anyway. For example, IRAs and 401(k) plans are exempt in all states although the exemption for IRAs is limited to $1,362,800 per person (this figure will adjust on April 1, 2022).

Inventory Your Property

If you decide to file for bankruptcy, you'll be required to list all property that belongs in your bankruptcy estate. Whether you can hold on to that property, or at least some of the property's value in dollar terms, depends on what the property is worth, which exemptions are available to you, and what type of bankruptcy you file. The best way to start finding out what you'll be able to keep in Chapter 7 or pay out in Chapter 13 is to create a list of your property and match it with the available exemptions.

The simplest strategy is to start with the property items that you are most interested in keeping and worry about the rest if you actually file for bankruptcy. Or, you can be more systematic and list everything in your bankruptcy estate. If you're married and plan to file jointly, enter all property owned by you and your spouse. Use Worksheet E: Personal Property Checklist located on this book's online companion page at www.nolo.com/back-of-book/ FIBA.html to identify the property in your bankruptcy estate.

Value Your Property

Use Worksheet F: Property Value Schedule to figure out what each item is worth. You'll find the form below and you can download it from this book's companion page at www.nolo.com/back-of-book/FIBA.html.

It's easy to enter a dollar amount for cash and most investments. If you own a car, start with the middle *Kelley Blue Book* price or, alternatively, the middle price calculated by the National Automobile Dealers Association. If the car needs repair, reduce the value by what it would cost you to fix the car. You can find the *Kelley Blue Book* at a public library or online at www.kbb.com. Alternatively, you can use the valuations provided at www.nada.com.

Worksheet F: Property Value Schedule

List the total replacement value of each item in your Personal Property Checklist.

Item	Replacement Value
1. Cash	$ _____
2. Bank accounts	_____
3. Security deposits	_____
4. Household goods and furniture	_____
5. Books, pictures, etc.	_____
6. Clothing	_____
7. Furs and jewelry	_____
8. Sports and hobby equipment	_____
9. Interest in insurance	_____
10. Annuities	_____
11. Pensions and profit-sharing plans	_____
12. Stock and interest in business	_____
13. Interest in partnership and ventures	_____
14. Bonds	_____
15. Accounts receivable	_____
16. Alimony and family support	_____
17. Other liquidated debts, tax refund	_____
18. Future interests and life estates	_____
19. Interests due to another's death	_____
20. Other contingent claims	_____
21. Intellectual property rights	_____
22. Licenses and franchises	_____
23. Vehicles	_____
24. Boats, motors, and accessories	_____
25. Aircraft and accessories	_____
26. Office equipment, furniture, and supplies	_____
27. Machinery, fixtures, etc.	_____
28. Inventory	_____
29. Animals	_____
30. Crops—growing or harvested	_____
31. Farm equipment	_____
32. Farm supplies, chemicals, and feed	_____
33. Anything not listed above	_____
TOTAL	$ _____

For bankruptcy purposes, compute the property's replacement value—what it would cost to buy identical property from a retail merchant taking into account its age and condition. When online, you can visit eBay (www.eBay.com) to get a fix on the going price for just about anything. Or briefly describe the item in Google or another search engine and see what turns up. You should use the lowest value you can find because you'll be more likely to be able to keep the property under your state's exemption laws.

If you own something jointly with someone other than a spouse with whom you're filing for bankruptcy, reduce the value of the item to reflect only the portion you own. For example, suppose you and your brother invest in craft brewing equipment worth $10,000. Your ownership share is 40% and your brother's is 60%. You should list the value of the property you own as $4,000, not $10,000.

If you are married and filing separately in a community property state, you'll need to include the total value of all the community property as well as the value of your separate property.

If you are married and own the property with your spouse as tenants by the entirety, your ownership interest might not be 50% for purposes of computing your exemption. Talk to a lawyer to find out what percentage of your tenancy by the entirety property you can claim as exempt.

Understanding Exemptions

Bankruptcy is intended to give debtors a fresh start—not to leave them utterly destitute. You are entitled to keep certain property that the laws applicable to your bankruptcy categorize as exempt. Creditors cannot take exempt property as part of their collection efforts, and the bankruptcy trustee can't take it, either. Exempt property can literally range from "the shirt on your back" to a million-dollar estate, depending on which exemptions you are entitled to use.

State Exemption Systems

Every state has its own fairly lengthy list of exempt property. You can find these lists on this book's online companion page at www.nolo.com/back-of-book/FIBA.html.

Also, some states offer bankruptcy filers an alternative choice of exemptions—a list of exempt property found in the federal Bankruptcy Code. States that allow filers to choose between state and federal exemptions include Arkansas, Connecticut, Hawaii, Massachusetts, Michigan, Minnesota, New Hampshire, New Jersey, New Mexico, Oregon, Pennsylvania, Rhode Island, Texas, Vermont, Washington, and Wisconsin. In these states, you must one exemption system—mixing and matching isn't allowed.

Although California doesn't make the federal Bankruptcy Code exemptions available, it has two separate exemption systems—both created by state law. Debtors who use the California exemptions must choose between System 1 (the regular state exemptions available to debtors in and out of bankruptcy) and System 2 (state exemptions available only in bankruptcy). Here, too, filers can't mix and match exemptions from both sets.

Be Careful of Joint Ownership Accounts

Joint accounts are often created for purposes other than ownership of the funds in the account. For example, a parent commonly puts an adult child on an account to provide an easy means of inheritance. When the parent dies, the account automatically goes to the adult child. Or, the adult child might be added to the account to handle economic transactions for the parent. In these situations, it's clear to the parent and adult child that the funds belong to the parent. But absent a formal statement of this fact when setting up the account, it might not be clear to anyone else. For instance, suppose the adult child filed for bankruptcy. A Chapter 7 bankruptcy trustee might reasonably view the account as belonging to the filer and the parent, and try to seize some or all of it as part of the bankruptcy estate. Fortunately, most trustees are sensitive to these issues and will work with filers who demonstrate proof of ownership.

How Exemptions Work

Under both the federal and state exemption systems, some types of property are exempt regardless of value. For example, in some states, home furnishings, wedding rings, or clothing are exempt without regard to value. In Washington, DC, homes are exempt regardless of the value of the bankruptcy filer's equity in the home. Your equity is the amount you would get to keep if you sold the property.

Other exemptions allow a filer to protect equity up to a limited value. For instance, the home equity exemption ranges from nothing in New Jersey to $15,000 in Missouri to $500,000 in Massachusetts, to no limit other than acreage in Florida, Texas, and a few Midwestern states. And exemptions for vehicle equity typically range from $2,500 to $5,000.

When there is a dollar limit on an exemption, any equity above the limit is considered nonexempt. Even though a portion of your ownership in these items is exempt, the trustee can seize and sell property in which your equity exceeds the exemption limit, give you your exemption amount, and distribute the remainder to your unsecured creditors.

Many states offer a "wildcard" exemption —a dollar amount that you can apply to any property, in order to make it (or more of it) exempt. This type of exemption typically runs from a few hundred to several thousand dollars (more than $30,000 in

California's System 2 exemptions). If you use the federal exemptions, the wildcard is up to $13,900 for individuals and $27,800 for couples.

Where You Make Your Home

When we refer to the state "where you make your home," we mean the place where you are living and intend to remain living for the indefinite future, the place where you work, vote, receive your mail, pay taxes, bank, own property, participate in public affairs, register your car, apply for your driver's license, and send your children to school. Congress refers to this state as your "domicile." Your domicile might be different from where you are actually living if you spend time in one state but consider another state to be your true home. For example, members of Congress or the military, professional athletes, and corporate officials all might spend significant amounts of time working in another state or country; their domicile is the state where they make their permanent home.

Domicile has been defined as "the place where a man has his true fixed and perma-nent home and principal establishment and to which whenever he is absent he has the intention of returning." This means some-thing more than your residence, which generally means wherever you are living at any given time. Even if you reside in one state, your domicile might be elsewhere—and your domicile determines which exemptions you can use.

EXAMPLE: Lucinda and Freddie file a joint bankruptcy petition in Vermont, which allows a choice between the Vermont state exemptions and the federal exemptions. Lucinda and Freddie rent their home but own a travel trailer with a value of roughly $20,000, which they want to keep. The Vermont state exemptions provide a wildcard allowance up to a maximum of $7,400, not nearly enough to protect the travel trailer. However, the federal exemptions provide a wildcard exemption for couples of $27,800 on any type of property. Lucinda and Freddie choose the federal exemptions, which also protect their other property, such as their furniture, animals, and tools of the trade.

When the Trustee Takes Property

As mentioned earlier, the trustee can seize and sell nonexempt property only in a Chapter 7 bankruptcy only. As a practical matter, the trustee won't seize and sell property unless the value of the nonexempt portion, after the costs of storage and sale are deducted, is high enough to make it worth the trustee's while. For example, even if your used furniture exceeds the exemption limit in your state, the trustee is unlikely to seize and sell the furniture unless it is quite valuable and could obviously be resold for an amount that will cover your exemption and still leave enough for your unsecured creditors to generate a decent commission for the trustee. (See "The Bankruptcy Trustee" in Ch. 1 for more on how trustees get paid.)

The kinds of property listed below typically are not exempt unless they can be covered with a wildcard exemption. If you are concerned about keeping any of these items, you should pay close attention to the exemptions that are available to you:

- interests in real estate other than your home (see Ch. 5 for more on residential property exemptions)
- substantial equity in a newer-model motor vehicle
- expensive musical instruments unrelated to your job or business
- stamp, coin, and other valuable collections
- cash, deposit accounts, stocks, bonds, and other investments
- business assets other than exempt tools of the trade
- valuable artwork
- expensive clothing and jewelry
- antiques, or
- IRAs that have been inherited and that no longer have any restrictions on withdrawal.

Residency Requirements for Exemption Claims

Some filers have to use the exemptions available in the state where they used to live—not the state in which they file. Congress became concerned about people gaming the system by moving to states with liberal exemptions just to file for bankruptcy. As a result, in 2005, it passed residency requirements filers must meet before claiming a state's exemptions. Here are the rules:

- If you have made your current state your home for at least two years, you will file in that state and use that state's exemptions (subject to the homestead cap explained in Ch. 5).
- If you have made your current state your home for more than 91 days but less than two years, you will file in that state and use the exemptions of the state where you lived for the better part of the 180-day period immediately prior to the two-year period preceding your filing.
- If you have lived in your current state for fewer than 91 days, you must wait until you have lived there for 91 days to file in that state. You'll still need to comply with other timing rules to determine which state or federal exemptions are available to you.
- If the state you are filing in offers the federal homestead exemption, you can use that exemption list regardless of how long you've been living in the state.
- If this system deprives you of the right to use any state's exemptions, you can use the federal exemptions, even if the state where you file doesn't offer this choice. For example, some states allow

their exemptions to be used only by current state residents, which might leave former residents who haven't lived in their new home for at least two years without any available state exemptions.

A longer residency requirement applies to homestead exemptions: If you acquired a home in your current state less than 40 months before your filing date, your homestead exemption could be subject to a $170,350 cap regardless of which state's exemption system you use. (Ch. 5 covers homestead exemptions in detail.)

RESOURCE

Find state exemptions online. You can search the exemptions for your state at Nolo.com.

EXAMPLE 1: Skyler lives in South Carolina from July 2019 until January 2020, when she gets lucky at a casino, moves to Texas, and buys a car for $15,000. In March 2021, Skyler files for bankruptcy in Texas. Because Skyler has been living in Texas for only 14 months —not two years—before she files for bankruptcy, she can't use the Texas exemption for cars, which can be up to $50,000 depending on the value of other personal property claimed as exempt. Because Skyler filed in March 2021,

the two-year period begins in March 2019. And because Skyler lived in South Carolina for the better part of the two-year period preceding the bankruptcy filing date, the South Carolina state exemptions are the only state exemptions available to her. As it turns out, the South Carolina exemption for cars is only $6,325, which means Skyler will probably lose her car if she uses the South Carolina state exemptions.

However, Texas offers federal exemptions as an alternative to its state exemptions. The state where a person files determines whether the federal exemptions are available, regardless of how long the person has lived in that state. So Skyler can use the federal exemptions instead of the South Carolina state exemptions. Under the federal exemptions, Skyler is entitled to exempt a motor vehicle up to $4,000— still not enough to cover her car, which is now worth $14,000. But wait. The federal exemptions also provide a wildcard of $1,325 plus $12,575 of unused homestead exemption. Skyler rents rather than owns her home so she doesn't need a homestead exemption and can add the entire wildcard of $13,900 to her $4,000 vehicle exemption, for a total exemption applicable to her car of $17,900. (The federal exemptions will adjust on April 1, 2022.)

EXAMPLE 2: Julia lives in North Dakota for many years until she moves to Florida on January 15, 2019. She files for bankruptcy in Florida on November 30, 2020. Because her two-year anniversary is January 14, 2021, Julia must use the exemptions from the state where she lived for the better part of the 180-day period preceding the two-year period—which is North Dakota. Julia's largest property item is a prepaid medical savings account deposit of $20,000. While this would be exempt under Florida law, North Dakota has no exemption for this item. Nor are the federal exemptions available in Florida. So the trustee will most likely seize the medical savings account and use it to pay Julia's creditors. Had Julia waited another month and a half to file, she would have been able to use Florida's exemptions and keep her medical savings account.

Using the Exemptions Charts

You can find the exemptions for all 50 states on this book's online companion page at www.nolo.com/back-of-book/FIBA.html. If you are considering filing for bankruptcy in one of the states listed below, you'll also want to look at the federal exemptions, which are listed right after Wyoming.

Use the exemption lists to find the applicable exemptions for your property, using the rules set out above to determine which exemptions to use. Do this by comparing the type and value of your property, and the amount of equity you have in the property, with the exemptions. (You can find definitions of many of the terms in the Glossary at the back of this book.)

States That Offer the Federal Exemptions	
Alaska	New Jersey
Arkansas	New Mexico
Connecticut	New York
District of Columbia	Oregon
Hawaii	Pennsylvania
Kentucky	Rhode Island
Massachusetts	Texas
Michigan	Vermont
Minnesota	Washington
New Hampshire	Wisconsin

Remember, if you are filing in a state that offers the federal bankruptcy exemptions, you should also check the federal exemption chart. Items that aren't exempt under the state exemptions available to you could be exempt under the federal system, and vice versa. However, you must pick one system or the other to use in your bankruptcy—you can't mix and match.

If you are married and filing jointly, you can double the federal exemptions and any state exemptions unless the chart says that you can't. This will be indicated either at the top of the chart for the particular state or next to a particular exemption.

Assuming you live in California and meet the residency requirements for claiming that state's exemptions, you can choose System 1 or System 2. If you file in California but don't meet the residency requirements, you can't use either California system—you'll have to use the rules set out above to figure out which exemptions you can use.

Federal Nonbankruptcy Exemptions

If you are using the exemptions of a particular state rather than the federal exemptions, you can also exempt property listed under Federal Nonbankruptcy Exemptions. Don't confuse those with the federal bankruptcy exemptions, which can be used only if a state allows, and only as an alternative to the state exemptions.

Your Home

One of the biggest worries most people face when deciding whether to file for bankruptcy is the possibility of losing a home. Whether you own or rent, you'll be relieved to know that the bankruptcy system is not designed to put you out on the street.

If you can get and stay current on your mortgage payments and the equity in your home is fully protected by an exemption, your chances of keeping your home in Chapter 7 are good. If, however, the equity in your home is more than you can protect, or you're behind on your payments, Chapter 7 wouldn't be a safe proposition—you'd likely lose the house. In both cases, Chapter 13 bankruptcy would likely be a better option.

If you are a renter facing eviction based on a court order, filing for bankruptcy is unlikely to improve your situation. However, if you owe back rent but your landlord hasn't obtained a judgment of eviction, you can use bankruptcy to temporarily postpone the eviction and discharge any liabilities arising from your tenancy.

In this chapter, you'll learn more about the issues homeowners and renters can expect to encounter in bankruptcy.

Homeowners Filing for Bankruptcy Under Chapter 7

If you aren't behind on your house payments, you can figure out how bankruptcy will affect your home by doing some simple math:

1. Compute your equity in your home.
2. Choose the appropriate homestead exemption.
3. Compare your equity to the homestead exemption.

If your equity is less than the homestead exemption, your home is protected. If your equity is more than the homestead exemption, your home is at risk. (See "If You Are Behind on Your Mortgage Payments," below, if you aren't current on your payments.)

Compute Your Equity

Your equity in your home is the amount you would end up with if you sold it. It's what it would cost you to sell the property *less* the amount you'd pay because of legal claims (liens) against the property by your mortgage lender, the county tax collector, or others. For now, don't include the costs of selling the house—such as closing costs or broker's fees—in your calculations. However, these costs will be important later when deciding whether your home is safe from being sold by the trustee for the benefit of your creditors.

> **EXAMPLE:** Your house will sell for $300,000. You have a mortgage for $200,000. If no other debts have to be paid out of the sales proceeds, your equity is $100,000. If there is a lien on your home, you must subtract that as

well. For example, if you didn't pay the contractor who remodeled your kitchen and the contractor put a $20,000 lien on your home, your equity would be reduced by that lien amount to $80,000.

If there's a money judgment lien on your home that would deprive you of your full homestead exemption if the property were sold, you can ask the bankruptcy judge to remove the lien. But even if you plan to petition to have the lien removed, don't include the amount of the lien when calculating your equity in the home. You can find out more about lien avoidance procedures in Ch. 10.

Assess the Fair Market Value of Your Property

When computing your equity, you must first assess your home's fair market value. When home values deteriorate, it's often difficult to know what a home is worth without actually selling it. Home values have traditionally been determined by comparables—what similar homes in the neighborhood have sold for. However, comparables are hard to come by when homes aren't being sold. And even when they are being sold, they aren't necessarily sold under normal market conditions. For example, homes that have sat empty for months as a result of a foreclosure sale might ultimately be sold to investors who

are looking for rock bottom prices. If you use sales under those conditions to judge your home's value, you might not get what you think your home is worth. Still, in the final analysis, its value can only be determined by what it would sell for, and it might not sell for much more than was paid for the distressed home down the street. Probably the best way to pin a value on your home is to find a real estate agent who can give you an estimate. The amount will be the agent's best guess at what they could get for it if you put it up for sale. Alternatively, you can use the information databases available online (see below).

Fortunately, most areas in the country have rebounded after the great recession of 2008. Now it's more likely that you'd run into the problem of having too much equity. If your home would sell for significantly more than what you owe, you have to determine whether your state's exemption laws protect the equity. Suppose the real estate market in your area appreciates quickly. In that case, you must make sure that you know the house value just before your bankruptcy filing date, so you can be sure your homestead exemption covers your equity.

Realtors in your area will know what similar homes have sold for and can give you a pretty accurate estimate of what they could get for your home. Most realtors will provide you with a written broker's price opinion free of charge.

Liens Exist Only If They're Recorded

A lien on real estate exists only if it has been recorded in the local land records office. For this reason, you can tell whether you have any liens against your property by paying that office a visit and searching its database. It's not uncommon for people to assert liens based merely on language in written agreements. For example, an agreement stating that Johnny owes Florence $2,000 and that Florence will have a lien on Johnny's home to secure repayment of the loan, does not by itself create the lien. The contract must be properly recorded.

RESOURCE

Using the Internet to find sales prices for comparable homes in your area. Information (purchase price, sales date, and address) is available free from sites including www.trulia.com, www.zillow.com, and www.realtor.com. Simply enter your home's address into the search bar.

Identify Liens on Your Property

When computing your equity, you must subtract any liens on the property. A lien is a legal claim on property that can only be removed voluntarily by the lienholder or by a court order. A mortgage, for example, is a debt that is secured by the property in the form of a lien.

Because a lien claims a right to some portion of the property's value, it "clouds" the owner's title to the property. Buyers don't want to buy property that is encumbered by liens—and insurance companies don't want to issue title insurance in this situation, either. As a practical matter, this means you will have to pay off liens to sell your house (unless you can get rid of the liens in your bankruptcy—which might be the case with liens arising from money judgments).

In addition to a mortgage, other typical liens arise from:

- second deeds of trust
- home equity loans and lines of credit
- money judgments issued by a court
- child support arrearages
- delinquent income or property taxes, and
- debts owed to people who improved the property but who weren't paid for some reason (these are called mechanic's and materialman's liens).

To compute your equity, deduct all liens on your home from its fair market value (what you could sell it for). If a lien doesn't secure a debt on your home, you don't have to count it when computing your equity.

As explained above, you shouldn't count liens that can be removed in bankruptcy when calculating your equity. See "Eliminating Liens in Chapter 7 Bankruptcy" in Ch. 6 and "Lien Avoidance Motions" in Ch. 10 for more information on lien avoidance.

Choose Your Homestead Exemption

Your homestead exemption is the amount of equity in your home you are entitled to keep if you file for Chapter 7 bankruptcy. Every state has its own homestead exemption rules—and the exemption available to you will help determine whether you keep or lose your home. However, because bankruptcy law imposes strict residency requirements on homestead exemptions, you might not qualify for the exemption you want to use. This section explains the various types of homestead exemptions available and how to figure out which one to use.

Types of Homestead Exemptions

Homestead exemptions vary tremendously from state to state. In fact, in a few states, the homestead exemption isn't a monetary amount at all—it's based on your lot size. On the other hand, in a handful of states there is no homestead exemption at all. Some states are at the other extreme and allow you to protect a very large amount of equity (for example, $500,000 in Massachusetts). In a few states, the homestead exemption is based on a combination of lot size and a monetary amount.

Homestead Exemptions Protect Only Residences

With very few exceptions, you must reside in the home as your primary residence when you file for bankruptcy to claim a homestead exemption. Homestead exemption laws do not protect second homes, vacation homes, or other real estate in which you aren't living when you file. However, they typically apply to a mobile home, an RV, or a boat used as your primary residence.

Declared Homesteads

In California and many other states, the homestead exemption automatically kicks in when you file for bankruptcy as long as you claim the exemption by listing the exemption statute in your paperwork. However, some states require you to file a Declaration of Homestead with the county recorder before using the state's homestead exemption in bankruptcy. In rare cases, some states will allow you to claim an exemption for a declared homestead even if you aren't living in the home when you file.

States That Require a Declaration of Homestead	
Alabama	Nevada
Idaho	Utah
Massachusetts	Virginia
Montana	Washington

States With Two Exemption Systems

In 19 states and the District of Columbia, you must choose between two different homestead amounts—one offered by the state and one offered under the federal Bankruptcy Code. California also offers a choice between two different amounts, but both amounts are offered under California state law. (See Ch. 4 for more on these dual systems.)

Wildcard Exemptions

In some states, you can increase the amount of your homestead exemption with a state "wildcard" exemption—that is, a dollar amount that your state allows you to apply to any property to exempt it. The chart below lists the state wildcard exemptions that you can apply to real estate; although other states have wildcard exemptions, they can be applied only to personal property.

> **EXAMPLE:** In Connecticut, the base homestead exemption is $75,000. In addition, Connecticut has a wildcard exemption of $1,000 applicable to any property. So if you don't use the wildcard exemption for another type of property, you can use it for your homestead, which would increase the exemption from $75,000 to $76,000.

State Wildcard Exemptions Applicable to Real Estate	
California	$1,550
Connecticut	$1,000
Georgia	$1,200
Indiana	$10,250
Kentucky	$1,000
Maine	$400
Maryland	$6,000
Mississippi (available if you are 70 years or older)	$50,000
Missouri ($1,250 if head of household)	$600
New Hampshire	$8,000
Ohio	$1,325
Pennsylvania	$300
Rhode Island	$6,500
Vermont	$7,400
West Virginia	$800

Tenancy by the Entirety

In 18 states, spouses are allowed to own property together in a form known as "tenancy by the entirety." If only one spouse files for bankruptcy, property the couple owns as tenants by the entirety is, generally, not part of the bankruptcy estate. In other words, the property is exempt in its entirety, regardless of its value. If both spouses file, the property will be part of their bankruptcy estate and will be subject to the appropriate homestead exemption available to the couple under the rules discussed below.

States That Allow Spouses to Own Property in Tenancy by the Entirety	
Delaware	Missouri
District of Columbia	North Carolina
Florida	Ohio
Hawaii	Pennsylvania
Illinois	Rhode Island
Indiana	Tennessee
Maryland	Vermont
Massachusetts	Virginia
Michigan	Wyoming

Choose the Appropriate Homestead Exemption

As explained in Ch. 4, residency requirements determine which exemptions filers can use. In addition to these general rules, Congress passed even stricter residency requirements for claiming a state's homestead exemption, to discourage people from moving to states with more generous homestead exemptions just to file for bankruptcy.

If You Have Been Domiciled in Your State for at Least Two Years and You Acquired Your Current Home at Least 40 Months Before Filing
You can use your current state's homestead exemption without restriction.

EXAMPLE: Marta and Peter are domiciled in Washington. They have owned their home for five years. They file for bankruptcy in Washington and can use Washington's homestead exemption without limitation because they lived in Washington for at least two years and acquired their home at least 40 months before filing their bankruptcy. Because Washington offers the federal exemption option, Marta and Peter can choose either the Washington state homestead exemption or the federal homestead exemption. As it turns out, the Washington state homestead exemption is $125,000 compared to a maximum federal homestead exemption of $50,300 for a couple filing together.

If You Have Been Domiciled in Your State for at Least Two Years and You Bought Your Home Within 40 Months of Filing, Using the Proceeds From the Sale of Another Home in the Same State
If you acquired your current home within 40 months of filing, but purchased it with the proceeds from the sale of another home in the same state that occurred at least 40 months earlier, you can use your current state's homestead exemption without restriction.

Choosing Between Exemption Systems Can Be Painful

As mentioned, California has two exemption systems and 17 states plus the District of Columbia give you a choice between the state exemptions and the federal exemptions. Sometimes it is an agonizing choice as to which system to use. For instance California System 1 allows up to $600,000 whereas System 2 only allows $29,275. On the other hand, not only does System 2 have a $1,550 wildcard exemption, but you can use any unused portion of the $29,275 homestead exemption to protect any property of your choice—essentially giving you a wildcard exemption worth $30,825. System 1 only lets you use the homestead exemption for home equity and doesn't provide a general-purpose exemption for personal property.

To see how this plays out, assume you have $50,000 worth of equity in your home and a car worth $15,000. If you use System 1, you can keep your home but you might have to give up your car, since that system only allows you to keep $3,325 worth of vehicle equity (more if your vehicle qualifies as a "tool of the trade"). In System 2, you could keep the car using the $5,850 motor vehicle exemption plus a portion or the $30,825 wildcard exemption to the $15,000 equity in your car, but you would likely lose your home. Since you can't mix or match, you'll ultimately have to choose one system or the other. However, most people elect to keep their home. In this situation, meeting with a bankruptcy attorney to find out how to minimize your loss will likely be well worth the cost.

EXAMPLE: Violet and Robin have lived in Nevada for six years. When they first moved there, they bought a home for $175,000. Three years later, they sold that home and bought another home for $250,000. Although they have owned their current home for less than 40 months, they bought it with the proceeds of another Nevada home that they purchased more than 40 months before filing. Violet and Robin can claim Nevada's homestead exemption without restriction.

If You Acquired Your Home Within 40 Months of Filing and Have Been Domiciled in Your State Two Years or More

If you acquired your current home within the previous 40 months and have made your home in your state for at least two years, you can use that state's homestead exemption, subject to a $170,350 cap.

EXAMPLE 1: Three years ago, John and Susie moved from Massachusetts to Texas, where they bought a home. If they file for bankruptcy in Texas, they can claim the Texas homestead exemption because they have lived there longer than two years. However, because they bought the Texas home within the 40 months before their bankruptcy filing, they will be limited to a homestead cap of $170,350. The Texas homestead exemption, which protects a home on up to ten city acres regardless of value, would typically protect John and Susie's equity. However, because they're subject to the cap, their protection will be limited to $170,350.

EXAMPLE 2: Massachusetts provides a homestead exemption of $500,000. After moving from Vermont to Boston in 2018, Julius and his family buy a fine old Boston home in 2019 for $700,000. After borrowing heavily against the home because of financial reversals, Julius files for bankruptcy in early 2020. At the time, Julius owns $250,000 equity in the house. Although the Massachusetts homestead exemption of $500,000 would easily cover Julius's equity, Julius can claim an exemption of only $170,350 because he acquired the Massachusetts house after moving from another state within the previous 40 months.

If You Have Lived in Your State for Less Than Two Years

If you moved to your current state within two years before filing bankruptcy, you must use the homestead exemption available in the state where you made your home for the better part of the 180-day period prior to the two-year period, subject to the $170,350 cap. However, if the state where you are filing offers the federal homestead exemption, you can use that exemption regardless of how long you've been living in that state or when you bought your home.

EXAMPLE: Eighteen months ago, Fred moved from Florida to Nevada, where he purchased his current home with $400,000 he received from a recent inheritance. Fred files for bankruptcy in Nevada, his current state. Because Fred has not lived in Nevada for two years, and because he lived in Florida for the 180 days before the two-year period preceding his bankruptcy filing, he must use Florida's homestead exemption, subject to the $170,350 cap. The cap imposes an extreme penalty on Fred. Florida's homestead exemption is unlimited while Nevada's is $550,000. However, because Fred can protect only $170,350, most of his equity in his home is nonexempt, so the trustee will sell the home, give Fred his $170,350, and distribute the balance to Fred's unsecured creditors.

If You Have Committed Certain Crimes, Torts, or Deception Against Creditors

Even if you qualify for an "uncapped" homestead exemption under the rules explained above, your exemption might be limited if you have engaged in particular types of misconduct. If you have committed a felony, a securities act violation, or certain crimes or intentional torts that have led to death or serious bodily injury, your homestead exemption might be capped at $170,350, depending on how the court sees your circumstances. For instance, the court might decide to lift the cap if it finds that the homestead in question is reasonably necessary to support yourself and your dependents.

Even if you haven't committed a crime or tort, your homestead exemption might be limited if you have tried to cheat your creditors. Suppose you have disposed of nonexempt property with the intent to hinder, delay, or defraud a creditor at any time within the ten years before you file for bankruptcy. In that case, the value of your interest in your current home could be reduced by the value of the property you unloaded, leaving you with little or no homestead protection. •

Find Your Homestead Exemption

Once you have decided which state's homestead exemption you can use, turn to this book's online companion page at www.nolo.com/back-of-book/FIBA.html to find out the homestead exemption amount for that state.

If you are married and filing jointly with your spouse, check to see whether you can double your state's homestead amount.

If the chart for your state indicates that the federal exemptions are available, compare your state's exemption with the federal homestead exemption, which currently is $25,150 for a single filer and double that for a married couple filing jointly, plus a general-purpose (wildcard) exemption of $1,325

for a single filer and double that for joint filers. So, under the federal exemptions, a married couple could exempt up to $50,300 plus $2,650 for a combined total homestead exemption of $52,950.

Compare Your Equity to the Homestead Exemption

Now that you've computed your equity and located the appropriate homestead exemption, it's time to put the two together. This comparison will help you decide whether you can safely file for Chapter 7 bankruptcy and keep your home, or whether you should consider other options—such as filing under Chapter 13.

If You Have No Equity in Your Home or Owe More Than It's Worth

If the total amount of debt against your home is equal to or more than its market value, you have no equity and aren't at risk of losing the home in bankruptcy as long as you keep current on your payments. This is true no matter how large or small the homestead exemption that's available to you and no matter how upside down you are. The trustee wouldn't get any money out of selling your home—all of the proceeds would go to the mortgage company and other creditors who have liens on the property.

EXAMPLE: Your home is worth $325,000. You still owe $335,000. The trustee cannot sell the home because there isn't any equity that could be used to repay the mortgage. So even if you live in a state that offers little or no homestead protection, you will still keep your home as long as you remain current on the mortgage payment. The trustee can't profit from selling it because the value is less than what you owe.

If You Have Some Equity in Your Home

If the total amount of debt against your home is less than its market value, you will want to compare the difference—your equity—with the homestead exemption available to you. As long as the homestead exemption covers your equity, the trustee won't have any interest in selling your home; there wouldn't be any equity left over to pay your unsecured creditors, and the trustee wouldn't get any commission for the sale. Even if your equity exceeds the homestead limit, the trustee will likely figure in about 6% of its selling price as costs of sale before deciding whether it makes sense to sell the home.

EXAMPLE: The real estate broker you used when you bought your home told you that it is currently worth $300,000. You owe your mortgage lender $250,000. The equity in your home is $50,000 ($300,000 minus $250,000).

Suppose selling your $300,000 home will net the trustee approximately $275,000 because of the costs of sale and the trustee's commission. After paying the mortgage, the trustee would clear $25,000. If your homestead exemption is equal to or greater than $25,000, the trustee will gain nothing by selling the home. If a significant chunk of the $25,000 is unprotected by a homestead exemption, however, your home is in danger of being sold for the benefit of your unsecured creditors.

Keep in mind that when you declare the value of your home on your bankruptcy paperwork, you don't get to subtract costs. Also, if the trustee gets a deal that will allow the sale of the house for less than 6%, you might still stand to lose the home. This is an example only. You can't rely on sales costs to prevent the sale of your home— only the exemption amount.

> **CAUTION**
>
> **Tax liens get priority over homestead exemptions.** Tax liens get priority over any exemptions that you can claim. In some cases, the bankruptcy trustee can sell your home for the benefit of the tax lien creditor and cut you out of receiving any homestead exemption. If you have a tax lien and your home is worth more than you owe on your mortgage, then Chapter 13 bankruptcy might be a better choice for you.

If Your Equity Is Significantly More Than Your Homestead Exemption

The homestead exemptions in some states are adequate to cover all or most of a person's equity, but not every state has an exemption.

As the economy has recovered, many homes have increased in value and equity that greatly exceeds the states' homestead exemption. These homes are at risk in Chapter 7 bankruptcy filings.

If you have nonexempt equity in your home (equity that isn't protected by your homestead exemption) and would lose it if you filed for Chapter 7 bankruptcy, you'll want to explore other options. For instance, if your home would sell for $300,000, the total liens are $100,000, and your state's homestead exemption is $100,000, you would have $100,000 of unprotected equity. The trustee would sell your home, pay off the $100,000 mortgage, pay you your $100,000 homestead exemption, and use the extra $100,000 minus sales costs and the trustee's commission to pay your creditors. If anything remained, you'd get the balance in addition to your homestead exemption.

If you have too much equity in your home, the better option might be to use some of it to pay off your debts and avoid bankruptcy altogether. There's no reason to pay the trustee a commission to do it for you.

If You Are on a Fixed Income

If you have excess equity in your home, you might be tempted to take out a loan and use it to pay your debts. However, if you are on a fixed income because of retirement or disability, you might not be able to make the payments on a loan. In other words, by borrowing to pay your debts, you could end up defaulting on the loan and losing your home to the lender.

> **EXAMPLE:** Trudy bought her home in 1956 for $56,000. Over the years, the value of the house has increased to $400,000. Trudy owes $175,000 in credit card debt and is considering filing for bankruptcy. Trudy wants to borrow against her home and pay off the debt, but her sole income is $800 a month from Social Security. She won't be able to make the payments on the loan.

Although this is a difficult situation, Chapter 7 bankruptcy is not the answer—you would lose your home to the trustee. You might be able to buy a new home with the proceeds from your homestead exemption, but for many, the loss of a home would be traumatic.

In Trudy's case, depending on her age, the best option might be a reverse mortgage she can use to pay off the debt and augment her fixed income while remaining in her home for the rest of her life. The downside to this is that she won't be able to pass the home down to her kids or other heirs when she dies.

If You Are Behind on Your Mortgage Payments

If you are behind on your mortgage payments when you file for Chapter 7 bankruptcy, you will almost certainly lose your home to foreclosure unless you can get current in a hurry. As a general rule, your mortgage lender will ask the bankruptcy court to lift the automatic stay (the court order that bars creditors from trying to collect their debts, discussed in Ch. 1), and the court will probably grant the request, allowing the mortgage lender to begin or resume foreclosure proceedings.

The only way Chapter 7 bankruptcy can help you is if you can stave off foreclosure for the length of your bankruptcy case—and this assumes that the lender won't ask the court to lift the automatic stay.

When the case is over and your other debts are wiped out or reduced, you might have an easier time remaining current on your mortgage payments if the lender hasn't yet accelerated (demanded full payment of the principal plus interest) the loan. Or, if

you have funds in a retirement plan, you might be able to borrow enough money from the plan so that you can reinstate your mortgage. To reinstate a mortgage, you pay all back and current mortgage payments, plus various costs incurred by the lender due to your default.

Keep in mind, however, that borrowing from retirement funds is usually a bad option. Tax-exempt retirement accounts are usually exempt in bankruptcy, so you'd be able to keep the funds after bankruptcy. If you borrow from those funds to catch up on your house payment, but you continue to have a problem keeping up on the payment, you could lose the house and the borrowed funds. Again, if you choose this route and run into this problem, you might want to consider a reverse mortgage.

Another option is to seek a loan modification from your lender that reduces your payments. You might qualify for a modification under a government program if you have a qualifying loan (a Fannie Mae, Freddie Mac, FHA, or VA loan) or you might be able to negotiate a workout directly with your lender or find another way to get caught up. Get Nolo's *The Foreclosure Survival Guide*, by Amy Loftsgordon, for more information on these options.

Get Some Help Negotiating Your Modification

If you are trying to make your mortgage more affordable, either temporarily or in the long term, consider using a free HUD-certified housing counselor. These nonprofit counselors typically are employed by local community action agencies, but also can be located through a couple of national networks. To become certified, these counselors must attend an intensive week-long training sponsored by HUD, which schools them in every aspect of the mortgage business and the various modification procedures used for mortgages insured or owned by the various federal housing entities. These counselors may have contacts within the various banks and companies involved in servicing mortgages and can assist you in working out a deal to make your mortgage more affordable. You can find a HUD-certified counselor by calling (800) 569-4287 or:

- HUD. Go to www.hud.gov and choose "What We Do" and then "Avoiding Foreclosure."
- The Homeownership Preservation Foundation. Go to www.995hope.org or call 888-995-HOPE.
- Making Home Affordable. Go to www.makinghomeaffordable.gov, choose "Get Expert Help."

Negotiating With the Lender

If you've missed only a few mortgage payments, your lender might be willing to negotiate. What the lender agrees to will depend on your payment history, the reason for your missed payments, and your financial prospects.

Here are the possible options your lender might agree to:

- spread out the missed payments over a few months
- reduce or suspend your regular payments for a specified time and then add a portion of your overdue amount to your regular payments later on
- extend the length of your loan and add the missed payments at the end
- suspend the principal portion of your monthly payment for a while and have you pay only interest, taxes, and insurance, or
- modify your loan to reduce the interest rate and monthly payments.

If the Lender Starts to Foreclose

If your debt problems look severe or long-lasting, the lender could take steps toward foreclosure. In most cases, the lender will accelerate the loan before foreclosure actually occurs. Usually this means you must pay the entire balance immediately, or else the lender will foreclose. However, many states give you additional time to bring your loan current and thereby avoid foreclosure.

States Where Judicial Foreclosure Is Customary	
Connecticut	New Jersey
Delaware	New Mexico
District of Columbia	New York
Florida	North Dakota
Hawaii	Ohio
Illinois	Oklahoma
Indiana	Pennsylvania
Iowa	South Carolina
Kansas	South Dakota
Kentucky	Vermont
Louisiana	Wisconsin
Maine	

The two main types of foreclosure are "judicial" and "nonjudicial" foreclosure. In a "judicial" foreclosure, the lender must file a lawsuit and obtain the court's approval before selling the home at a foreclosure sale. Connecticut and Vermont follow another foreclosure procedure called "strict" foreclosure wherein a judge can order a transfer of the home's ownership directly to the lender without a foreclosure sale.

Depending on several factors, including state law and whether the borrower files a response to the lawsuit, a judicial foreclosure can take several months or even years to complete. If you file Chapter 7 bankruptcy, you will add two or three extra months to that period depending on whether your lender gets permission from the judge to proceed with the foreclosure before your bankruptcy runs its course. And, if you are putting away at least a portion of your mortgage payment each month, even a three-month delay can result in a substantial increase in your savings.

Most Lenders Must Wait 120 Days Before Starting to Foreclose

Under federal law, a waiting period of 120 days exists between payment delinquency and the first notice or filing. This waiting period gives homeowners time to apply for a program with the mortgage lender that will allow the owner to stay in the home or give up the property without going through foreclosure. If a homeowner submits a complete application, the lender must finish the review process before starting the foreclosure—a protection that is especially important in states with a short foreclosure period. See www.nolo.com/back-of-book/ FIBA.html—as changes occur.

States Where Nonjudicial Foreclosure Is Customary	
Alabama	Nevada
Alaska	New Hampshire
Arizona	North Carolina
Arkansas	Oklahoma (homeowner can request judicial)
California	
Colorado	
District of Columbia (sometimes)	Oregon
	Rhode Island
Georgia	South Dakota (homeowner can request judicial)
Idaho	
Maryland	Tennessee
Massachusetts	Texas
Michigan	Utah
Minnesota	Virginia
Mississippi	Washington
Missouri	West Virginia
Montana	Wyoming
Nebraska	

This trustee is the person or business named in the deed of trust that you signed (or their successors in interest) instead of a traditional mortgage when you purchased or refinanced your property. In some states, especially in the South, nonjudicial foreclosures can happen within a month or two, while in other states nonjudicial foreclosures might take as long as or longer than judicial foreclosures—a year or more in some cases.

When the Automatic Stay Will Be Lifted to Permit Foreclosure

If you file for Chapter 7 bankruptcy and are behind on your payments, expect the mortgage lender to come to court and ask the judge to lift the automatic stay. (See Ch. 1 for more on the automatic stay.) If you have nonexempt equity in your home, the bankruptcy trustee is likely to successfully oppose the motion and sell the property for the benefit of your unsecured creditors. If you have no equity, however, the trustee will probably not oppose the motion to lift the stay and will let the foreclosure go through.

The other common type of foreclosure is called "nonjudicial" foreclosure, so named because the lender does not have to go to court in order to foreclose. Instead, in most cases a third-party trustee (not the bankruptcy trustee) sells your property after sending the borrower one or more notices. The exact process varies from state to state.

During a foreclosure, you have several options (although if the creditor begins a nonjudicial foreclosure, some of them might not be available to you simply because of time constraints):

- **Sell your house.** If you don't get any offers that will cover what you owe your lender, the lender might agree to take less. This is called a "short sale."

- **Get a new loan.** A new loan could pay off all or part of the first loan and put you on a new schedule of monthly payments. If the original lender has accelerated the loan, you'll need to refinance the entire balance of the loan to prevent foreclosure. Unfortunately, refinancing can be difficult without good credit and home equity.
- **Reinstate the loan.** State law or your loan contract might give you the right to prevent foreclosure simply by paying the missed payments (principal and interest), taxes, insurance, plus fees and costs. If you don't have a legal right to reinstate, your lender might agree to let you complete a reinstatement.
- **File for Chapter 13 bankruptcy.** The section below explains how Chapter 13 bankruptcy can save your home if you are behind on your mortgage.
- **Plan to lose your home.** Take advantage of the foreclosure procedures—and delays inherent in bankruptcy—to stay in your home for as long as possible. (See "If Foreclosure Is Unavoidable," below.)
- **Use faulty mortgage documents as a negotiating tool.** If you suspect that a lender is wrongfully foreclosing on your home, it's a good idea to have a knowledgeable attorney review your case as soon as possible.

Homeowners Filing for Bankruptcy Under Chapter 13

If you own your home and file for bankruptcy under Chapter 13, you won't face the same issues as you would under Chapter 7. Chapter 13 repayment plans are funded out of your projected disposable income, not your nonexempt property. As long as you can propose a legal plan out of your projected disposable income, you can keep your home no matter how much equity you have—or how large the homestead exemption available to you. In other words, you get to keep your property, but you'll have to pay an amount equivalent to your nonexempt property through your plan—perhaps more, depending on your other debt. As always, however, the devil is in the details. Here's how it works.

Under the law governing Chapter 13, you must propose a repayment plan that pays your unsecured creditors at least as much as they would have received if you had filed for Chapter 7 bankruptcy. For example, if your creditors would have received $100,000 worth of unprotected (nonexempt) home equity in Chapter 7, you will have to pay your unsecured creditors at least $100,000 over the life of your plan minus what it would cost to sell the property and pay the trustee's commission. If you don't have adequate projected disposable income to pay that amount, the court will not confirm your plan and you'll find yourself in Chapter 7, or outside of bankruptcy if you choose to dismiss your Chapter 13 case. (See "Chapter 13 Eligibility Requirements," in Ch. 2, for more on how projected disposable income is computed.)

In this situation, an experienced bankruptcy attorney might be able to come up with a creative solution so that you afford your plan payments although it's the exception, not the rule. For example, the court might approve a plan whereby you have an affordable monthly plan payment, and then later make up the difference with one, large balloon payment. To come up with the cash for the balloon payment, you could sell or refinance property that you own.

Determining Which State's Exemptions Apply

The starting point is to figure out which exemptions are available to you. "Choose Your Homestead Exemption," above, helps you make that determination for homestead exemptions in a Chapter 7 case. The same rules apply in a Chapter 13 case for the purpose of deciding the minimum amount your unsecured creditors must be paid. These rules are:

- If you acquired your home at least 40 months before filing, and have been domiciled in your state for at least two years, you can use your state's homestead exemption without restriction.

- If you acquired your home less than 40 months ago but you have made your home in your current state for at least 40 months and you purchased your current home with the proceeds from the sale of a former home in your current state, you can use your current state's homestead exemption without restriction.

- If you have made your home in your current state for at least two years but you acquired your home less than 40 months previous, you must use your current state's homestead exemption subject to a $170,350 cap.

- If you have made your home in your current state for less than two years, you must use the homestead exemption of the state where you were living for the better part of the 180-day period prior to the two-year period, subject to the $170,350 cap.

- If the state you are filing in offers the federal homestead exemption, you can use that exemption regardless of how long you've been living in the state or when you bought your home.

- If you don't qualify for any state's homestead exemption, you can use the federal homestead exemption.

For a discussion and examples of these rules, review "Choose Your Homestead Exemption," above.

CAUTION

You must count all your nonexempt property. In most cases, the equity you own in your home will be the big-ticket item that determines how much you must pay your unsecured creditors in a Chapter 13 bankruptcy. However, if you own other valuable property that is nonexempt, you must add in the value of that property to determine how much your unsecured creditors must get paid under your repayment plan. Chs. 4 and 6 discuss exemptions for other kinds of property; residency requirements apply to those exemptions as well.

Selling or Refinancing Your Home to Increase Your Disposable Income

As discussed in Ch. 2, you qualify for Chapter 13 only if you have enough projected disposable income to remain current on certain obligations and pay 100% of any arrearages owed on them. For instance, your repayment plan must propose to pay:

- usually 100% of all support arrearages owed to a child or an ex-spouse, as well as your current required payments on those obligations
- 100% of all arrearages on a mortgage as well as the current monthly payments
- 100% of recent tax debt, and
- an amount to your unsecured creditors equal to the value of your nonexempt property.

These and other requirements often make it difficult, if not impossible, for some people to propose a viable Chapter 13 plan. In this situation, you might wish to use some or all of the equity in your home to help fund your Chapter 13 plan— particularly if your equity, when added to your projected disposable income, is sufficient to make your plan confirmable, but isn't enough to make a serious dent in your debt load.

EXAMPLE: Ethan owes $125,000 in credit card debt and is contemplating bankruptcy. However, his income is insufficient to propose a confirmable Chapter 13 plan because he owes back child support and taxes that he must pay in full. Chapter 7 also isn't an attractive option for Ethan because he would lose nonexempt property that he really wants to keep: stock options and shares in a family corporation. Fortunately, Ethan owns a home that would produce $50,000 after costs of sale. If Ethan sells his home and devotes the proceeds to his plan, the plan will then become confirmable.

In order to use property to fund a Chapter 13 plan, you either must have:

- the sale proceeds in hand when you file your bankruptcy petition or shortly afterwards, or

- a feasible plan of sale that will convince the judge that you really will be able to sell the property and devote the proceeds to the plan.

Of course, if refinancing or borrowing against your home would pay off your debts outside of bankruptcy and still leave you with a manageable loan payment, this might be your best option. In fact, if you can get a sizeable sum of money to pay toward debt, some courts might find your Chapter 13 filing an abuse of the bankruptcy process. If you find yourself in this situation, you'll want to speak with a local bankruptcy attorney before filing your case. If your debts are already delinquent, your creditors may be willing to settle them for less than what you owe. In this situation, you might be able to use the refinance funds or sale proceeds to negotiate lump-sum payments on your debts at a large discount, and avoid filing for bankruptcy.

If Your Mortgage Is in Arrears but Foreclosure Hasn't Started

If you are behind on your mortgage and want to keep your home, immediately apply for a loan modification if time permits. If that is not feasible, then Chapter 13 will likely be your bankruptcy chapter of choice. As discussed above, filing for Chapter 7 bankruptcy usually won't prevent a lender from ultimately foreclosing on a mortgage default. But Chapter 13 is different. If you

have enough disposable income to propose a plan that (a) makes your regular payments on your mortgage and (b) pays off your arrearage in a reasonable period of time, you will be allowed to keep your home as part of your Chapter 13 case.

EXAMPLE: Kenny and Zoe, a married couple, pay $2,000 a month on their mortgage. They have fallen five payments behind and owe an arrearage of $10,000. If they file for Chapter 7 bankruptcy, the lender will get the bankruptcy stay lifted and proceed to foreclose on the loan. Because they want to keep their home, Kenny and Zoe file a Chapter 13 bankruptcy and propose a repayment plan that will, among other things:

- pay their monthly mortgage of $2,000, and
- pay another $300 a month toward the arrearage.

If the judge confirms their plan and they remain current on their repayment plan payments, they'll be able to stay in the home.

Mortgage Modifications Under Chapter 13

In Chapter 13, the court can reduce the amount of your secured mortgage debt to the value of the property. The remaining mortgage debt becomes unsecured property. This is often referred to as a "cramdown." Unfortunately, you cannot cram down the mortgage on your principal residence. Therefore, this is helpful only for investment and vacation properties and is used infrequently. Additionally, you must pay the entire crammed down amount of your mortgage over the life of your Chapter 13 plan, which cannot exceed 60 months. This makes many real estate cramdowns unworkable; most people cannot afford to pay off such a large sum in just five years.

EXAMPLE: John and Quinn, a married couple, own their residence and a rental unit. The home is currently worth $200,000, and their mortgage is $250,000. Their rental unit is currently worth $100,000, and the mortgage is $125,000. If John and Quinn file for Chapter 13 bankruptcy, they cannot cram down the mortgage on their residence. However, they can cram down the mortgage on the rental unit to $100,000. But they would need to pay the entire $100,000 through their Chapter 13 plan.

Stripping Off Liens in Chapter 13

Chapter 13 provides another useful tool to homeowners with junior mortgages on their property, called lien stripping. With lien stripping, you are allowed to get rid of junior liens on your home if they are wholly unsecured.

Beware of Foreclosure "Rescue" Scams

Beware of foreclosure "consultants," lawyers, and other services claiming they can help you avoid foreclosure. Many of these services claim you have a legitimate defense to the foreclosure, when in fact you don't. Examples of what scammers tell frustrated homeowners include:

- If their lenders won't work with them, they have a legitimate defense to foreclosure (as discussed above, this is not true).
- If the homeowners cannot afford to pay the loans, it must be the lenders' fault.

Other foreclosure consultants claim they will help you avoid foreclosure—and then do nothing.

How do scammers get away with this? They are savvy enough to promise things the homeowner would desperately like to be true. And there just aren't enough resources available to prevent these scams or catch all of the scammers. The end result: You pay the consultant lots of money, and still lose your home.

You can find more information about foreclosure scams in *The Foreclosure Survival Guide*, by Amy Loftsgordon (Nolo).

What exactly does this mean? Junior liens are anything other than your first mortgage. So they would include second or third mortgages, HELOCs, and home equity loans. A lien or security interest is wholly unsecured if the equity in your property does not cover any of the lien amount. For example, say your home is worth $500,000, your first mortgage is $550,000, and your second mortgage is $50,000. Since your first mortgage is greater than the equity in your home, there is no equity left to cover your second mortgage. If a lender were to foreclose on your home, the first mortgage holder would get $500,000 and the second mortgage holder would get nothing. If a junior mortgage or home equity line is eligible for lien stripping, the formerly secured debt becomes unsecured debt. As we discussed earlier in this book, most Chapter 13 filers pay pennies on the dollar when it comes to unsecured debt.

You should be aware that you cannot strip junior liens in Chapter 7 bankruptcy. If you keep real estate in a Chapter 7 case, you'll remain responsible for all the associated debt.

If Your Mortgage Is in Arrears and the Lender Has Started to Foreclose

If your lender has started to foreclose, you can file for Chapter 13 bankruptcy and take up to five years to make up your missed payments, reinstate the loan, and keep making the payments under the original contract. This is called "curing the default."

Your right to cure the default depends on how far along the foreclosure proceeding is. If the lender has accelerated the loan or obtained a foreclosure judgment, you usually can still cure the default. If the foreclosure sale has already occurred, however, Chapter 13 usually won't help. Cases have held that the bankruptcy court has no jurisdiction to undo a sale, even if state law might otherwise allow it.

Raising Defenses to Foreclosure in Bankruptcy

If you have a legitimate defense to the foreclosure of your home, in most cases you can raise and litigate the issue in bankruptcy court. For example, if you are not in arrears on your mortgage as the servicer claims, you can raise this defense within your bankruptcy case. However, you will almost always need a lawyer to do this because the process is so complicated.

Some people erroneously believe that if their lender won't "work with" them, for example, by agreeing to a loan modification or some other way to avoid foreclosure, they have a legitimate defense to foreclosure. This is not true. Your mortgage loan is a contract and you and your lender must live up to the original bargain. If the agreement no longer works for you, the lender is under no obligation to modify your loan to help you out. If it refuses to do so, you can't raise this as a defense against the foreclosure.

Don't Walk Away From Home Equity —Let the Bankruptcy Trustee Help

Unfortunately, a homeowner who can't meet a mortgage payment or sell a home before a foreclosure can face losing a home with equity. If you find yourself in this situation, you might have another avenue to explore—filing for Chapter 7 bankruptcy. Although this approach won't help you keep the house, it might allow you to retain a portion of your equity—which is better than nothing when you're out of options. Here's how it works: The automatic stay will stop the foreclosure and give the bankruptcy trustee time to sell the home. Once sold, the trustee must pay off the mortgage. Then, in most cases, the trustee must give you the amount of equity that you're entitled to protect (exempt) in your state. After taking a percentage as a fee, the trustee will distribute the remaining proceeds to your creditors. Of course, this plan won't work unless there will be something left over for creditors. If the math doesn't work, it might make sense to give the trustee incentive to sell the house by claiming less than the full exemption amount. Finally, as with any unusual plan, you'll want to speak with a local bankruptcy attorney before proceeding forward. Not only will you want to make sure that you aren't doing anything inappropriate, but the attorney will likely have a working relationship with the trustee and will know the best way to approach the trustee on your behalf.

If Foreclosure Is Unavoidable

If you owe significantly more on your mortgage than your home is worth, or you can't afford your mortgage perhaps because of a reset in interest rates or a loss of income, consider using your state's foreclosure procedures to your best advantage. Depending on your state and your mortgage lender's policies, you can easily remain in your home for many months without paying a dime to anyone. By paying yourself all or a part of your mortgage instead of sending it to your lender, you can easily amass a savings of many thousands of dollars that will be available to you when you seek out new shelter. For example, assume that Kenny's mortgage payment increases from $1,200 to $1,500 because of a mortgage interest reset. Kenny has been able to afford the $1,200, but he can't meet the $300 monthly increase. Kenny decides to walk away from the mortgage. He stops making his mortgage payments and instead puts $1,200 a month into his own bank account. Kenny will probably have months of payment-free shelter before he has to move, meaning he will be able to save just by living in his house payment free.

Importantly, if you react to foreclosure by selling your home (typically in a short sale) or offering the lender the deed back "in lieu of foreclosure," you will have to move out of the house much earlier than if you just wait out the foreclosure procedures in your home, and you will thus forgo this unique opportunity to amass a considerable savings. For more information on your state's foreclosure laws and strategies for remaining in your home payment free for the maximum period of time, see *The Foreclosure Survival Guide,* by Amy Loftsgordon (Nolo).

The Risk of Deficiency Judgments

In most states and with certain property and types of loans, the lender can get a deficiency judgment following a foreclosure. A "deficiency judgment" is a judgment for the difference between what you owe and what the lender gets for the property at auction. The creditor can use this deficiency judgment to collect the rest of the debt by seizing your other available property.

The possibility of a deficiency judgment could affect your strategy when facing a foreclosure. For instance, if you are at risk of a deficiency judgment, you might try to deed the property back to the lender, in exchange for a release from liability (commonly called a "deed in lieu of foreclosure"). But if your state doesn't permit deficiency judgments (called nonrecourse states), or your property is not subject to a deficiency judgment, you might benefit from fighting the foreclosure as long as possible without making any payments in the meantime.

These laws vary from state to state, which is one reason you may need to consult a real estate or bankruptcy attorney if you get a notice of foreclosure.

 SEE AN EXPERT

If your lender has sent you a foreclosure notice, it might be time to consult with a bankruptcy or real estate attorney — quickly. You might have special legal options —and risks—in your state that are not discussed above. (See "The Risk of Deficiency Judgments," above.) If you think you can't afford an attorney, remember that you won't be paying your mortgage. For most people, just one month's mortgage payment is enough to buy an attorney's advice, if not outright representation. And if the attorney can help you stay in your home, payment free, for longer than you could stay there without the attorney's help, which is frequently the case, the attorneys' fees would be well worth it.

Renters Filing for Bankruptcy

If you're current on your rent payments and you file for either Chapter 7 or Chapter 13 bankruptcy, your bankruptcy should have no effect on your tenancy. Although your landlord might not like the idea that you filed for bankruptcy, the chances are good that the landlord won't even find out about it. Because you are current on your rent, you don't have to list your landlord as a creditor entitled to notice of the proceeding. Although you have to list on your bankruptcy papers any security deposits held by your landlord, you will probably be able to claim those deposits as exempt.

If You Are Behind on Your Rent When You File

Back rent is dischargeable in both Chapter 7 and Chapter 13 bankruptcies. However, if you get very far behind on your rent, your landlord will likely file an action in court to evict you. If you file for bankruptcy before the court issues a judgment for possession (an eviction order), the automatic stay will prohibit your landlord from trying to evict you on the basis of your prefiling rent default during your bankruptcy—unless the landlord files a motion to lift the stay. However, if you don't stay current on your rent after you file, the landlord is free to seek your eviction on the basis of the postfiling rent default.

> **EXAMPLE:** Aldo owes two months' back rent when he files for bankruptcy. At the time Aldo files, his landlord hasn't yet obtained a judgment of possession. The landlord can't evict him for this debt while the bankruptcy is pending unless he files a motion to lift the stay. However, if Aldo fails to pay rent on time after he files for bankruptcy, the landlord can give him a delinquency or "pay or quit" notice and file an eviction action in court if he doesn't move and the rent isn't paid as required. Also, many states and localities give landlords the right to evict tenants for no reason at all, as long as the tenant receives adequate notice and the landlord strictly complies with the state's eviction procedures. So, even if Aldo faithfully pays his rent on time after his bankruptcy, he might still lose his apartment.

If the Landlord Already Has a Judgment

If your landlord has already obtained a judgment of possession (or "eviction") against you when you file for bankruptcy, the automatic stay won't help you (with the possible exception described below). The landlord is entitled to proceed with the eviction just as if you never filed for bankruptcy.

If the eviction order is based on your failure to pay rent, you might be able to have the automatic stay reinstated. However, this exception applies only if your state's law allows you to stay in your rental unit and "cure" or pay back the rent delinquency after the landlord has a judgment for possession. Here's what you'll have to do to take advantage of this exception:

Step 1: As part of your bankruptcy petition, you must file a "certification" or statement under oath stating that your state's laws allow you to cure the rent delinquency after the judgment is obtained and to continue living in your rental unit. Very few states allow this. To find out whether yours is one of them, ask the sheriff or someone at legal aid if you have legal aid in your area. In addition, when you file your bankruptcy petition, you must deposit with the court clerk the amount of rent that will become due during the 30-day period after you file.

Once you have filed your petition containing the certification and deposited the rent, you are protected from eviction for 30 days unless the landlord successfully objects to your initial certification before the 30-day period ends. If the landlord objects to your certification, the court must hold a hearing on the objection within ten days, so theoretically you could have less than 30 days of protection if the landlord files and serves the objection immediately.

Step 2: To keep the stay in effect longer, you must, before the 30-day period runs out, file and serve a second certification showing that you have fully cured the default in the manner provided by your state's law. However, if the landlord successfully objects to this second certification, the stay will no longer be in effect and the landlord can proceed with the eviction. As in Step 1, the court must hold a hearing within ten days if the landlord objects.

SEE AN EXPERT

If you really want to keep your apartment, talk to a lawyer. As you can see, these new rules are somewhat complicated. If you don't interpret your state's law properly, file the necessary paperwork on time, and successfully argue your side if the landlord objects, you could find yourself put out of your home. A good lawyer can tell you whether it's worth fighting an eviction—and, if so, how to go about it.

Endangering the Property or Illegal Use of Controlled Substances

Under bankruptcy law, an eviction action will not be stayed by your bankruptcy filing if your landlord wants you out because you endangered the property or engaged in the "illegal use of controlled substances" on the property. And your landlord doesn't have to have a judgment in hand when you file for bankruptcy: The landlord can start an eviction action against you or continue with a pending eviction action even after your filing date if the eviction is based on property endangerment or drug use.

To evict you on these grounds after you have filed for bankruptcy, your landlord must file and serve on you a certification showing either of the following:

- The landlord has filed an eviction action against you based on property endangerment or illegal drug use on the property.

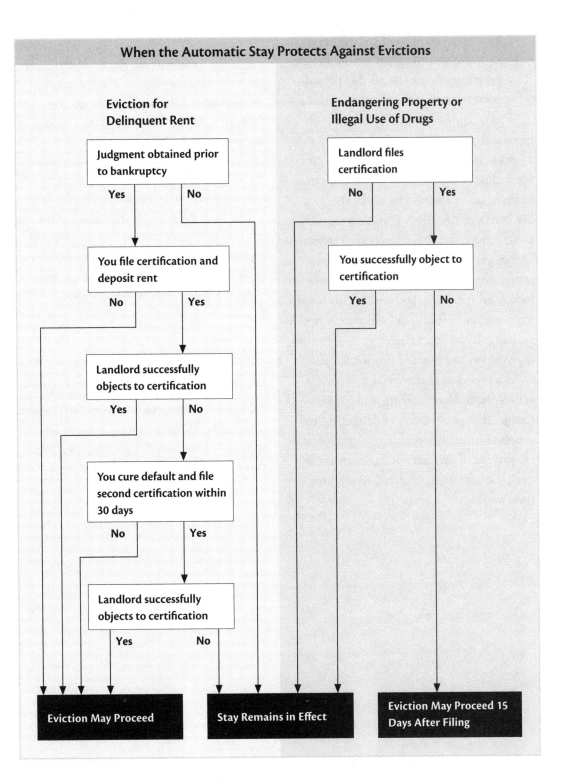

- You have endangered the property or engaged in illegal drug use on the property during the 30-day period prior to the landlord's certification.

If your landlord files this certification, he or she can proceed with the eviction 15 days later unless, within that time, you file and serve on the landlord an objection to the truth of the statements in the landlord's certification. If you do that, the court must hold a hearing on your objection within ten days. If you prove that the statements in the certification aren't true or have been remedied, you will be protected from eviction while your bankruptcy is pending. If the court denies your objection, the eviction can proceed immediately.

As a practical matter, you will have a very difficult time proving a negative—that is, that you weren't endangering the property or using drugs. Similarly, once allegations of property endangerment or drug use are made, it's hard to see how they would be "remedied."

CAUTION

Landlords can always ask the court to lift the automatic stay to begin or continue an eviction on any grounds. Although the automatic stay will kick in unless one of these exceptions apply, the judge can lift the stay upon the landlord's request. And many courts are willing to do so, because most evictions will have no effect on the bankruptcy estate—that is, your tenancy isn't something that the trustee can turn into money to pay your creditors. As a general rule, bankruptcy courts are inclined to let landlords exercise their property rights regardless of the tenants' debt problems.

RESOURCE

Need help with your landlord? For more information on dealing with landlords —including landlords who are trying to evict you—see *Every Tenant's Legal Guide,* by Janet Portman and Marcia Stewart (Nolo). ●

What Happens to Personal Property That Secures a Loan

This chapter explains what happens to personal property you are making payments on when you file for bankruptcy—typically, a car or major household furnishings, such as living room or bedroom sets. It also covers other collateral: property you already owned that you pledged as security for a personal or business loan.

What Are Secured Debts?

Almost without exception, if you are making that the property will serve as collateral for repayment of the debt. If you default on your payments, the lender can repossess the property, sell it, and obtain a court judgment against you called a deficiency judgment for the difference between what you owe and what the property sold for. In bankruptcy, debts secured by collateral are known as "secured debts."

How Secured Debts Are Handled in Chapter 7 Bankruptcy

Secured debts are treated differently in bankruptcy than other kinds of debts. Unlike credit card debt or medical bills, a secured debt has a piece of property attached to it. Although the debt itself will be discharged, the creditor will still have a right to take the property back if you default on the payments.

A secured debt has two parts:

- **Personal liability.** You have personal liability for a secured debt just as you would for any other debt. This is what obligates you to pay the debt to the creditor. Chapter 7 bankruptcy wipes out this personal liability if the debt is otherwise dischargeable. Once your personal liability is eliminated, the creditor cannot sue you to collect the debt.

- **Security interest.** The second part of a secured debt is the creditor's legal claim (lien or security interest) on the property that serves as collateral for the debt. The lien gives the creditor the right to repossess the property or force its sale if you do not pay the debt. And liens are not affected by the bankruptcy discharge. In other words, by failing to remain current on payments, you can lose the property, even if the debt itself is discharged. (In some cases, however, you can ask the bankruptcy court to remove the lien as part of your bankruptcy case.)

If You Are Current on Your Payments

If you are current on your payments for a secured debt when you file Chapter 7 bankruptcy, but you no longer want to keep the property, you can surrender the property and discharge the underlying debt. You'll be able to walk away from the property and the contract free and clear.

If you want to keep the property, you can do so if all of the following apply:

- Your equity in the property, if any, is protected by an applicable exemption (see below).
- You are current on your payment.
- You are willing to take one of the two available options for secured debts—reaffirmation or redemption, although you might not need to in every case (see below).

Does an Exemption Protect Any Equity You Have in the Property?

You have equity in property serving as collateral if it could be sold for more than you owe. For instance, if you owe $3,000 on a car loan and the car could be sold for $6,000, you have $3,000 worth of equity. This equity is part of your bankruptcy estate (see Ch. 4), which means the trustee can take it unless it's protected by an exemption. In this example, if you have $3,000 equity in your car and the exemptions available to you allow $1,000 for motor vehicles, the trustee could sell the car, pay your secured creditor the $3,000 you still owe, give you your $1,000 exemption in cash, and distribute the remaining $2,000 minus sales costs and the trustee's commission to your unsecured creditors.

RELATED TOPIC

Information for homeowners.
See Ch. 5 for information on computing your equity in a home.

Debtors frequently owe more on secured loans than the property securing the debt is worth—which by definition means they have no equity in the property. But that's not always the case. If you have equity that you can't exempt, the Chapter 7 trustee will sell the property, pay off the loan, return your exemption amount to you, and use the remaining amount minus sales costs and trustee fees to pay creditors.

If you have no equity in the property, or if your equity is fully protected by an available exemption, the trustee will have no interest in the property. You can either surrender it to the secured creditor or take one of the actions explained in "Redemption and Reaffirmation," just below, if you want to hold on to the property.

Redemption and Reaffirmation

Even if the trustee isn't interested in taking your property, that doesn't mean you get to keep it. The creditor still has that lien on the property. You might lose it to repossession unless you are current on your payments and use one of the remedies explained in this section.

Of course, you always have the option of simply giving the secured property to the creditor. Surrendering the property completely frees you from the debt, quickly and easily: The lien is satisfied by your surrender of the property, and your personal liability is discharged by bankruptcy. The downside, obviously, is that you lose the property.

If you want to hang on to secured property, and you're current on the payment, you have two options: redemption or reaffirmation.

The exception is that some creditors will allow you to continue to pay on the loan without entering into a reaffirmation agreement or repurchasing the property through redemption. The downside is that you won't have a contract to stop the creditor from repossessing or foreclosing on the property for any reason. There is an upside, however—if you fall behind on the payment or damage the property and the lender recovers it, you won't be liable for a deficiency judgment—the difference between the value of the property and what you owe. For this reason, some courts prefer this approach and are hesitant to sign reaffirmation agreements for any type of property.

Redeem the Property

In Chapter 7 bankruptcy, you have the right to "redeem" property—that is, to buy it back from the creditor with a lump sum, rather than have the creditor take it and sell it to someone else. Under bankruptcy law, if the property is used for personal, family, or household purposes, you can redeem it by paying the replacement value—the price

Negotiate for Better Terms

There is no requirement that your reaffirmation agreement contain the same terms as your current agreement, although you have a right to reaffirm under the same terms if you can't get better terms through negotiation. While your lender ultimately has the right to hold you to the same terms, bankruptcy law gives you the right to surrender the property and walk away from the note without paying a penny. Because the lender will lose money if it has to auction off the property after you surrender it, you do have some leverage to negotiate a better deal.

Assume you are paying $350 a month on a 2018 Ford F-250 truck. When you file bankruptcy in 2021, the truck is worth $14,000 but you still owe $22,000. The lender sends you a reaffirmation agreement containing the same terms as the old note. You call the lender back and explain that you won't be able to afford $350 a month but that you are willing to reaffirm if the lender reduces the principal to the current value of the truck, and the payment from $350 to $250 a month. The lender rejects your offer but counteroffers with a plan that will require payments of $300 a month and a longer time to pay off the note. Because you really do want to keep the truck, you accept the offer and the lender sends you a new reaffirmation agreement to be signed and filed with the court.

a retail merchant would charge for property of that kind, considering the age and condition of the property at the time you redeem it. This means, for example, that you can redeem a car for the middle price listed in the *Kelley Blue Book* at www.kbb.com or similar car valuation systems, such as www.nada.com.

At first glance, redemption doesn't seem like much of a remedy. After all, if you are filing for bankruptcy, how can you afford to buy the property outright? The answer is that all cash and other property you acquire after your bankruptcy filing date is yours to do with as you please (with the few exceptions explained in Ch. 4) and can be used to redeem property. For instance, you can sell some of your exempt property (with the trustee's permission if you're still in bankruptcy), get a loan from family or friends, or work overtime to raise the money. Also, some lenders specialize in redemption loans, so it might make sense to refinance the property if the amount you would pay in payments and interest will be less overall than the amount owed before bankruptcy.

Redemption is a great option if your debt substantially exceeds the property's value. The creditor must accept the replacement value of the item as payment in full, even if you owe much more. However, you do have to come up with the replacement value of the property in a lump sum. If you can't afford to do that or can't find affordable financing, you might be able to file a Chapter 13 case and pay off the property's

replacement value over the life of your plan rather than through a lump sum payment.

You have the right to redeem property in a Chapter 7 bankruptcy only if all of the following are true:

- The debt is a consumer debt on goods used for personal or household purposes. This means you cannot redeem property that secures business debts or a car that you use for business purposes.
- The property is tangible personal property. "Personal property" includes everything but real estate. "Tangible property" is property you can touch, such as a car or stereo system. (Examples of intangible personal property, for comparison purposes, include investments, like stocks and bonds, or intellectual property rights, like patents, trademarks, and copyrights.)
- You have either claimed the property as fully exempt or the trustee has abandoned it because it has little or no equity.

Reaffirm the Debt

When you "reaffirm" a debt, you and the creditor use an official form to set out the amount you owe and the terms of the repayment. In essence, this restores the old debt with the same terms set out in the original contract. You might even be able to negotiate better terms. Although getting better terms is rare for car loans, many debtors can negotiate much better terms for loans on appliances, jewelry, furniture, and electronics. In return, you get to keep the property as long as you keep current on your payments under the new agreement. If the debt is reaffirmed, both the creditor's lien on the collateral and your personal liability under the new contract survive bankruptcy.

Reaffirmation can be used when redemption is unavailable or impractical. It provides a sure way to keep property, as long as you abide by the terms of the reaffirmation agreement. But because reaffirmation leaves you personally liable, there is no way to walk away from the debt after your bankruptcy, even if the property becomes worthless or you simply decide you no longer want it. You'd have to wait eight years to file another Chapter 7 bankruptcy case or explore the options available in Chapter 13.

As a general rule, you should sign a reaffirmation agreement only if it is the sole way to keep property you can't be without, and you have good reason to believe you'll be able to pay off the balance. For example, many people use reaffirmation to keep a car, one of the few essential items of property in today's world.

The reaffirmation agreement form contains a number of disclosures about what you are getting into by reaffirming the debt. If you are represented by an attorney, the agreement becomes effective upon its signing unless the attorney refuses to approve the reaffirmation. The attorney must believe that the payments would not pose a substantial hardship to you and your family. If you are not represented

by an attorney, or the attorney refuses to sign off on it, the agreement will become effective only after it has been filed with the court and approved by the bankruptcy judge in a court hearing near the end of your bankruptcy that you must attend.

At the hearing, the judge will only approve the agreement if he or she determines that it is in your best interest. To that end, the judge will look at the income and expense schedules you filed with your other bankruptcy paperwork and consider whether continuing to make payments on the debt will be a substantial hardship or interfere with your ability to get a fresh start through bankruptcy. While the judge will probably be sympathetic to your desire to keep your vehicle, the judge might nevertheless disapprove the reaffirmation agreement. Some courts have ruled that if you do everything you are supposed to do to reaffirm—that is, agree to reaffirm in your Statement of Intention, sign and file the reaffirmation agreement in court, and appear at the reaffirmation hearing— bankruptcy law authorizes you to retain possession of the car as long as you remain current, regardless of whether the judge approves or disapproves the agreement. As discussed above, many courts feel you will be better off if the judge disapproves the agreement because then you won't owe a deficiency if you have to return the car after bankruptcy. But you'll be able to keep the car as long as you remain current on your payments. However, this approach won't help your credit. To do that, you'll need to sign a reaffirmation agreement. That's because the creditor won't report your on-time payments to the credit reporting agencies unless you have a reaffirmation agreement. The same holds true if you don't sign a reaffirmation agreement for a home. The lender won't report your payments for credit purposes.

TIP

Most bankruptcy judges won't approve the reaffirmation of an unsecured debt. Some debtors want to keep a credit card that has a balance and are told by the credit card company that they can do that if they agree to reaffirm the debt. While this might technically be true, very few judges would approve such a reaffirmation agreement. Why not? From the judge's viewpoint, a reaffirmation agreement on an unsecured debt provides no benefit to the bankruptcy debtor and therefore doesn't support the goal of giving the debtor a fresh start.

The Statement of Intention for Individuals Filing Under Chapter 7

As part of your bankruptcy case, you are required to file an official form called a "Statement of Intention for Individuals Filing Under Chapter 7," which tells your secured creditors what you plan to do with the collateral. That is, you must tell them whether you plan to surrender the collateral, redeem it, or reaffirm the debt.

Keeping Property Without Reaffirming or Redeeming

Prior to the 2005 changes in the bankruptcy law, many bankruptcy courts allowed a debtor to keep secured property without going through the reaffirmation process, provided he or she remained current on payments under the contract with the creditor. If the debtor fell behind, the creditor could take the property, but the debtor's personal liability for the debt was wiped out by the bankruptcy. This method was often referred to as the "retain and pay" or "ride through" option.

According to recent court decisions, this remedy is no longer available under bankruptcy law, however, many creditors allow the practice informally. Plus, you might be protected in another way. If the law of your state forbids creditors from enforcing a lien on your property as long as you are current on your payment, your creditors might have to let you keep the property as long as you remain current, no matter what the new bankruptcy law says. Many creditors are perfectly happy with this arrangement to this day; they would rather have a steady payment stream on the original contract than repossess used property that has to be sold at auction. This approach doesn't come without risk, though. Some creditors—especially credit unions—have increased repossessions even when the debtor's payment is current.

If you don't file the Statement of Intention within 30 days after you file your bankruptcy petition, your creditor can repossess the property in the manner permitted by state law. Repossession could also occur if you fail to carry out your stated intention within 45 days of filing the statement.

If You Are Not Current on Your Payments

If you're behind on your payments to a secured creditor and don't have the ability to get current, Chapter 7 bankruptcy won't prevent the creditor from repossessing the property. While your bankruptcy filing will initially stop any repossession activity, the creditor can ask the court to lift the automatic stay during your bankruptcy case, or wait to repossess the property after your bankruptcy case is closed. If you are behind on your payments, most courts will lift the stay in order to let the creditor proceed with repossession. Whether the court grants the lender's motion often comes down to the amount of equity in the property. If there isn't much equity and the lender stands to lose money as time progresses, the court will likely lift the stay. (For more on the automatic stay, see Ch. 1.)

If you want to keep the property, you'll need to reinstate the loan outside of bankruptcy, by making up the missed payments and fees associated with the default, and by resuming your regular payments.

If your lender has already accelerated the loan (declared the entire balance due) and won't let you reinstate it, you can file for Chapter 13 bankruptcy. You can make up the missed payments in your plan as long as you also make the regular payments called for under your original agreement. (See Ch. 2.) Also, in Chapter 13, you might be able to reduce the total amount of your payments to the property's actual value.

Eliminating Liens in Chapter 7 Bankruptcy

During your Chapter 7 bankruptcy case, you might be able to eliminate a lien on an item of secured property. If you can eliminate, or "avoid," a lien, you get to keep the property free and clear, without paying anything more to the creditor. To avoid a lien, you must be able to claim an exemption in the property that is impaired by the lien—that is, that the lien deprives you of your right to benefit from the exemption because you can't sell the property without paying off the lien. (See Ch. 4 for more on exemptions.)

For the purpose of lien avoidance, there are two types of liens: (1) judicial liens, and (2) liens you agree to have placed on property you already own in exchange for a personal loan. A judicial lien is one that was placed on your property to collect a court judgment for money. The second type of lien is called a nonpossessory, nonpurchase money lien because the lienholder doesn't possess the collateral (as would be the case if the lien were owned by a pawnbroker), and you didn't use the loan to buy the collateral.

A judicial lien can be "avoided" (wiped out) on any type of property, including real estate, to the extent the lien "impairs an exemption." A nonpossessory, non-purchase money lien, on the other hand, can be avoided only on certain types of personal property (see below).

In most courts, lien avoidance actions are relatively simple. Most of the time, the lien owner doesn't contest the motion, so you'll just have to make sure you get the paperwork right. On occasion, however, a lien owner might object, which means you will have to participate in one or more court hearings, depending on the type of objection. (The procedural steps necessary for lien avoidance are described in more detail in Ch. 10.)

Avoiding Judicial Liens

Most judicial liens occur when:

- You've been sued for money and lost.
- The judgment creditor (the winner of the lawsuit) obtains a judgment against you for a sum of money.
- The judgment is recorded against your property in the form of a lien.

Most often, judicial liens are imposed on real estate. Judicial liens can also be imposed on business assets; almost all states provide a way to do this under the Uniform Commercial Code. However, liens are seldom, if ever, attached to consumer goods because ownership of consumer personal property is rarely recorded in public documents.

If paying a judicial lien would deprive you of any part of the exemption you are entitled to claim on the property, you can get rid of the lien by following the lien avoidance process outlined in Ch. 10. A few courts have ruled that you can avoid a judicial lien even if you have no equity in the property. Be sure to speak to an attorney about the possibility of avoiding the lien even if you are underwater on the mortgage.

Avoiding Nonpossessory, Nonpurchase Money Liens

A nonpossessory, nonpurchase money security lien is almost always created when a consumer obtains a personal loan from a finance company. These liens can be avoided only on the following types of property and only if the property is exempt without regard to your equity in the property:

- household furnishings, household goods (see the list below), clothing, appliances, books, musical instruments, or jewelry
- health aids professionally prescribed for you or a dependent

- the first $6,825 of a lien attaching to animals or crops held primarily for your personal, family, or household use, and
- the first $6,825 of a lien attaching to tools used in your trade.

Under bankruptcy law, the term "household goods" is limited to:

- clothing
- furniture
- appliances
- one radio
- one television
- one VCR (the statutory language hasn't been updated to take DVDs into account)
- linens
- china
- crockery
- kitchenware
- educational equipment and materials primarily for the use of your minor dependent children
- medical equipment and supplies
- furniture exclusively for the use of your minor children or elderly or disabled dependents
- your personal effects and those of your dependents (including the toys and hobby equipment of your dependent children and your wedding rings), and
- one personal computer and related equipment.

The following are not considered to be household goods, and you cannot avoid liens on them:

- works of art unless they are by you or a relative
- electronic entertainment equipment with a fair market value of more than $725 in the aggregate (excluding the one television, one radio, and one VCR listed above)
- items acquired as antiques with a fair market value of more than $725 in the aggregate
- jewelry with a fair market value of more than $725 in the aggregate (excluding wedding rings), and
- a computer (excluding the computer equipment listed above), a motor vehicle (including a tractor or lawn tractor), a boat, or a motorized recreational device, conveyance vehicle, watercraft, or aircraft.

To avoid a nonpossessory, nonpurchase money lien, you must have owned the property before the lien was "fixed" on it. This will almost always be the case with this type of lien. See Ch. 10 for more on lien avoidance.

How Secured Debts Are Handled in Chapter 13 Bankruptcy

Secured debts are handled completely differently in Chapter 13 than in Chapter 7. By filing for Chapter 13 bankruptcy, you can keep property subject to a secured debt even though you are behind on your payments when you file. Under your Chapter 13 plan, you can pay off the arrearage or defaulted payments over the course of the plan, as long as you meet your current payment obligations during that time.

Surrendering Property

If you don't want to keep property that is subject to a secured debt, you can surrender it to the creditor and schedule what you still owe on the contract as an unsecured debt. This means that you might have to pay a portion of the debt over the life of your plan, depending on the factors described in Ch. 2, under "Chapter 13 Eligibility Requirements."

Reducing Secured Debt to the Property's Value (Cramdowns)

If you want to keep property that is worth less than what you owe on it, instead of paying the balance, you can propose a plan that pays the replacement value of the property over the life of the plan. For example, if you owe $20,000 on the property and its replacement value is $10,000, you can propose a plan that pays only $10,000. If you complete your plan, then you'll own the property free and clear. This remedy of reducing a secured debt to the replacement value of the collateral is known as a "cramdown," a most descriptive term.

EXAMPLE: Dave owes $13,000 on his car, and its replacement value is $8,000. Dave can propose to pay $8,000 in equal payments over the life of his plan, and then own the car outright once he obtains a discharge.

If you fail to complete your Chapter 13 plan, the cramdown is canceled and you must pay the full balance of the debt before obtaining title.

There are three important exceptions to the cramdown rule:

- You can't cram down a debt owed on a motor vehicle purchased within 30 months of your filing date if you bought the car for your personal use. However, if you use the car as part of your business, you can cram down the debt without regard to the 30-month restriction.
- You can't cram down a debt owed on other personal property purchased within a year of your filing date.
- You can't cram down a mortgage that is used exclusively for your primary residence.

The purpose of these restrictions is to prevent people from purchasing cars or other property with the intent to file for bankruptcy and use the cramdown remedy. The good news is that, because you can't cram down the debt, you might be able to surrender the vehicle and perhaps get off the hook for the entire debt. However, the majority of the courts that have decided this issue require you to include the deficiency as an unsecured debt when you formulate your plan.

Continuing the Contract

If you want to continue the secured debt as before, all you have to do is provide in your proposed plan that you will remain current on the contract during the life of the plan. If you don't complete your Chapter 13 plan, but are still making payments on the secured debt, you can either convert to Chapter 7 and use one of the remedies described in "How Secured Debts Are Handled in Chapter 7 Bankruptcy," above, or continue making the payments outside of bankruptcy. Keep in mind, however, that if you have crammed down a debt in Chapter 13 and then convert to Chapter 7, you'll lose the benefit of the cramdown. This means you'll owe the the creditor the original amount of the debt minus any amount paid through the plan. If you want to keep the property, you'll have to cure the default or make some other arrangement with the creditor. If you are still in Chapter 13 and something happens to the collateral—for example, it is destroyed in an accident—it is usually possible to amend your plan and reschedule what you still owe as unsecured debt.

Making the Decision

The previous chapters explain how bankruptcy works to stop collection efforts and give you a fresh start. You also learn how the two main types of consumer bankruptcy—Chapter 7 and Chapter 13—will affect your debts and property and how to determine your eligibility for each. It's a lot of information to absorb, especially when making a choice between chapters.

To help you sort through this information and reach a decision, you'll find a transcript of a consultation between a debtor and a lawyer in this chapter. The debtor, Georgia Cox, consulted with the lawyer to figure out whether filing under Chapter 7 or Chapter 13 would be best. The lawyer's questions illustrate factors you should consider as you evaluate your own situation.

Lawyer: Hi, Georgia. How can I help you today?

Debtor: Well, I've run up quite a bit of debt, and I might want to file for bankruptcy. I know there are different types of bankruptcy, but I need some help figuring out what my options are.

Lawyer: Okay, I can help you with that. The two basic types of bankruptcy for individuals are Chapter 7 bankruptcy and Chapter 13 bankruptcy. There are a couple of major differences between them. In a Chapter 13 bankruptcy, you pay down some or all of your debts over a three- to five-year period and discharge, or "cancel" whatever is left over at the completion of your plan. In a Chapter 7 bankruptcy, you don't pay down any of your debt, and the entire process takes between three and four months. But you might have to give up property you own so it can be sold and the proceeds distributed to your creditors.

In either type of bankruptcy, some types of debts aren't discharged and survive your bankruptcy. For instance, overdue child support and many tax debts must be paid in full as part of a Chapter 13 bankruptcy. Also, some debts that can be discharged in Chapter 13 will survive a Chapter 7 bankruptcy. But we'll get to that later. Do you have any questions so far?

Debtor: I kind of already knew most of what you just told me and I'm leaning toward Chapter 7 since it's over a lot sooner and seems simpler. But I still wonder whether Chapter 13 would be the better choice—which would you suggest?

Lawyer: Okay. Well, some people aren't eligible to file for Chapter 7 bankruptcy, so let's start by determining whether you qualify. Then, if both options are available to you, we can talk about which one makes more sense.

Debtor: Sounds good.

Lawyer: First, have you lived in New Hampshire for more than two years?

Debtor: Yes.

Lawyer: Who lives with you as part of your household? Tell me about relatives, dependents, and anyone else whose income and expenses are regularly combined with yours to maintain your home.

Debtor: Just me and my two children. One is eight and the other just turned 12.

Lawyer: Okay. And do you operate a business?

Debtor: Actually, I do. Does it matter?

Lawyer: Well, business debts are sometimes treated differently than consumer debts when it comes to deciding your eligibility for filing Chapter 7. Also, Chapter 13 is often the better type of bankruptcy for an ongoing business if you're the sole owner because you can keep your business assets and use your business earnings to make your required payments, but we'll get to that later.

Debtor: Okay. I run my own business, repairing used electronic equipment.

Lawyer: Have you incorporated your business or is it a partnership?

Debtor: No, just me, a sole proprietor.

Lawyer: And do you have other work? Do you have a regular job and operate your business on the side?

Debtor: No, just the business.

Lawyer: Is your income pretty steady?

Debtor: It was until recently. Near the end of the year, my business dropped off and I'll be lucky to bring in half of what I was earning not too long ago. Also, I receive alimony and child support, which helps stabilize my income, but my ex told me just last week that his company is starting to lay people off and he may be next.

Lawyer: Looking at your debts as a whole, were more of them due to your business or more due to your personal needs? When making this assessment, your mortgage counts as a consumer debt and back taxes count as a business debt.

Debtor: Why are you asking?

Lawyer: If your debts were primarily incurred for your business, you wouldn't have to worry about something we call the means test—essentially a questionnaire that determines whether you can afford to pay back some of your debts in a Chapter 13 bankruptcy.

Debtor: I would say about 40% were from my business and 60% were personal.

Lawyer: Okay, too bad. That makes you a consumer debtor rather than a business debtor and we'll have to evaluate your income to see whether you need to take the means test. For starters, how much did you earn in the last six months? That's gross earnings less your reasonable business expenses.

Debtor: About $3,000 a month after expenses for the last six months.

Lawyer: You mentioned that you receive child support and alimony. How much, and do you have any other income?

Debtor: About $1,000 a month in alimony and $800 a month for child support. That's it.

Lawyer: Have those amounts been steady over the last six months?

Debtor: Yes, there haven't been any changes.

Lawyer: So, it looks like your average monthly earnings over the past six months are $3,000 from your business, $1,000 in alimony, and $800 for child support, for a total of $4,800. Does that sound right?

Debtor: Yes.

Lawyer: Under the bankruptcy law, if your income is less than the median annual income for a family of your size in your state, you are presumed to be eligible to file for Chapter 7 bankruptcy. You don't have to go fill out a lengthy form comparing your income to your expenses and your deductions for contractual obligations, such as a car note and mortgage. Does any of this sound familiar to you?

Debtor: Yes, I remember reading a few years ago that higher-income people aren't able to file for Chapter 7. Is that what you are talking about?

Lawyer: Yes, that's it. Also, if your income is less than the median for your state and you decide to file a Chapter 13 bankruptcy anyway, your repayment plan can last for three years instead of five. If, on the other hand, your income is more than the median, your plan would have to last for five years.

Debtor: I didn't know that.

Lawyer: So, let's see how these numbers work out. Your annual income based on your gross income for the last six months is $57,600. The New Hampshire median income for a household of three people is $107,942. So, you're well under the median income and don't have to take the means test to prove your eligibility for Chapter 7 bankruptcy. And if you decide to use Chapter 13, you can repay your debts over three years, instead of five.

Debtor: I guess that's good news, but when it comes right down to it, I wish I earned more, even if that meant I had to take the means test and have a Chapter 13 case last longer. Of course, if I had more money, I guess I wouldn't be talking to you about filing for bankruptcy in the first place.

Lawyer: Even though you qualify for Chapter 7 bankruptcy on the basis of your average income over the past six months, you can still be disqualified if, going forward, your actual monthly net income is substantially more than your actual monthly expenses, leaving you with some extra income every month to pay down your debt under a three-year Chapter 13 repayment plan.

Debtor: I wish I did have some extra income. When I recently compared my net income to my expenses, I definitely didn't have any money left over. Of course, there are probably ways I could reduce my expenses if I had to.

Lawyer: Well, your income is below the state median income, so as long as your basic living expenses are more or less equal to your net income, you have the option of filing for Chapter 7 bankruptcy.

Let's turn now to your residence. How long have you lived in New Hampshire?

Debtor: About three years.

Lawyer: Have you lived there continuously for the last three years, or did you live or maintain a residence somewhere else?

Debtor: I've lived here the whole time. I moved here from Vermont because of a job, but I didn't keep a home in Vermont. I vote and get my mail here.

Lawyer: Great. Because you've been living in New Hampshire for more than two years, we'll use our state's property exemptions. These will determine what property you can keep if you file a Chapter 7, and the minimum amount you'll have to pay your unsecured creditors if you file a Chapter 13 bankruptcy.

Debtor: Why do the exemptions matter in a Chapter 13 bankruptcy? I thought I could keep all of my property if I use Chapter 13.

Lawyer: Yes, you're right about that. But the law doesn't want your creditors to be worse off because you use Chapter 13. So a Chapter 13 repayment plan has to give your unsecured, nonpriority creditors at least as much they would have received had you filed a Chapter 7 bankruptcy. Roughly speaking, you have to pay for any nonexempt property that you keep.

Debtor: Okay, I guess that's fair.

Lawyer: Also, priority creditors have to be paid 100% in Chapter 13 cases. This would include back taxes, child support and alimony, and a portion of wages owed to employees. Nonpriority creditors are the rest of your creditors, typically credit card issuers, banks, doctors and lawyers, and holders of money judgments for repossessed and foreclosed property. For example, in your case, if you owed your employees wages or you owed contributions to a retirement plan, these would be priority debts and those creditors would be paid first in a Chapter 7 case if you have nonexempt assets. In a Chapter 13 case, priority debts must be paid in full over the life of your plan.

Debtor: Thanks for explaining that.

Lawyer: You're welcome. Let's figure out what you can protect. Do you own a home?

Debtor: Yes.

Lawyer: Are you making payments on a mortgage?

Debtor: Yes.

Lawyer: What's your monthly payment?

Debtor: $1,200.

Lawyer: Are you current on your payments?

Debtor: Yes.

Lawyer: What's your home worth?

Debtor: $150,000.

Lawyer: And how much do you owe on it?

Debtor: About $100,000.

Lawyer: That's a total?

Debtor: Yes.

Lawyer: Okay. Under the New Hampshire homestead exemption, you are entitled to protect $120,000 of equity in your home. You have $50,000 of equity, so all of your equity is protected.

Debtor: What's a homestead exemption?

Lawyer: That's an exemption that protects equity in your home. You are entitled to keep that much equity, even if you file for Chapter 7 bankruptcy. If your equity exceeded the exemption, you might lose the extra equity if you filed for Chapter 7. The trustee could sell your home, pay off the mortgage, pay you your exemption, and distribute the balance among your creditors. But because your equity is protected by the exemption, there wouldn't be anything left for your creditors after you got your exemption amount and the mortgage was paid. That's how exemptions work.

In Chapter 13, if you have property that isn't exempt, your repayment plan must pay unsecured creditors an amount equal to the nonexempt portion of the property's value at a minimum.

Debtor: I remember reading back in 2005 that the new bankruptcy law makes it harder for people to keep their homes. Will that affect me?

Lawyer: No. The law puts a cap of $170,350 on the exemption amount for people who bought their home within the 40 months before they filed for bankruptcy. So it affects only people who bought homes more recently, and then only if their states would otherwise allow them to take higher exemptions. For example, even if you bought your home in New Hampshire within the previous 40 months, the New Hampshire homestead is only $120,000, so the $170,350 cap wouldn't make any difference.

Debtor: So, I don't have to worry about it.

Lawyer: Right. Your exemption might be affected if you used nonexempt property in the last ten years to buy your home in order to cheat your creditors but that probably didn't happen. I guess I should ask how you got the money to pay for your home, just in case.

Debtor: I borrowed money from my parents.

Lawyer: Great. Your home equity is covered by your state's homestead exemption and you can keep it if you file for Chapter 7 bankruptcy.

Debtor: What happens to my home if I file for Chapter 13 bankruptcy?

Lawyer: As long as you keep making your mortgage payments and the other payments required by your Chapter 13 plan, there won't be a problem. However, if you fall behind on your payments, your lender could foreclose, just as if you hadn't filed bankruptcy. On the other hand, if you have reason to believe that the mortgage or foreclosure papers are defective, you can challenge the mortgage or foreclosure as part of your Chapter 13 case.

Debtor: So unless I have some basis to challenge the mortgage, I have to keep my mortgage payments current, no matter which type of bankruptcy I file?

Lawyer: That's right. What other debts do you owe?

Debtor: Mainly credit card debts. And one SBA bank loan for my business.

Lawyer: Is the SBA loan secured by any of your property?

Debtor: No, it's just a bank loan.

Lawyer: How much are you paying on that loan?

Debtor: About $300 a month.

Lawyer: And how much credit card debt do you owe?

Debtor: About $23,000.

Lawyer: What were the credit card debts for?

Debtor: About $14,000 for personal expenses and $6,000 for paying off back taxes. Also, $3,000 for a credit card charge by my husband that I assumed in our divorce.

Lawyer: Oh yeah? What period did you owe the taxes for?

Debtor: The last couple of years.

Lawyer: That's interesting. I'll come back to this later, but bankruptcy law allows you to discharge credit card charges used to pay off taxes in a Chapter 13 bankruptcy but not in a Chapter 7 bankruptcy. So, if there is no other reason to choose one type of bankruptcy over the other, you would be wise to choose Chapter 13.

So, having paid those taxes, are you now current on your taxes for the past four years?

Debtor: Yes.

Lawyer: That's good. You can't file for Chapter 13 unless you have filed your state and federal taxes for the previous four years. How much was the bank loan for?

Debtor: $40,000.

Lawyer: Did anybody cosign on that loan?

Debtor: As matter of fact, my mother cosigned that loan.

Lawyer: Did any of the money from the loan go to your mother? Or did you get all of it?

Debtor: All of the loan money was received by me and used by me.

Lawyer: Hmm. Even if you could get rid of that debt in bankruptcy, your mother would still be on the hook to repay it if you filed under Chapter 7. Even though you wouldn't be responsible for the debt going forward, she would be.

But if you file for Chapter 13 bankruptcy, your mother won't have to repay it while your plan is in place, as long as your plan provides for payment of some or all of that debt. So, assuming your plan lasts for three years, your mother won't be on the hook during that period. However, she will still be responsible for any amount you haven't paid when your plan ends. So, again, if there is no other reason to choose one type of bankruptcy instead of the other, it looks like Chapter 13 might be a good choice.

Do you have any other debts?

Debtor: Nothing significant, maybe a total of $2,000 in miscellaneous bills. And, oh, does child support count?

Lawyer: I thought you were receiving child support.

Debtor: I am, but I also owe child support for a child from a previous marriage. I never paid because my ex never asked, but now he's seeking current support as well as $5,000 in back support.

Lawyer: How much will you owe?

Debtor: Under the court order, $300 a month.

Lawyer: Have you started paying the support?

Debtor: No. I have to start paying it next month.

Lawyer: If you decide to file for Chapter 13, you will have to remain current on your child support payments throughout the life of your plan. If you don't, your case will be dismissed or converted to a Chapter 7 bankruptcy.

Debtor: I understand.

Lawyer: Let's talk later about the back support you owe. When were you divorced?

Debtor: A couple of years ago.

Lawyer: Did you assume any of the debts in the course of your divorce?

Debtor: Yes, I assumed the credit card charges for personal expenses in exchange for my ex-husband's share of our home.

Lawyer: Okay. How much were these charges?

Debtor: About $3,000.

Lawyer: Hmmm, in a Chapter 7 bankruptcy you can discharge this debt with regard to the creditor, but your ex can come after you for this debt if he is sued by the creditor. In Chapter 13 bankruptcy, the debt would be fully discharged, both in respect to the creditor and your ex.

Debtor: It sounds like I should probably file for Chapter 13.

Lawyer: Maybe, but we're not through yet. Let's talk about your other property. And this is where exemptions will become important. Other than your home, do you have any other property you would want to keep in your bankruptcy?

Debtor: Oh, yes. I have a concert piano and some copyright interests in several songs I wrote. Also, I have a car I want to hold on to and the tools I use in my business.

Lawyer: How much are the tools worth?

Debtor: About $3,000.

Lawyer: Great. New Hampshire allows you to keep up to $5,000 worth of tools for your occupation, so those are covered. How much is the car worth?

Debtor: About $4,000 according to *Kelley Blue Book*.

Lawyer: Are you making payments on it?

Debtor: Yes.

Lawyer: How much is left on your note?

Debtor: About $8,000.

Lawyer: When did you buy it?

Debtor: Three years ago.

Lawyer: If you file for Chapter 13, you can pay off the value of the car rather than what you still owe on the note. This is called a cramdown, and it's another great reason to file for Chapter 13. And it's a good thing you didn't buy your car more recently: You couldn't use this cramdown procedure if you bought the car within 2½ years of your bankruptcy filing date.

Now let's take a look at the New Hampshire exemptions to see whether your other property is covered. Remember, exemptions like the homestead exemption and the tools of your occupation exemption are laws that determine what property you can keep in your bankruptcy. As I read them, the car is covered because you owe more than it's worth, so your creditors wouldn't get anything if it were sold. Because you don't have any equity in the car, you don't need to protect it with an exemption. As for the piano and your copyright interests, there are no state exemptions that specifically cover those items.

Debtor: Does that mean I'll lose my piano?

Lawyer: Not necessarily. Remember, if you file for Chapter 13, you don't lose any property—you just have to make sure you pay your creditors at least what they would have received from a sale of the piano in a Chapter 7 bankruptcy. And even though New Hampshire doesn't specifically exempt pianos, it has a $3,500 exemption for all your furniture. So depending on your piano's value, it might be covered by the furniture exemption.

Debtor: I think my piano would sell for about $8,500 and I guess my copyrights are pretty much worthless.

Lawyer: Why do you say your copyright interests are worthless?

Debtor: Well, they belong to three songs I wrote, but I've never had the songs published, so there is no one to sell them to.

Lawyer: Okay, let's forget about the songs. We're only talking about the piano.

Looking at the New Hampshire exemptions, in addition to the portion of the piano's value arguably covered by the $3,500 furniture exemption, there are also some wildcard exemptions. This type of exemption can be used to protect any property you choose. New Hampshire's wildcard exemptions will provide an additional $8,000 that you can put toward the piano: That takes into account a $1,000 straight wildcard, plus a $7,000 wildcard that you can use if you don't fully take advantage of certain other exemptions. If you use these wildcards for your piano, only about $500 of its value is not exempt. Since the costs of sale and the trustee's commission, on top of the exemptions, would more than eat up that $500, there is a chance that you won't have to pay any of the piano's value to your creditors in a Chapter 13 case. Of course, if you need part of the furniture exemption for other pieces of furniture, that would take away from the exemption available for your piano. And, the trustee might object to classifying a piano as furniture.

Debtor: Okay.

Lawyer: Here is a copy of the New Hampshire exemptions. (Lawyer hands Georgia a page showing the New Hampshire bankruptcy exemptions.) Other than the piano, do you have any property that exceeds the exemption limit or isn't on the exemption list?

Debtor: No, the piano is the only problem. But if I use the furniture exemption for my piano, my furniture won't be exempt. It's old furniture I bought at Goodwill. I have nothing that would be of any value.

Lawyer: Well, that's up to the trustee. If you choose to use the entire furniture exemption for your piano, you might have to place some value on your furniture equal to what it would cost you to replace it.

Debtor: That would probably be about $1,000.

Lawyer: Okay, so you might have a couple of thousand dollars in nonexempt property depending on how you use the wildcard. That's under the New Hampshire state exemptions. If your state allows it, you can choose to use a different set of exemptions set out in the bankruptcy code termed the "federal exemptions." As it turns out, New Hampshire does allow filers to use the federal exemptions. You can choose from the federal exemption list or the New Hampshire state list, but you can't mix or match.

Let's take a look and see if the federal exemptions would do you any good. The federal exemptions protect only $25,150 in your home equity. You have $50,000 equity to protect, so you wouldn't want to choose the federal exemptions.

So, we know you can file for Chapter 7 bankruptcy if you wish. You could keep your home and perhaps your piano, even though it isn't wholly exempt. If you can't use the furniture exemption for the piano, the trustee would probably sell it and use the proceeds to pay your unsecured creditors. Or, you could keep the piano if the trustee were willing to sell it to you for a negotiated price. But that's all in a Chapter 7 bankruptcy.

Debtor: It still sounds like Chapter 13 is a good idea. But you said I have to make sure I'm eligible. What are the requirements?

Lawyer: Before we get to that, I have a few more questions.

Debtor: Okay.

Lawyer: During the previous year, have you made payments on any loans you owe to relatives?

Debtor: Nope.

Lawyer: Good. If you had, the trustee might require the relative to return the money and increase the amount your creditors would get.

Debtor: I wouldn't want that to happen.

Lawyer: Have you given away or sold any property to anyone within the past two years?

Debtor: No.

Lawyer: That also simplifies things. If you had given away some property, or you had sold some property for less than what it was worth, the difference in value would be considered nonexempt property. You'd have to add that to the amount you have to pay under your Chapter 13 plan. But you didn't sell any property, so this rule doesn't affect you.

Debtor: Wow, there's a lot to consider here. Are we done—isn't it clear that Chapter 13 is the correct choice for me?

Lawyer: Bear with me; just a few more issues to consider. Chapter 13 has some limitations on how much debt you can owe. Let's see, you owe a total of $69,000 of unsecured debt: a $40,000 bank loan, $23,000 in credit card debts, $5,000 in child support arrearage, and $2,000 in other debts. You owe a total of $108,000 secured debt for your home and car. This means you fall within the eligibility guidelines, which are $1,257,850 for secured debts and $419,275 for unsecured debts.

Debtor: That's good.

Lawyer: Now let's see what debts you would have to pay in your Chapter 13 bankruptcy. Some debts have to be paid in full while others can be paid in part, depending on your income. The debts you would have to pay in full include at least the $5,000 arrearage for your child support

and the $500 for the nonexempt portion of your piano and your furniture, or $5,500 total debt payable in full over the course of your Chapter 13 plan.

Debtor: So how much would that be a month?

Lawyer: People whose average gross income for the preceding six months is less than the state median income—which is your situation—can propose a three-year repayment plan. If your income were higher than the median, you'd have to propose a five-year payment plan.

So, when spreading out $5,000 over three years, you would have to pay at least $139 a month, plus the monthly payment on your car as modified downwards to reflect its value ($111), your current mortgage payment, and other expenses related to Chapter 13 bankruptcy, such as the trustee's fee and your attorney's fee if you use an attorney. If you don't have enough income to pay that after you subtract your living expenses—including your mortgage payment and your car payment—you won't qualify for a three-year Chapter 13 plan.

Debtor: How can I tell whether I have enough income to meet the Chapter 13 requirements?

Lawyer: If you decide to file a Chapter 13 bankruptcy, you have to fill out some forms to determine your income and your expenses. These forms will basically show whether you can afford a Chapter 13 bankruptcy. If you don't have enough income to pay all necessary debts in three years, you can ask the judge to let you propose a five-year plan and pay less each month. If you still don't have enough to make your payments, you probably won't be able to use Chapter 13.

Debtor: So, do you suggest that I file for Chapter 7? Or should I use Chapter 13?

Lawyer: Well, before I answer that, I've saved the best for last. Let's talk about attorneys' fees. I charge $3,500 for a Chapter 13 and $1,500 for a Chapter 7. So, by filing a Chapter 7, you'll save at least $2,000 in legal fees. But in Chapter 13 cases, I charge only $2,000 up front; the additional $1,500 can be paid through your plan. Overall, it will cost less up front for you to file a Chapter 7 bankruptcy. Also, in your case, I see no reason why you couldn't handle your own Chapter 7 bankruptcy with the help of the ABC Bankruptcy Petition Preparation Service down the street. They have the same computer program as I use, but all they do is help you complete your paperwork. They can't give you legal advice. If you are up to handling your own case, which I think you are from this conversation, you should explore the self-help option.

If you do decide to do it yourself, I would be happy to consult with you for a flat rate of $150. Under my consultation agreement you could ask me as many questions as you want, over the telephone. Even with a good

self-help book, you might miss important information that you need to have a good result in your bankruptcy.

Debtor: I want you to handle my case. I don't think I'm up for self-representation.

Lawyer: Okay, now I'm ready to answer your basic question. If you have enough income in your budget to use Chapter 13, it would be an excellent choice because:

- It will protect your codebtor—your mother—for the life of the plan.
- It will allow you to keep your car and pay it off at market value rather than reaffirming the current note, which is twice what it's worth.
- Unlike Chapter 7, it fully discharges the credit card debts you assumed in your divorce.
- Unlike Chapter 7, it will allow you to discharge the credit card debts you incurred to pay off your taxes.
- It will allow you to pay off your child support arrearage—that is, the back child support you owe—over the life of your plan, without worrying about wage garnishments and bank levies.

So, assuming you have enough income to propose a confirmable Chapter 13 plan, and pay my fees, I recommend Chapter 13. If you can't propose a confirmable Chapter 13 plan even over a five-year period, or you can't afford my fees, I suggest you go with Chapter 7. ●

CHAPTER

8

Your Credit Cards

What will happen to your credit cards when you file for bankruptcy depends largely on the current status of your accounts, and to a lesser degree on the creditors. For this discussion, most credit cards fall into three possible categories:

- cards on which you have a zero balance—that is, you're all paid up
- cards on which you have a balance but are current—that is, you make at least the minimum payment each month, and
- cards on which you are in default— that is, you haven't made any payments in a while.

If Your Balance Is Zero

On your bankruptcy papers, you'll have to list your creditors—all of the people and businesses to whom you currently owe money. If you have a balance of zero on a credit card, you don't currently owe the card issuer any money, and you don't have to list it on your bankruptcy papers, you might come through bankruptcy still owning that credit card. But don't get your hopes up because it's unlikely. One of several things will probably happen.

The Trustee Might Take Your Card

It's possible that the bankruptcy trustee might confiscate your credit cards, ask you about the creditors with whom you have a zero balance, or demand that you write to them and tell them about your bankruptcy. However, this is much more likely to happen in a Chapter 13 case because the trustee must supervise your finances for three to five years. In a Chapter 7 case, the trustee won't care about debts incurred after filing.

The Credit Card Issuer Could Find Out About Your Bankruptcy

Most credit card companies constantly review your credit reports for any sign of economic weakness. For example, credit card companies often raise interest rates on cards if the cardholder makes a late payment on another card or to another creditor although the Credit Card Accountability and Disclosure Act of 2009 placed some restrictions on interest rate hikes and requires companies to provide a certain amount of notice before increasing your interest rate. Therefore, even if you have a zero balance and you don't list the creditor on your paperwork, a credit card company might find out about your bankruptcy.

EXAMPLE: You file for bankruptcy and include the following debts, among others: BigBank Visa, MediumBank MasterCard, and LittleBank Visa. Your balance on your TinyBank MasterCard is $0, so you don't include that creditor on your bankruptcy papers. TinyBank learns of your bankruptcy from the credit bureaus it checks to monitor the creditworthiness of its customers and closes your account.

Your Credit Card Issuer Could Cancel Your Zero-Balance Card

On learning of your bankruptcy, the company that issued your credit card might decide to terminate your account, even though you don't owe that business a penny, on the ground that you are no longer a good credit risk. On the other hand, some credit card companies will consider you an excellent credit risk and be happy to continue doing business with you because you won't be able to receive a Chapter 7 discharge for another eight years. Often enough, you will be able to keep your zero-balance credit card account.

Even if you lose all your credit cards in your bankruptcy, don't worry too much over it—especially if you file for Chapter 7 bankruptcy. There are other ways to get a credit card if you think you need one. Many people receive credit offers shortly after filing for bankruptcy. In the meantime, you should be prepared to use your debit card. You can learn more about rebuilding your credit after bankruptcy in *Credit Repair*, by Amy Loftsgordon and Cara O'Neill (Nolo).

The Trustee Might Recover Recent Payments on Your Credit Card

If you're thinking that you should pay off a credit card before filing for bankruptcy so you can keep it, think again. When you file for bankruptcy, you must indicate on your papers all of your recent financial transactions.

For filers whose debts are primarily consumer debts, payments of more than $600 to any single creditor in the 90 days before filing could be retroactively canceled. For filers whose debts are primarily business debts, payments of more than $6,825 to any single creditor in the 90 days before filing could be retroactively canceled. (These figures will adjust on April 1, 2022.)

These "eve of bankruptcy" payments are called "preferences." The trustee can recover preferences from the creditor you paid and use the money for the benefit of all your creditors, not just the creditor who received the payment. There are exceptions to this rule for business debtors who make the payment in the normal course of their business. Another exception exists for payments made for regular ongoing expenses like your mortgage or utilities as opposed to one-time expenses, like paying off a delinquent bill.

If You Owe Money But Are Current

If you owe money on a credit card but have managed to pay at least a minimum payment each month, you will have to list this creditor on your bankruptcy papers even though you aren't behind. Your bankruptcy—Chapter 7 or Chapter 13—might come as a surprise to the creditor.

If you file for Chapter 7 bankruptcy and want to keep your credit card, you might be able to do so by offering to sign a reaffirmation agreement with the credit card issuer. In a reaffirmation agreement, you agree to repay the balance in full, as if you never filed for bankruptcy. However, you will have to convince the court that reaffirming the debt is in your best interest. Most courts will likely be unwilling to sign such an agreement. (See Ch. 6 for more on reaffirming debts.)

If you file for Chapter 13 bankruptcy, your plan will propose to repay your nonpriority unsecured creditors, including your credit card issuers, some percentage of what you owe. Chapter 13 plans are sometimes referred to by this percentage—for example, "this couple filed a 55% plan."

If this doesn't immediately make sense, remember that, unlike credit card debts, some types of debts, including priority debts and secured debts, must be repaid in full, even in Chapter 13. They'd be paid first. Then your disposable income—the amount remaining after paying your secured and priority creditors—gets divided between the nonpriority unsecured creditors. The percentage each receives is the percentage we refer to here. (For more on secured debts, see Ch. 6.)

In most cases, even if you propose to pay 100% of what you owe on a card, the creditor will cancel your account. And the Chapter 13 trustee could confiscate your card anyway.

Reaffirming a Credit Card Debt Might Not Be a Good Idea

Before you reaffirm a credit card debt, ask yourself whether it really makes sense. For most people, it doesn't. The purpose of filing for bankruptcy is to get rid of debts, not to still owe money. Admittedly, some people choose to file, even though they know that they won't be able to eliminate certain debts. But even in that situation, it almost never makes sense to come out of bankruptcy owing a credit card balance you had before you filed. And it's unlikely that a bankruptcy judge would approve the agreement. More likely, you will come out of bankruptcy still owing taxes or a student loan. If you want to have a credit card after bankruptcy, chances are very good that you'll be able to get one (but one that starts with a zero balance, not with the amount you owed before you filed). A debit card will probably serve all of your needs—and won't get you back into debt.

Your Job, Freedom, and Self-Respect

For most people, the thought of filing for bankruptcy raises a number of troubling questions. Many of these have to do with eliminating debts. Other questions concern the potential loss of property. (You'll find answers in Chs. 3, 4, 5, and 6.)

But many of the questions go beyond debts and assets and hit at the core of what it means to be a member of our society—earning a living, bringing up your children, and keeping your freedom and self-respect.

Will You Lose Your Self-Respect?

Americans learn almost from birth that it's a good thing to buy all sorts of goods and services. A highly paid army of persuaders surrounds us with thousands of seductive messages each day that say "Buy, buy, buy." Available credit makes living beyond our means easy—and resisting the siren sounds of the advertisers difficult. But we're also told that if we fail to pay for it all right on time, we're failures. In short, much of American economic life is built on a contradiction.

Adding to this contradiction is the system of high interest and penalties employed by most credit card companies that cause our debt to soar beyond any reasonable expectation. In many cases, the interest rates are so high that the companies involved would have been prosecuted for loan sharking in the not-too-distant past—before the credit card industry

systematically lobbied to do away with usury laws or to create exceptions to those laws for credit card interest rates.

Credit card companies keep this system working by encouraging us to make the minimum payment, which stimulates us to make more credit purchases and eases us into debt loads far beyond our ability to ever pay them off. To feel guilty about being caught in this deliberately contrived economic trap is nonsense. There's much more to life than an 800 point credit rating and bigger things to feel guilty about than the failure to pay bills on time.

What About Friendly Creditors?

While you might not care about discharging your credit card debts in bankruptcy, you might feel bad about doing the same to the debts you owe to friends, family, or business creditors in your community—such as a doctor, dentist, chiropractor, pharmacist, accountant, lawyer, contractor, or hardware store. Even so, you have to list all debts in your bankruptcy papers, including those obligations that you'd rather pay. While qualifying debts you owe to creditors close to you will get discharged, there's nothing to prevent you from voluntarily paying the debts after you file. Communicating your intent to repay these friendly creditors will make everybody involved feel a whole lot better about your bankruptcy.

Fortunately, it's been recognized that debts can get the better of even the most conscientious among us. Bankruptcy provides a sensible way for debt-oppressed people to start new economic lives. It's a truly worthy part of our legal system, based as it is on forgiveness rather than retribution. Certainly, it gives people a fresh start in our increasingly volatile economy, helps keep families together, reduces suicide rates, and keeps the ranks of the homeless from growing even larger. So, don't let the word "bankruptcy" cause you stress.

Will You Lose Your Job?

No employer—government or private—can fire you because you filed for bankruptcy. An employer can't discriminate against you in other terms and conditions of employment either—for example, by reducing your salary, demoting you, or taking away responsibilities —because of your bankruptcy.

Termination for Other Reasons

If there are other valid reasons for taking these actions, the fact that you filed for bankruptcy won't protect you. In other words, an employer who wants to take negative action against you can do so provided there are other valid reasons to explain the action—such as tardiness, dishonesty, or incompetence. But if you are fired shortly after your bankruptcy is brought to your employer's attention, you might have a case against the employer for illegal discrimination because of your bankruptcy.

How Employers Find Out About Bankruptcy Filings

In practice, employers rarely find out about Chapter 7 bankruptcy filings. However, if a creditor has sued you, obtained a judgment, and started garnishing your wages, you or your attorney must notify your employer about the bankruptcy to stop the garnishment. In that case, your employer will get the news. Given that the payroll department already knew you were having financial problems, your employer will probably welcome that you are taking affirmative steps to put your problems behind you by filing for bankruptcy. Most employers prefer it because it lessens the temptation to embezzle funds—or, in security-related fields, to accept a bribe— to pay off debt.

An employer that doesn't know about your bankruptcy case might learn about it if you fall behind on your Chapter 13 bankruptcy payments. Some jurisdictions allow judges to order Chapter 13 payments automatically deducted from your wages and sent to the bankruptcy court. In effect, if you default on your payments, your employer will act as a sort of collection agency to make sure you honor your Chapter 13 plan.

Income Deduction Orders Work

You might not like the idea of the income deduction order, but the bankruptcy court could deny your Chapter 13 plan if you refuse to comply with it. And the order will probably make it easier for you to complete your plan. The success rate of Chapter 13 cases is higher for debtors with income deduction orders than for debtors who pay the trustee themselves, for the very obvious reason that it's hard to spend money you never receive.

Security Clearances

Many jobs require a security clearance. If you are a member of the armed forces or an employee of the CIA, FBI, another government agency, or a private company that contracts with the government, you might have a security clearance. Do you risk losing your security clearance if you file for bankruptcy? Probably not—in fact, the opposite could be true. According to credit counselors for the military and the CIA, a person with financial problems— particularly someone with a lot of debt— is at high risk of being blackmailed. By filing for bankruptcy and getting rid of the debts, you substantially lower that risk. Bankruptcy usually works more in your favor than to your detriment.

Effect of Bankruptcy on Job Applicants

Federal, state, and local government agencies cannot consider your bankruptcy when deciding whether to hire you. However, a corresponding rule for private employers doesn't exist, and some people find that having a bankruptcy comes back to haunt them. This is particularly true when applying for jobs involving money handling, such as bookkeeping, accounting, payroll, and so on.

Many private employers conduct a credit check on job applicants as a matter of course and will find out about your bankruptcy from the credit report. While employers need your permission to run credit checks, employers can also refuse to hire you if you don't consent. If you're asked to give this authorization, consider speaking candidly about what the employer will find in your file. Being honest up front about problems that are truly behind you could outweigh any negative effects of the bankruptcy filing itself.

Other Forms of Discrimination Because of Bankruptcy

Federal, state, and local governmental units can't legally discriminate against you because you filed for bankruptcy.

Discrimination by Government Agencies

Governmental units might not deny, revoke, suspend, or refuse to renew a license, permit, charter, franchise, or another similar grant based on your bankruptcy. Judges interpreting this law have ruled that the government cannot:

- deny or terminate public benefits
- deny or evict you from public housing
- deny or refuse to renew your state liquor license
- exclude you from participating in a state home mortgage finance program
- withhold your college transcript
- deny you a driver's license
- deny you a contract, such as a contract for a construction project, or
- exclude you from participating in a government-guaranteed student loan program.

In general, once any government-related debt has been discharged, all acts against you arising from that debt must also end. If, for example, you lost your driver's license because you didn't pay a civil court judgment that resulted from a car accident, you must be granted a license once the debt is discharged. However, if the debt isn't discharged, you can still be denied your license until you pay up.

Discrimination by Private Entities

Prohibitions against private discrimination aren't nearly as broad as prohibitions against government discrimination. As mentioned above, private employers cannot fire you or punish you because you filed for bankruptcy. However, other forms of discrimination in the private sector, such as denying you rental housing or a surety bond or withholding a college transcript, are legal.

The best way to confront this type of discrimination is to build a solid credit history after bankruptcy. You can find sound strategies for getting back on your financial feet in *Credit Repair*, by Amy Loftsgordon and Cara O'Neill (Nolo).

If a potential landlord does a credit check, sees your bankruptcy, and refuses to rent to you, there's not much you can do except try to show that you'll pay your rent and be a responsible tenant. You probably will need to go apartment hunting with a "renter's résumé" that shows you in the best possible light. Be ready to offer a cosigner, find roommates, offer to pay more rent, or even pay several months' rent up front in cash.

Effect of Bankruptcy on Child Custody

Bankruptcy and divorce are so often related these days that one frequently follows the other. Bankruptcy judges are becoming experts on family law matters, and family law judges are becoming bankruptcy experts. Don't worry about your bankruptcy affecting your custody status. Keep in mind, however, that bankruptcy does not relieve you of your child support and spousal support obligations, past or present.

Effect of Bankruptcy on Your Freedoms

We Americans are used to some basic freedoms, and many people fear losing those freedoms if they file for bankruptcy. Relax. Except in some unusual cases, this is just not going to happen.

Consequences of Dishonesty

When you file for bankruptcy, you swear, under "penalty of perjury," that everything in your papers is true to the best of your knowledge. If you deliberately commit a dishonest act, such as failing to disclose property, omitting material information about your financial affairs, unloading nonexempt assets just before filing—especially if you don't disclose the transfer—or using a false Social Security number to hide your identity as a prior filer, you can be criminally prosecuted for fraud.

Bankruptcy law streamlines the process by which fraud-related cases can be referred to the U.S. Attorney's office for prosecution. Also, the law requires the government to audit one out of every 250 bankruptcy cases. It is important to disclose all of your property and debts in your bankruptcy papers, provide accurate answers to the questions in your Statement of Financial Affairs for Individuals Filing for Bankruptcy (see Ch. 10), and not try to hide property from the trustee or your creditors before filing.

Examples of criminal prosecutions abound. A debtor in Massachusetts went to jail for failing to list on his bankruptcy papers his interest in a condominium and $26,000 worth of jewelry. Another Massachusetts debtor served time for listing her home on her bankruptcy papers as worth $70,000 when it had been appraised for $116,000. An Alaska debtor was jailed for failing to disclose buried cash and diamonds. A Pennsylvania debtor omitted from her papers $50,000 from a divorce settlement and was sentenced to some time in prison.

The message is simple: Bankruptcy is geared toward the honest debtor who inadvertently gets in too deep and needs the help of the bankruptcy court to get a fresh start. A bankruptcy judge will not help someone who has played fast and loose with creditors or tries to do so with the bankruptcy court. If you lie, hide, or cheat, it might come back to haunt you in ways much worse than your current debt crisis ever could.

Moving

You are free to change your residence after you file. Just be sure to send the trustee and court a written notification of change of address if your case is still open. If your move involves selling your house and you've filed for Chapter 13 bankruptcy, the trustee will likely want to use sales proceeds that you can't protect with a bankruptcy exemption to pay off your creditors if your plan doesn't already propose full payment.

Changing Jobs

You can certainly change jobs while your bankruptcy case is pending and after it ends. If you've filed a Chapter 13 case, let the trustee know so the trustee can transfer the income deduction order.

Divorce

No one can force you to stay married, not even a bankruptcy judge. Here's what you can expect to happen.

Chapter 7. If you've filed for Chapter 7 bankruptcy and want to end your marriage, it shouldn't be a problem. Your bankruptcy case will probably end long before your divorce case does. Usually, it's beneficial to file for divorce while you're still married because it allows you to erase joint and individual debt leaving you less to divide in family court. However, sometimes it makes sense to wait to file for bankruptcy until after the divorce. For instance, if your joint income is too high to qualify for Chapter 7 while married, you might have a better chance of qualifying as a single person once the divorce is final.

Keep in mind that if you assume responsibility for debts in a divorce, you will still owe those debts after your bankruptcy to the extent that the creditor goes after your ex. For instance, if you agree in your divorce agreement to pay off a particular credit card and then you file bankruptcy, your liability to the creditor is discharged, but you are still responsible to your ex if the credit card company sues him or her for the amount owed. For this reason, it sometimes makes sense to file bankruptcy before you assume responsibility for any debt in the course of your divorce. Another approach is to divide the debt so that the person who took out the credit remains responsible, not the other spouse. That will allow a post-divorce bankruptcy to wipe out the debt completely and avoid the issue of the other spouse remaining responsible for payment.

Note that unlike the situation in Chapter 7, in Chapter 13, you are permitted to fully discharge the debt you've assumed responsibility for in your divorce as long as it's not for support. For instance, you can eliminate debt related to property division.

Chapter 13. If you've filed a Chapter 13 case with your spouse, you might face some complications if you want to continue your case and get divorced. Bankruptcy law states that you must be a married couple to be eligible to file a joint case. If you have a "final decree" of divorce, you are no longer eligible to file a joint bankruptcy.

TIP

Who's going to know? It's highly unusual for anyone to find out about your bankruptcy other than your creditors, businesses that obtain a copy of your credit report, and the people you tell. Although your bankruptcy filing might be listed in a local newspaper, these notices often appear in low-circulation papers, and few people sit around reading such notices anyway. Bankruptcy filings aren't broadcast on local television or radio unless you are very famous.

Bankruptcy Forms and Procedures

Chapter 7 bankruptcy is a relatively straightforward process for most filers. You can look forward to smooth sailing—whether you represent yourself or are represented by a lawyer— if all of the following are true in your situation:

- Your average gross monthly income over the six-month period prior to the month you file doubled (you'll multiply the six-month figure by two) is less than the yearly median income for a household of your size in the state where you are filing.
- If you are in business for yourself and your business has few or no assets or inventory.
- Your only real estate is your home, you have little or no equity in it, and you're current on your mortgage payment if you'd like to keep it.
- You have lived in the state where you are filing for at least two years.
- Your net monthly income doesn't exceed your reasonable living expenses by more than a few hundred dollars.
- You haven't given any property away or sold it for less than it's worth during the previous two years.
- Property you care about keeping can't be taken by the trustee because it's protected by exemption laws.
- You haven't repaid a debt owed to a relative or business associate within the previous year.

- All of your debts are dischargeable, such as credit card bills, medical balances, and personal loans.

If you meet all of these criteria, it is unlikely that your case will produce any disputes that will have to be resolved by a bankruptcy judge, rather than by agreement between you and the trustee or your creditors. Your only personal appearance is likely to be at the creditors' meeting (see Ch. 1). However, if you are reaffirming a car note or another debt connected to collateral, you might have to appear at a brief hearing where the bankruptcy judge will decide whether reaffirmation is in your best interest (see Ch. 6 for more on the reaffirmation hearing). But, to the extent that your case is more complex—perhaps because of multiple real estate holdings, an ongoing retail business, or inappropriate prebankruptcy transfers of property—it makes good sense to hire a lawyer in order to achieve the best possible result.

Some brief descriptions of the Chapter 7 proceedings that might require some legal help are explained in this chapter. (Ch. 11 explains what type of help is available and how to find it.)

While many Chapter 7 filers successfully represent themselves, most people who file for Chapter 13 bankruptcy hire an attorney to represent them. Chapter 13 bankruptcy is almost always too difficult for people to complete successfully without representation. Some of the trouble points are outlined later in this chapter.

If, after you file your bankruptcy, you want to change course and convert to another type of bankruptcy or get out of bankruptcy altogether, you'll find the rules that apply in this chapter. And, no matter what type of bankruptcy you file, you can look forward to completing plenty of paperwork. The basic forms required in both types of bankruptcy are explained in this chapter as well.

The Means Test

A single dollar's difference in your income can have a large impact on your bankruptcy plans. If your "current monthly income" (CMI defined and described in Ch. 2) multiplied by twelve is one dollar less than your state's median yearly income, you can:

- file for Chapter 7 bankruptcy without completing the Chapter 7 Means Test Calculation (Form 122A-2)
- use your actual expenses to compute your disposable income rather than the IRS's expense standards, which are often lower, and
- propose a three-year plan if you file for Chapter 13 bankruptcy.

The Means Test Forms

The means test consists of three bankruptcy forms, but you won't have to fill out all of them. Here's how it works:

- Form 122A-1, Chapter 7 Statement of Your Current Monthly Income. Everyone filing for Chapter 7 bankruptcy must complete this form. It calculates your CMI and compares it to the median income in your state for the same family size. If your income is above the state median, you must also complete Form 122A-2. If your income is below the state median, then you don't have to complete Form 122A-2.
- Form 122A-1Supp, Statement of Exemption from Presumption of Abuse Under § 707(b)2). There are several instances when you do not have to

pass the Chapter 7 means test in order to be eligible for Chapter 7 bankruptcy. If any of these apply to you, you must complete Form 122A-1 Supp.

- Form 122A-2, Chapter 7 Means Test Calculation. If your income is above the median income in your state, you must complete Form 122A-2. If you pass this part of the test, you can file for Chapter 7 (assuming you meet other eligibility criteria). If you don't pass, you cannot file for Chapter 7.

Although all filers used to use the same forms, this has changed. You'll want to be sure that you're using the individual version for your filing (businesses use the "non-individual" forms).

On the other hand, if your CMI multiplied by 12 is even one dollar more than the state's median yearly income, you must:

- complete the Chapter 7 Means Test Calculation (Form 122A-2) and produce results showing that you have insufficient funds in your budget to support a Chapter 13 repayment plan
- use the IRS standards to compute your disposable income if you decide to file a Chapter 13 bankruptcy, and
- propose a five-year plan if you file for Chapter 13 bankruptcy.

For many filers, this won't be a close call: It will be fairly easy to figure out where you stand. But how should you proceed if a modest change in your income or expenses would put you below the median income or change the outcome of the means test?

Sometimes waiting a month or two before filing will take care of the problem. For example, if you have recently become unemployed but your income for the months prior to your unemployment put you over the top, just waiting another month might sufficiently lower your average income for the six-month period to squeeze you under the bar. Let's see how this works. Assume Dennis makes an average monthly gross income of $5,000 for the five-month period of March through July 2021. He gets laid off in August and receives $1,800 in unemployment insurance payments. His average gross monthly income for the

entire six-month period (March to August) is $4,466. If Dennis files for bankruptcy in September, his average gross monthly income for the preceding six-month period multiplied by twelve ($53,592) will exceed the median yearly income for his family's size ($48,000). However, if Dennis waits another month to file, his average monthly income for the six-month period preceding his filing date will decrease to $3,933, putting him under the median income level applicable to his case.

If waiting to file bankruptcy won't solve the problem, the stakes might well be worth the cost of a consultation with a bankruptcy attorney who will be familiar with the categories and definitions of income and expenses. In addition to appreciating the nuances contained within the means test, attorneys in close cases can help clients decide the best course of action.

Challenges for Abuse

Bankruptcy law describes two kinds of abuse that can sink your Chapter 7 filing:

- failure to pass the means test (presumptive abuse), and
- abuse under the totality of the circumstances (general abuse).

If abuse is presumed because you fail the means test, you won't be allowed to proceed with your Chapter 7 bankruptcy unless you can rebut the presumption by showing special circumstances (see "Defending a Motion to Dismiss or Convert," below). If you are accused of abuse under the totality of the circumstances, however, the party bringing the charge—usually the U.S. Trustee—has the burden of proving abuse. Needless to say, you are much more likely to be barred from Chapter 7 when abuse is presumed than when it must be proved.

TIP

Abuse laws apply only to consumer cases. If your business is filing for bankruptcy, or if you're filing but the majority of your debts stem from your business, you won't need to take the means test. The law on abuse, both general and presumed, applies only to filers with primarily consumer debts. Filers who have primarily business debts are not subject to abuse motions on either general or presumptive grounds. Your debts are primarily business debts if more than half of the total value of your debt arises from the operation of a business.

If you file under Chapter 7, you won't know for sure whether your bankruptcy filing will be challenged on abuse grounds until the trustee, or in some cases, a creditor, asks for a court hearing to dismiss or convert your case. However, if your filing is accurate, or if you consult with an attorney, it would be unusual for this issue to catch you by surprise.

Presumed Abuse

If your bankruptcy paperwork demonstrates that you don't pass the means test, you likely won't file for Chapter 7 bankruptcy. You'd file for Chapter 13 instead.

If you do file for Chapter 7, you can expect the U.S. Trustee to file a motion to dismiss your case or convert the case to Chapter 13. The bankruptcy trustee or any creditor can also file a motion to dismiss or convert your case on the grounds of abuse, but the U.S. Trustee will probably be the one bringing the motion. The U.S. Trustee is legally responsible for assessing your eligibility for Chapter 7 bankruptcy and otherwise seeing that the bankruptcy laws are complied with.

General Abuse

If your average monthly income (calculated according to the formula explained in Ch. 2, under "Calculating Your Income Status") is less than the state's median income, you aren't subject to the means test and your filing won't be presumed to be abusive. Your Chapter 7 filing can still be challenged on the ground of general abuse, but only if the judge or U.S. Trustee files the motion. Again, absent the presumption, the court or U.S. Trustee must prove abuse under the totality of the circumstances.

Motions to Dismiss for Abuse Under All the Circumstances

As we've explained, it's possible to have your case dismissed if it appears that your Chapter 7 filing is an abuse of the bankruptcy code under all the circumstances. Motions to dismiss for this reason tend to focus primarily on whether the debtor's expenses are unnecessarily extravagant. For example, one very strict Ohio bankruptcy court ruled that a mortgage expense on a $400,000 home and an expense for repayment of a 401(k) loan should not be allowed. Without those expenses, the debtors had adequate income to fund a Chapter 13 plan, which made their case an abuse under all the circumstances. (*In Re Felske*, 385 B.R. 649 (N.D. Ohio 2008).)

The grounds for dismissal don't necessarily have to exist when you file for bankruptcy. A motion to dismiss for abuse can be brought on the basis of events occurring before the discharge. So if you get a new job or win the lottery, or some other event happens while your case is pending that would enable you to proceed under Chapter 13, you might face a challenge to your Chapter 7 case. (See also *In re Littman*, 370 B.R. 820 (Bankr. D. Idaho 2007).)

If you face dismissal on this ground, you will need to explain why it's unlikely you could complete a Chapter 13 bankruptcy, or why expenses that are challenged by the trustee are really necessary for you to get a fresh start. There is no clear test of what constitutes abuse under all the circumstances. The judges will know it when they see it. Fortunately, the U.S. Trustee—the party who usually brings these motions—has the burden of proving the abuse. If you pass the means test, your eligibility for Chapter 7 bankruptcy is presumed and the trustee has to overcome that presumption.

The most common reason a filing might be objected to is if it appears that you have enough money to make a reasonable payment to your creditors even though you passed the means test.

The trustee is likely to challenge the Chapter 7 bankruptcy filing on general abuse grounds if you could easily propose a feasible Chapter 13 plan even though you weren't subject to the means test or you passed the means test. For instance, if you otherwise qualify for Chapter 13 and can pay $13,650 or more over a five-year period toward a Chapter 13 plan—or you could pay at least 25% of your unsecured, nonpriority debt—you might face an abuse motion (amounts subject to adjustment April 1, 2022).

For instance, suppose that you pass the means test using standard deductions, but your bills are actually quite less. This discrepancy would show up when you list your actual income and expenses on Schedules I and J. If you have a sufficient amount of disposable income remaining after subtracting your income from your expenses, the trustee might object on the grounds that you should be using those funds to pay creditors through a Chapter 13 plan.

For example, during the previous six months, suppose Julian and Edna's combined average monthly gross income is $7,000, which is $1,500 a month over the median income for a similar size family. They pass the means test because they have a number of large deductions, including $1,000 a month for two car notes and $3,500 for their mortgage. As it turns out, shortly before filing, Julian gets a large raise, and his and Edna's actual monthly net income exceeds their actual living expenses by $700 (well over the $13,650 for a five-year period). The trustee files a motion to dismiss or convert the bankruptcy on the ground that a Chapter 7 filing would constitute abuse under all the circumstances. The reasoning is that there is enough excess income to fund a Chapter 13 plan, and because Julian and Edna are spending more for their car notes and mortgage than is reasonable in their particular situation. Following other cases decided by courts in his district, the bankruptcy judge grants the motion, giving Julian

and Edna 15 days to either convert their case to Chapter 13 or have it dismissed.

Charitable Contributions

Assuming you have a record of making set charitable contributions to a qualified religious or charitable entity or organization, a court may not consider these contributions as part of your disposable income. In other words, the trustee cannot argue that you should pay your money into a Chapter 13 repayment plan rather than to the charity of your choice.

EXAMPLE: You pass the means test but the U.S. Trustee files a motion to dismiss your case for abuse because you give 25% of your income to your church (and have over a substantial period of time). The U.S. Trustee argues that if you only tithed 15% of your income, you could propose a feasible Chapter 13 repayment plan. Following this law, the court dismisses the U.S. Trustee's motion and allows your Chapter 7 bankruptcy to proceed.

In some cases, you can avoid an abuse motion when your income and expenses are unequal.

EXAMPLE: Roberto files for bankruptcy after receiving unemployment income for eight months. He passed the means test because his current monthly income was $1,400 per month. He kept his bills to a minimum by sleeping on a friend's couch. A week before filing, he accepted a good job offer and declared his new salary of $3,500 per month on Schedule I. Because it appeared that he had a substantial amount of disposable income, the trustee filed an objection.

In Roberto's case, his best bet would be to explain his need to rent an apartment and pay for vehicle expenses to and from his new job in the section provided on Schedule I. Most trustees would see the new anticipated expenses as reasonable and not object to Roberto's case.

Other less common reasons you might be subject to an abuse motion exist, too. For instance, if you seek to reject a personal services contract—a contract in which you've agreed to provide services to another person or business—without adequate financial justification. For instance, if you sign a three-year recording contract and then file for Chapter 7 bankruptcy just to get out of it, your case could be challenged on general abuse grounds.

Court Procedures

If you fail the means test, the U.S. Trustee must file a statement indicating whether your filing should be considered an abuse within ten days after your meeting of creditors. (See Ch. 1 for more on this meeting.) Five days after the U.S. Trustee's statement is filed, the court must send the notice to all of your creditors, to let them know about the U.S. Trustee's assessment and to give them an opportunity to file their own motions to dismiss or convert on abuse grounds, if they desire.

Within 30 days after filing this statement, the U.S. Trustee must either:

- file a motion to dismiss or convert your case on the grounds of abuse, or
- explain why a motion to convert or dismiss isn't appropriate (for example, because you passed the means test).

If your income is below the state median income, the U.S. Trustee doesn't have to file either statement, because abuse will not be presumed. However, your filing can still be challenged for general abuse, as explained earlier.

Note that these duties and time limits apply only to the U.S. Trustee. If your income is more than the state median, your creditors can file a motion to dismiss or convert after you file, but no later than 60 days after the first date set for your creditors' meeting.

Defending a Motion to Dismiss or Convert

If the U.S. Trustee, trustee, or creditor files a motion to dismiss or convert your case, you are entitled to notice of the hearing at least 20 days in advance. You will receive papers in the mail explaining the grounds for the motion and what you need to do to respond. If the motion to dismiss or convert is based on presumed abuse, the burden is on you to prove that your filing is not abusive. If the motion is based on general abuse, the burden of proof is on the party bringing the motion.

Presumed Abuse

If the motion to dismiss or convert is based on your actual failure to pass the means test, your only defense is to show "special circumstances." However, it's not enough to show that these circumstances exist: You must also show that they justify additional expenses or adjustments of current monthly income "for which there is no reasonable alternative."

In order to establish special circumstances, you must itemize each additional expense or adjustment of income and provide:

- documentation for the expense or adjustment, and
- a detailed explanation of the special circumstances that make the expense or adjustment necessary and reasonable.

You will win only if the additional expenses or adjustments to income enable you to pass the means test.

> **EXAMPLE:** Nicole and Chris have a child, Sarah, with Autism Spectrum Disorder. Sarah is making remarkable progress in her private school, for which Nicole and Chris pay $1,000 a month. No equivalent school is available at a lower tuition. Under the means test guidelines, Nicole and Chris are entitled to deduct only $1,875 a year from their income for private school expenses. If Nicole and Chris were allowed to deduct the full $1,000 monthly tuition, they would easily pass the means test. By documenting Sarah's condition, the necessity for the extra educational expense, and the fact that moving her to a less expensive school would greatly undermine her progress, Nicole and Chris would have a chance of convincing the court to allow the $1,000 expense, which would, in turn, rebut the presumption of abuse.

Keep in mind that the bankruptcy court views any special circumstance as creditors "funding" the expense. Therefore, you'll want to be conservative in this area. Indeed, the above example might not fly. There's a good chance that Nicole and Chris might have to file for Chapter 13 instead.

Bankruptcy courts have issued written decisions on a variety of special circumstance claims. If you need to prove special circumstances to pass the mean test, you will want to check with a local attorney or do your own research to find out how bankruptcy court or the courts in your state have treated the special circumstances you're claiming.

A frequently addressed issue is whether payments on nondischargeable student loans can be considered a special circumstance. While a few courts have held that they can be, more courts have gone the other way and ruled that student loan payments do not constitute special circumstances. (See, for example, *In re Champagne*, 389 B.R. 191 (Bankr. Kan. 2008) and *In re Pageau*, 383 B.R. 221 (S.D. Ind. 2008).)

Here are some cases in which the court has allowed a particular special circumstances claim, but remember that courts in your area might see the issue differently:

- unusually high transportation expenses (*In re Batzkiel,* 349 B.R. 581 (Bankr. N.D. Iowa 2006); *In re Turner,* 376 B.R. 370 (Bankr. D. N.H. 2007))
- mandatory repayment of 401(k) loan (*In re Lenton,* 358 B.R. 651 (Bankr. E.D. Pa. 2006))
- birth of a child and student loan debt (*In re Martin,* 371 B.R. 347 (Bankr. C.D. Ill. 2007))
- reduction in income due to voluntary job changes (*In re Tamez,* No. 07-60047 (Bankr. W.D. Tex. 2007))

- joint debtors who have two separate households (*In re Graham,* 363 B.R. 844 (Bankr. S.D. Ohio 2007)
- unusually high rent expenses (*In re Scarafiotti,* 375 B.R. 618 (Bankr. D. Colorado 2007)), and
- court-ordered child support payments (*In re Littman,* 370 B.R. 820 (Bankr. D. Idaho 2007)).

In addition, the U.S. Trustee's office recently provided some guidance on this issue, noting that it might consider as special circumstances the following:

- job loss or reduction in income for which there is no reasonable alternative
- a one-time "bump" in prepetition income that is not likely to happen again
- debtors who have separate households due to pending divorce or job relocation, and have filed a joint bankruptcy petition, and
- a postpetition household size increase due to pregnancy or a reasonable need to support an additional person.

General Abuse

If your filing is challenged for general abuse, the party bringing the motion to dismiss or convert has the burden of proof. If the motion is based on your ability to fund a Chapter 13 plan even though you passed the means test, you can raise any special expense you have—for example, necessary private tuition, extraordinary child care expenses, or legal fees associated with a continuing legal action—to demonstrate your inability to fund a Chapter 13 plan.

Valuation Hearings

There are two situations when you might need to ask the court to assign a value to a car or other personal property. In a Chapter 7 bankruptcy, you might need a valuation if you propose to redeem property that you are making payments on. (See Ch. 6 for more on redemption.) If the property's replacement value—the amount the property could be purchased for in a retail market, considering its age and condition—is less than the debt, you can pay the replacement value in a lump sum and own the property outright.

Common Motion Procedures

There are many types of motions. The two main varieties are called "*ex parte*" motions and "noticed" motions. *Ex parte* motions are easier to bring because you don't have to send formal notice to all of the parties or schedule a court hearing. These are used primarily for administrative issues that are not controversial, such as a request to reopen a case or to get permission to shorten the required time for giving notice.

Noticed motions are more complex. One party files the motion and sends notice of what is requested to the appropriate parties (this is called "serving" the parties). The notice is accompanied by a legal argument (points and authorities) and a declaration—a sworn statement that sets out the facts of the case under penalty of perjury.

The notice typically includes the date and time at which the court will hear the motion. Sometimes, the notice states that a hearing will be set only if the party served with the motion wants to oppose it. If a hearing is set, all parties must receive notice at least 20 days in advance. The party against whom the motion is brought typically can file a written opposition to the motion at any time up to five days before the hearing. Other parties in all bankruptcy motion proceedings are the U.S. Trustee and the regular trustee.

The bankruptcy judge will hear argument on the motion and either rule right then and there (from the bench) or take the matter under submission (take it back to chambers and think about it for a while). The judge typically issues a written decision and orders the prevailing party to prepare a formal order.

Either party can appeal the motion to a U.S. District Court or a Bankruptcy Appellate Panel (if one has been established in the district where the case is heard). Notice of appeal must usually be filed with the bankruptcy court *within ten days* of the date the court's decision or order is "entered." If you don't file this notice on time, you will almost surely lose your right to appeal.

In a Chapter 13 bankruptcy, you might want the court to determine the replacement value of property that is collateral for a secured debt. If the replacement value is less than the debt, your repayment plan can pay the replacement value. This is called a "cramdown." (See Ch. 6 for more on cramdowns.)

RESOURCE

Getting evidence of value. For cars, *Kelley Blue Book* appraisals are a good start (www.kbb.com). Another good place to look is the website of the National Automobile Dealers Association, www.nada.com, which is recommended by the courts. However, you and the creditor might disagree about the car's value because of its condition, something these websites can't shed much light on. In that case, a private appraisal would be persuasive.

To get a valuation hearing, you or a creditor must file a motion. These motions are handled in the same way as the other motions discussed in "Common Chapter 7 Motions and Proceedings," just below. If you or a creditor requests a valuation hearing in Chapter 13, the court will either postpone your confirmation hearing or hold the valuation hearing immediately before the confirmation hearing.

Common Chapter 7 Motions and Proceedings

In very simple Chapter 7 cases, you will probably have to attend only one official proceeding: the creditors' meeting, supervised by the trustee. But if your Chapter 7 case involves issues that must be decided by a bankruptcy judge—for example, if you are facing a motion to dismiss or convert for abuse—you, or someone helping you, must know the required court procedures. You will have to either take the time to learn how to represent yourself or consult an attorney who already knows what needs to be done. You can also get help from bankruptcy petition preparers, but they are allowed only to fill in the bankruptcy forms in accordance with your instructions—they can't give you legal advice or appear for you in court. (See Ch. 11 for more information on bankruptcy petition preparers.)

This section briefly describes some of the more common court proceedings that might be required in a Chapter 7 bankruptcy in addition to the abuse motion to dismiss or convert discussed above. This will give you an idea of what you'll be facing if one of these issues pops up in your case.

RESOURCE

Use Nolo resources to help you through the litigation maze. Nolo's *How to File for Chapter 7 Bankruptcy*, by Cara O'Neill and Albin Renauer, provides guidance for some of these procedures. *Represent Yourself in Court*, by Paul Bergman and Sara J. Berman (Nolo), also has an excellent chapter on litigating in bankruptcy court. For a plain-English guide to making your way through law books and other resources, see *Legal Research: How to Find & Understand the Law*, by the editors of Nolo.

Hearing on Relief From Stay

A creditor who wants to collect from you or your property directly can request relief from the automatic stay in order to do so. This is called a "relief from stay" hearing. (For more on the automatic stay, see Ch. 1.) This could come up, for example, if you are behind on your mortgage or car payments.

The creditor asks for this type of hearing by filing a motion in the bankruptcy case. The creditor doesn't need to file a separate lawsuit, as it would with some other types of disputes within a bankruptcy case. The work you have to do to oppose the request and get your side of the case heard in court is not all that difficult. However, you might need to do some legal research.

Dischargeability Hearing

Ch. 3 explains that some types of debts survive your bankruptcy only if the creditor comes into court and challenges the proposed discharge of the debt. In addition, student loans and certain other types of debts will be discharged if you (the debtor) file a separate action in the bankruptcy court against the creditor and convince the judge that the debt should be discharged. These court procedures that determine whether debts survive bankruptcy are called "dischargeability" actions.

Debtors are most likely to bring dischargeability actions to discharge a student loan on the basis of hardship, or to cancel a tax debt on the basis that it meets the requirements for discharge under the bankruptcy code. Creditors are most likely to bring a dischargeability action alleging that a debtor incurred a debt through fraudulent means or caused personal injury through drunk driving or a willful and malicious act.

To start a dischargeability action, a creditor (or you) must file a separate complaint in the bankruptcy court, formally serve the complaint on the other party, and move the case forward to trial before the bankruptcy judge. This requires considerable research and knowledge of court rules. You are likely to have one or two false starts, in which the clerk returns your paperwork or the court tells you to try again. Dealing with formal court procedures can be quite frustrating for self-represented people. On the other hand, if there is enough money at stake, it could be worth your while to spend the time and deal with the frustration that comes with formal court litigation.

Of course, you can hire a bankruptcy attorney just for this part of your case, if there is enough at stake to justify paying the attorney's fees and you are able to find an attorney willing to provide limited services. (See Ch. 11.)

Reaffirmation Hearing

If you aren't represented by an attorney and have agreed with a creditor to "reaffirm" a debt (to recommit yourself to personal liability for a car note or another secured debt, despite your bankruptcy discharge), you will have to attend a hearing at which the judge will warn you of the consequences of reaffirmation: You'll continue to owe the full debt, you might lose the collateral if you default on your payments, and in many states, the creditor can sue you for any balance due after the property is sold at auction.

In some cases, the court will decide that because of the debtor's income and expenses, making the payments would be too much of a hardship to the debtor after bankruptcy, and will disallow the reaffirmation agreement.

The bankruptcy laws state that you have to enter into an agreement with the lender if the lender requires it but say nothing about what happens if the judge disallows the agreement. Courts have ruled that you are entitled to keep your vehicle if the only reason the car note is not reaffirmed is that the judge wouldn't allow it. Along this line, when disapproving reaffirmation agreements, some judges order lenders to refrain from repossessing cars as long as debtors are current on their payments. As a general rule, you are better off having the judge disapprove the reaffirmation agreement since you'll then be able to keep the vehicle as long as you remain current, but you won't owe the car note if you have to give the car back sometime after your bankruptcy is over.

Lien Avoidance Motions

Ch. 6 explains that certain types of liens can be removed from your property in a Chapter 7 bankruptcy case. To do this, you need to file a motion to "avoid" the lien. As with other motions, you must mail the lienholder a written explanation indicating that you want to avoid the lien and why you are entitled to it. You must also provide the lien owner with a notice explaining what the lien owner must do to respond if the holder wants to keep the lien. If there is no response, you can obtain an order to avoid the lien by default. If the creditor responds, you can set the matter for hearing. Sometimes, you set the matter for hearing in your initial notice—it all depends on the rules for your bankruptcy court's district.

Converting From One Chapter to Another

The bankruptcy law allows you to change your bankruptcy from one chapter to another in many circumstances. This process is called conversion. If you want to remain in bankruptcy and you convert, you won't have to pay another filing fee and your creditors are still prevented from taking action against you.

Conversions From Chapter 7

You can voluntarily convert a Chapter 7 case into a Chapter 11 (usually only businesses do this), Chapter 12 (for farmers), or Chapter 13 bankruptcy *at any time* unless you already converted to your Chapter 7 case from one of the other chapters. Some cases have held that a court can deny permission to convert if the conversion is made in bad faith, while other courts have upheld the plain language of the statute, which doesn't mention such a condition.

Upon a creditor's request, after notice and hearing, the court can convert a Chapter 7 case to a Chapter 11 case at any time. The court can convert your Chapter 7 case to a Chapter 13 case only if you consent. For example, as explained earlier, if you file for Chapter 7 and your filing is found to be abusive, the court can convert the case to Chapter 13 if you consent. If you don't consent, the court will dismiss your case outright.

Your case cannot be converted unless you qualify for relief under the new chapter. For example, you can't convert to Chapter 13 unless you fall within the debt guidelines for that chapter (secured debts not exceeding $1,257,850 and unsecured debts not exceeding $419,275; figures subject to change April 1, 2022).

Conversions From Chapter 13

Just like a Chapter 7 bankruptcy, you can convert your Chapter 13 case to another chapter, but only if you qualify for relief under that chapter. And your Chapter 13 case can also be converted against your wishes, in some situations.

Voluntary Conversion

You can convert your Chapter 13 case into a Chapter 7 case at any time, as long as you qualify to file for Chapter 7 under the rules discussed in Ch. 2. As mentioned earlier, some courts don't require you to take the Chapter 7 means test upon such a conversion.

Involuntary Conversion

The U.S. Trustee, the trustee, or a creditor can request that the court, after notice and hearing, dismiss your Chapter 13 case or convert it to Chapter 7, whichever is in the best interest of your creditors. Your case might be converted to Chapter 7 rather than dismissed if your Chapter 13 filing was in bad faith and you have valuable nonexempt property that the trustee could seize for the benefit of your creditors. If, on the other hand, you have no nonexempt property, the creditors would benefit more from an outright dismissal.

The court might order the dismissal of your Chapter 13 case, or convert it to Chapter 7, only for cause, such as your:

- unreasonable delay that is prejudicial to your creditors
- nonpayment of any court fees or charges
- failure to file a repayment plan in a timely manner
- failure to start making your plan payments on time
- failure to comply with your plan
- failure to file your bankruptcy papers on time
- failure to stay current on your alimony or child support payments after your filing date, or
- failure to file your state and federal tax returns with the court.

Any time prior to confirming the Chapter 13 plan, the court, after notice and hearing, can order your case converted to Chapter 11 or 12 upon request by the U.S. Trustee, the trustee, or a creditor. If you are a farmer, the court can't order a conversion to Chapter 7, 11, or 12 unless you request it. As with Chapter 7, no conversion can be ordered to another chapter unless you qualify for relief under that chapter.

Effect of Conversion From Chapter 13 to Chapter 7

One issue that often arises in the course of a conversion from Chapter 13 to Chapter 7 is how you treated your property between your filing date and your conversion date. As explained in Ch. 4, the trustee technically owns all of the property in your bankruptcy estate—which is essentially everything you own when you file, except pensions.

If you start out in Chapter 13 and don't sell any property, you'll be able to keep your exempt property after the Chapter 7 conversion. The Chapter 7 trustee will sell your nonexempt property. If you start out in Chapter 13 and sell some of your nonexempt property, then convert to Chapter 7, what happens to the property you got rid of? Not a problem. When you convert from Chapter 13 to Chapter 7, the property of the estate is the property that remains in your possession or under your control on the date of conversion.

Creditors should receive payments equivalent to the value of your nonexempt property when you filed for Chapter 13.

What about property you got after you filed for Chapter 13 bankruptcy but before you converted to Chapter 7? In most cases, this property will not be part of your Chapter 7 bankruptcy estate. However, if you acted in bad faith when converting from Chapter 13 to 7, then the court may find that it is part of your bankruptcy estate.

If you can cram down a debt in Chapter 13, the lien remains on the property until you complete the plan or the claim is paid in full without regard to the cramdown. If you don't complete the plan, the cramdown becomes ineffective and you will still owe the entire debt with lien attached, less money you have paid to the creditor during your Chapter 13 plan. In Chapter 7, you'll have the opportunity to surrender or redeem the property.

Potential Problems in Chapter 13

As with Chapter 7 cases, there are some potential bumps in the road in Chapter 13 cases. These typically come up in the context of the confirmation hearing, where the judge approves or rejects your proposed repayment plan.

Confirmation Hearing

Unlike Chapter 7, a Chapter 13 bankruptcy requires at least one appearance before a bankruptcy judge—the confirmation hearing. At the confirmation hearing, the court approves or rejects your proposed repayment plan. (Rejecting a plan is also called "denial of confirmation.")

The confirmation hearing must be held between 20 days and 45 days after your meeting of creditors. However, the hearing can be held earlier if no one objects. It's also common for the confirmation to be continued if you need to make adjustments to your plan.

Although a judge technically presides over the confirmation hearing, the trustee usually runs the show. If the trustee has no objection to your plan, and no creditor files a motion arguing that your plan is unfair, the judge will most likely approve the plan without a further hearing. But if the trustee has a problem with your plan, or a creditor raises issues of fairness, the judge will most likely send you back to the drawing board and reschedule ("continue," in legalese) the confirmation hearing to another date, giving you time to submit a modified plan. Each time you submit a modified plan, you must notify all of your creditors listed in the mailing matrix prepared by the court.

If it becomes obvious that Chapter 13 bankruptcy isn't realistic for you—for example, you don't earn enough money to pay into a plan—the judge will typically order that your case be dismissed unless you want to convert it to Chapter 7 bankruptcy before the date set for the dismissal.

Objections to Your Plan

The trustee or a creditor might raise objections to your proposed plan. (See Ch. 2, "Chapter 13 Eligibility Requirements.")

Listed below are some objections you might face in Chapter 13.

The plan was not submitted in good faith. The bankruptcy law explicitly requires you to file for Chapter 13 in good faith. In determining whether you filed in good faith, courts will look to see whether your proposed plan has any purpose other than sincerely trying for a fresh start. For example, one bankruptcy court ruled that a Chapter 13 filing was not in good faith because the debtor filed for the sole purpose of getting around a judge's decision in an ongoing state court case. If you are filing your papers with the honest intention of getting back on your feet, and you really can make the payments required by the plan, you probably will be able to overcome a good-faith objection.

Most bankruptcy courts will look at the following factors:

- How often you have filed for bankruptcy. Filing and then dismissing multiple bankruptcies does not, in itself, show bad faith. However, if you've filed and dismissed two or more other bankruptcy cases within one year, the court could find a lack of good faith if there are inconsistencies in your papers or you can't show that your

circumstances have changed since the previous dismissal.

- The accuracy of your bankruptcy papers and oral statements. The court is likely to find a lack of good faith if you misrepresent your income, debts, expenses, or assets, or if you lie at the creditors' meeting.

- Your efforts to repay your debts. If your plan will pay your unsecured creditors a small percentage of what you owe, or nothing at all, you might have to show the court that you are stretching as much as you can. The court will want to see that you are not living luxuriously and that you are making substantial efforts to pay your unsecured creditors, even if it means trading in your fancy new car for a used model.

The plan is not feasible. Probably the most common objection is that your plan is not feasible—that is, you won't be able to make the required payments or comply with the other terms of the plan. To overcome this type of objection, your monthly income must exceed your monthly expenses by at least enough to allow you to make the payments required under Chapter 13 bankruptcy. For instance, a debtor who owes a $50,000 tax arrearage as well as $25,000 in credit card debts must propose a plan that, at a minimum, pays the $50,000 in full over the life of the plan because taxes are usually a priority debt and must be paid in full.

The trustee or a creditor might also question your job stability, the likelihood that you'll incur extraordinary expenses, and whether you have any outside sources of money. If your plan seems to reflect too much wishful thinking, and your sources of money are uncertain, the court will probably reject the plan on the ground that it isn't feasible. Possible scenarios leading the court to find that your plan isn't feasible include:

- You have a business that has been failing, but you've predicted a rebound and intend to use business income to make your plan payments.
- You propose making plan payments from the proceeds of the sale of certain property, but nothing points to the likelihood of a sale.
- Your plan includes a balloon payment (a large payment at the end), but you have not identified a source of money from which the payment will be made.

The plan fails to promote the "best interest" of the creditors. Under your Chapter 13 repayment plan, you must pay your unsecured creditors at least as much as they would have received had you filed for Chapter 7 bankruptcy—that is, you must pay the greater of either all of your priority debts, the value of your nonexempt property less the costs of sale and the trustee's commission, or your disposable income. (Exemptions are discussed in Ch. 4 and the method for determining what the creditors would have received in a Chapter 7 bankruptcy is explained in Ch. 2.) This is called the "best interest of the creditors" test.

If the trustee or a creditor raises this objection, you will have to provide documents showing the values of the potentially nonexempt portions of your property, such as a recent appraisal of a home in which your equity is equal to or exceeds your state's homestead exemption, or a publication stating the value of an automobile of the same make, model, and year as yours. In determining property value, keep in mind that costs of sale also take into consideration the fact that at an auction (the way a trustee liquidates property in Chapter 7 bankruptcy), property sells for about 60% of wholesale.

The plan unfairly discriminates. Chapter 13 bankruptcy is intended to treat all unsecured creditors fairly, relative to each other. You might be inclined to pay some unsecured creditors more than others—for example, you might propose to pay 100% of a student loan but only 35% of your credit card debts (which are dischargeable). In this situation, the trustee or the credit card issuers are likely to object to your plan on the ground that they are unfairly being discriminated against.

The plan doesn't provide adequate protection for collateral. Plans must provide that payments to secured creditors on property serving as collateral will be distributed in equal monthly amounts and will be sufficient to provide the creditor with adequate protection of its interest in the collateral.

You have not provided documents that the trustee requested. Not only must you turn over tax returns, but you should expect to provide bank statements, paycheck stubs, and any other reasonable request for documents made by the trustee. For instance, it's common to give the trustee copies of the following your:

- most current mortgage or auto statement
- marital settlement agreement, and
- life or liability insurance policy.

When you find out which trustee will be handling your case, you can call the office or review the website to find out which documents you'll need to turn over.

Filling Out the Bankruptcy Forms

When you file bankruptcy, you'll need to complete a large number of official forms. Although all filers used to use the same forms, this has changed. You'll want to be sure that you're using the individual version for your filing. Businesses use the "non-individual" forms.

You have several options for completing the forms. You can:

- download the forms from the Internet and fill them in yourself
- hire a bankruptcy petition preparer to complete the forms under your direction (see Ch. 11)
- get limited advice from a lawyer, or
- hire an attorney to handle everything.

If you use an attorney, the papers will be filed electronically in most courts. If you represent yourself, you will mail the forms to the court or file them in person.

Chapter 7 Documents

There are a number of documents you will have to file in a Chapter 7 case.

The Voluntary Petition

You start a Chapter 7 case by filing a Voluntary Petition for Individuals Filing for Bankruptcy, the official court form that asks for some basic information, including:

- your name(s), address, and the last four digits of your Social Security number
- whether you have lived, maintained a residence, maintained a business, or had assets in the district for the better part of 180 days before filing (this establishes your right to file in a particular district)
- the type of bankruptcy you are filing (Chapter 7, 11, 12, or 13)

- whether your debts are primarily consumer or business
- whether you own a business
- how you will be paying your filing fee (in installments or by fee waiver)
- the estimated number of creditors
- the estimated amount of your debts
- the estimated value of your property
- whether you have nonexempt assets
- whether a judgment for eviction has been entered against you
- whether you are aware of some bankruptcy basics
- your history of bankruptcy filings within the past eight years, if any, and
- whether you have completed your debt counseling or obtained a waiver.

Additional Documents

A number of additional documents must be filed within 14 days after filing the petition. The best practice is to file all the documents when you file your petition, to keep your case under control and make sure you don't miss the 14-day deadline.

Here are the documents you must provide:

- a list of all of your creditors, including each one's name, mailing address, and account number (this is called the "creditor matrix")
- lists of your assets (Schedule A/B: Property)
- a schedule of liabilities (Schedule D: Creditors Who Hold Claims Secured By Property and Schedule E/F: Creditors Who Have Unsecured Claims)

> **CAUTION**
>
> **You must list all of your debts.** Some people think they don't have to list debts that they intend to pay in full, for example, car loans. Not so. You must list each and every debt you have. And remember, just because you list a secured debt doesn't mean you'll lose the property that guarantees payment of the debt. (See Ch. 6 for more on secured debts.)

- a statement of your financial affairs for up to ten years prior to your filing date
- a schedule of your current income (Schedule I) and current expenditures (Schedule J)
- wage stubs for the 60 days prior to filing
- a statement of your average monthly gross income over the previous six months, and a means test calculation if your income exceeds the median income for a similar size family in your state
- a certificate showing that you received credit counseling from an authorized provider within the six months prior to filing
- a copy of any debt repayment plan you developed during your mandatory credit counseling
- a form showing that you received counseling in personal financial management from an authorized provider during the course of your bankruptcy case; this is due after filing and before you receive your discharge

- a copy of your most recent tax return or a transcript of the return obtained from the IRS (due seven days prior to the creditors' meeting)
- a schedule indicating which assets you are claiming as exempt (Schedule C)
- a schedule of any executory contracts (contracts that are still in force and require action by one or both parties) and leases you have signed (Schedule G)
- a schedule of your codebtors, if any (Schedule H)
- a form called Statement of Intention for Individuals Filing Under Chapter 7, in which you tell your secured creditors how you plan to deal with your secured debt (see Ch. 6)
- if you are being evicted and want your bankruptcy filing to hold the eviction off, the certification and rent described in Ch. 5, and
- a form setting out your full Social Security number.

Chapter 13 Documents

Almost all of the documents required for a Chapter 7 bankruptcy are also required in a Chapter 13 bankruptcy, with the exception of the Statement of Intention for Individuals Filing Under Chapter 7.

In addition to these documents, you must file a proposed Chapter 13 repayment plan. Most local courts have a mandatory form that you must use for your plan.

You'll also file a form that you use to calculate your disposable income available to repay your unsecured creditors. You must also provide evidence that you have filed tax returns (or transcripts from the IRS) for the previous four tax years, prior to the creditors' meeting. The trustee can keep the creditors' meeting open for 120 days after the first date for which it is scheduled to allow you extra time to obtain and file your returns. And the court can give you 30 additional days, if necessary.

While your Chapter 13 case is pending, the trustee might ask you to file with the court:

- any new tax returns and amendments that you file with the IRS
- a statement under oath of your income and expenditures for each tax year, and
- a statement of your monthly income that shows how income, expenditures, and monthly income are calculated.

These statements must show:

- the amount and sources of your income
- the identity of any person who is responsible for the support of any of your dependents, and
- the identity of any person who contributed, and the amount contributed, to your household.

Upon request, you must provide the tax returns to your creditors, the U.S. Trustee, and the bankruptcy trustee.

Basic Requirements for Completing Bankruptcy Documents

Whether you file on your own or with the help of a professional, you have a duty to make sure that your papers meet these requirements:

- **You must be thorough.** Always err on the side of giving too much information rather than too little.

- **You must respond to every question.** If a question doesn't apply to you, check the "none" box. If there isn't one, you will have to type "N/A" for "not applicable." Make sure to list and value all of your property, even if you think it has no value. List the property, and either put zero for its value, or check the "unknown" box. Then be prepared to explain your answer at the creditors' meeting.

- **You must be willing to repeat yourself.** Sometimes different forms—or different questions on the same form—ask for the same or overlapping information. You will have to provide the same information multiple times.

- **You must be scrupulously honest.** You must swear, under penalty of perjury, that you've been truthful on your bankruptcy forms. The most likely consequence for failing to be scrupulously honest is a dismissal of your bankruptcy case, but you could be prosecuted for perjury if it's evident that you deliberately lied.

 RESOURCE

Finding the forms. You can find samples of the basic forms described in this section on the online companion page of this book at www.nolo.com/back-of-book/FIBA.html. You can also view the current official forms online at www.uscourts.gov/forms/bankruptcy-forms. These forms can be filled in online and downloaded, but you can't save them. Consider downloading the forms, before filling them in and printing them out.

At first glance, you might think that there's no way you can deal with all of this paperwork. However, in Chapter 7 cases, it really isn't as difficult as it looks—especially if you have a simple case. Nolo publishes excellent, up-to-date, line-by-line guides for the forms. To paraphrase the old saying, just take it one document at a time.

Getting Help With Your Bankruptcy

Y ou will have three sources of outside help if you wish to file for bankruptcy:

- a debt relief agency, as both lawyers and nonlawyer bankruptcy petition preparers are now called
- a book that gives you step-by-step instructions on how to file for bankruptcy, such as those published by Nolo, or
- a combination of bankruptcy books, Internet sites, and lawyers.

Debt Relief Agencies

Any person or entity that you pay or otherwise compensate for help with your bankruptcy is considered a debt relief agency. The two main types of debt relief agencies are lawyers and bankruptcy petition preparers (BPPs). Credit counseling agencies and budget counseling agencies are not debt relief agencies. Nor are any of the following:

- employers or employees of debt relief agencies
- nonprofit organizations that have federal 501(c)(3) tax-exempt status
- any creditor who works with you to restructure your debt
- banks, credit unions, and other deposit institutions, or
- an author, publisher, distributor, or seller of works subject to copyright protection when acting in that capacity (in other words, Nolo and the stores that sell its books aren't debt relief agencies).

Lawyers and BPPs are covered separately below. This section explains what the bankruptcy law requires of debt relief agencies generally.

Lawyers Are Debt Relief Agencies

In *Milavetz v. United States*, 130 S. Ct. 1324 (2010), the Supreme Court ruled that lawyers are considered debt relief agencies under the bankruptcy code and, therefore, are subject to the various notice and contract requirements imposed on all debt relief agencies. As to the rule which prohibits debt relief agencies from advising clients to undertake new debts, the Supreme Court said this section only prohibits lawyers from advising their clients to load up on debt that could later be discharged—and, therefore, did not infringe on lawyers' free speech rights.

Mandatory Contract

A debt relief agency must enter into a contract with you within five days that explains, clearly and conspicuously:

- what services the agency will provide you
- what the agency will charge for the services, and
- the terms of payment.

The agency must give you a copy of the completed, signed contract.

Mandatory Disclosures and Notices

The debt relief agency must inform you, in writing, that:

- All information you provide in your bankruptcy papers must be complete, accurate, and truthful.
- You must completely and accurately disclose your assets and liabilities in the documents you file to begin your case.
- You must undertake a reasonable inquiry to establish the replacement value of any item you plan to keep before providing that value on your forms.
- Your current monthly income, the amounts you provide in the means test, and your computation of projected disposable income in a Chapter 13 case, as stated in your bankruptcy papers, must be based on a reasonable inquiry into their accuracy.
- The U.S Trustee might audit your case and your failure to cooperate in the audit could result in dismissal or some other sanction, including a possible criminal penalty.

In addition to these stark warnings, a debt relief agency must also give you a general notice regarding some basic bankruptcy requirements and your options for help in filing and pursuing your case.

The agency must provide you this within three business days after the agency first offers you services. Failure to give you this notice can land the agency in big trouble.

Restrictions on Debt Relief Agencies

A debt relief agency cannot:

- fail to perform any service that the agency informed you it would perform in connection with your bankruptcy case
- counsel you to make any statement in a document that is untrue or misleading or that the agency should have known was untrue or misleading, or
- advise you to incur more debt in order to pay for the agency's services.

Any contract that doesn't comply with the requirements on debt relief agencies cannot be enforced against you. A debt relief agency is liable to you for costs and fees, including legal fees, if the agency negligently or intentionally:

- fails to comply with the law's restrictions on debt relief agencies, or
- fails to file a document that results in dismissal of your case or conversion to another chapter.

In sum, debt relief agencies are on the hook if they are negligent in performing the services required by the bankruptcy law or other services they have agreed to provide.

Bankruptcy Petition Preparers

Bankruptcy petition preparers (BPPs) are typing services. Under the law, they are permitted to enter data onto the official bankruptcy forms, print them out, and file them with the court. BPPs cannot provide any legal advice, nor can they tell you what information to include on the forms.

What a Bankruptcy Petition Preparer Cannot Do

BPPs are very different from lawyers. BPPs are legally prohibited from giving you legal advice, which includes information such as:

- whether to file a bankruptcy petition or which chapter (7, 11, 12, or 13) is appropriate
- whether your debts will be discharged under a particular chapter
- whether you will be able to keep your home or other property if you file under a particular chapter
- information about the tax consequences of a case brought under a particular chapter or whether tax claims in your case can be discharged
- whether you should offer to repay or agree to reaffirm a debt
- how to characterize the nature of your interest in property or debts, and
- information about bankruptcy procedures and rights.

This ban on providing legal advice is important because BPPs are not trained or licensed to provide legal advice. Relying on a BPP's advice or recommendation can cause you to suffer serious consequences in your bankruptcy case, such as losing assets or being denied a discharge of debts.

Fees

Each bankruptcy district imposes a strict cap on the fees that BPPs can charge, usually between $100 and $200. The reasoning is that BPP fees should be set according to what general typists in the community charge per page because BPPs are not supposed to do anything other than type forms.

Regulation of Bankruptcy Petition Preparers

Anyone can be a BPP. Yes, anyone. There is nothing in the bankruptcy code that requires BPPs to have any particular level of education, training, or experience. Unlike most other jobs, a prison record is no handicap to becoming a BPP. How, then, are BPPs regulated? The U.S. Trustee's office reviews all bankruptcy petitions prepared by BPPs. BPPs must provide their name, address, telephone number, and Social Security number on bankruptcy petitions and other bankruptcy documents they prepare.

At the creditors' meeting, the bankruptcy trustee might ask you questions designed to determine if the BPP gave you legal advice. For example, the trustee might ask how you chose your exemptions or how you decided which chapter to file.

BPPs can be fined for certain actions and inactions spelled out in the bankruptcy code (11 U.S.C. § 110). These are:

- failing to put their name, address, and Social Security number on your bankruptcy petition
- failing to give you a copy of your bankruptcy documents when you sign them
- using the word "legal" or any similar term in advertisements, or advertising under a category that includes such terms, and
- accepting court filing fees from you.

You must pay the filing fee yourself or, in some districts, give the BPP a cashier's check made out to the court.

Finally, a BPP must submit a statement under oath with each petition they prepare stating how much you paid in the previous 12 months and any fees that you owe but haven't yet paid. If BPPs charge more than permitted, the court will order the return of the excess fees.

If a BPP provides legal advice, engages in any fraudulent act, or fails to comply with the above rules, the court can also require the BPP to pay a fine for each violation. In cases of serious fraud, the penalty can be up to three times your fee. Plus, the court might order the BPP to stop providing services.

Can a BPP Give You Written Information?

Under the Bankruptcy Code, BPPs can prepare your bankruptcy forms only under your direction. You must tell the BPP what exemptions to choose, whether to file under Chapter 7 or Chapter 13, what approach to take in respect to your secured debts (car note, mortgage), and the values to place on your property. While fine in theory, unless you have the benefit of a self-book or another source of legal information, it's unlikely that you would have adequate bankruptcy expertise to tell the BPP how to proceed. In an attempt to bridge this gap, many BPPs hand their customers written materials that contain information their customers need (although some skirt the law altogether by providing legal advice directly to you—which they are not authorized or trained to do). However, providing a customer with written legal information about bankruptcy has itself been held to be the unauthorized practice of law in many states (California is an important exception).

A Bankruptcy Petition Preparer Cannot Represent You

If you decide to use a BPP, remember that you are representing yourself and are responsible for the outcome of your case. Not only must you learn about your rights under the bankruptcy law and understand the proper procedures to be followed, but also accept responsibility for correctly and accurately filling in the bankruptcy petition and schedules. If, for example, you lose your home because it turned out to be worth much more than you thought, and the homestead exemption available to you didn't cover your equity, you can't blame the BPP. Nor can you blame the BPP if other property is taken from you because you didn't get the necessary information— from a lawyer or a self-help book—to properly claim your exemptions. The point is unless you hire a lawyer to represent you, you are solely responsible for acquiring the information necessary to competently pursue your case.

Bankruptcy Lawyers

Bankruptcy lawyers are regular lawyers who specialize in handling bankruptcy cases.

When You Might Need a Lawyer

Most Chapter 7 bankruptcies sail through without a hitch if prepared correctly.

However, there are some situations in which you might need some help from a bankruptcy lawyer:

- Your average income during the six months before you file is more than your state's median income, and it looks like you won't be able to pass the means test. (See Ch. 2 for more information on these calculations.)
- You want to hold onto a house or motor vehicle and the information we provide on these subjects doesn't adequately address your situation or answer all of your questions.
- You want to get rid of a student loan or income tax debt that won't be wiped out in bankruptcy unless you convince a court that it should be discharged.
- A creditor files a lawsuit in the bankruptcy court claiming that one of your debts should survive your bankruptcy because you incurred it through fraud or other misconduct.
- The bankruptcy trustee seeks to have your whole bankruptcy dismissed because you didn't give honest and complete answers to questions about your assets, liabilities, and economic transactions.
- The U.S. Trustee asks the court to dismiss your case—or forces you into Chapter 13—because your income

is high enough to fund a Chapter 13 repayment plan, or because the trustee believes that your filing is an abuse of the Chapter 7 bankruptcy process for other reasons.

- You have recently given away or sold valuable property for less than it is worth.
- You went on a recent buying spree with your credit card and charged more than $725 on luxury goods within the past 90 days or took out cash advances in excess of $1,000 in the last 70 days (figures subject to change on April 1, 2022).
- You want help negotiating with a creditor or the bankruptcy court, and the amount involved justifies hiring a bankruptcy lawyer to assist you.
- You have a large lien on your property because of a court judgment against you, and you want to remove the lien in your bankruptcy case.
- A creditor is asking the court to allow it to proceed with a foreclosure, repossession, or another collection action despite your bankruptcy filing and you object to it.
- You are being evicted by your landlord because you have fallen behind on your rent and you believe you have grounds to stay in the residence.

Even if you aren't facing one of these complications, you might still want the convenience and comfort of having a lawyer to guide you through your case. If you find the thought of going through the process overwhelming, a lawyer can take charge of your matter and relieve you of the responsibility to get everything done. The lawyer will accompany you to the creditor's meeting, work with you to ensure that your documents are complete and accurate, get all your paperwork filed on time, and generally handle all of the little details that go into a successful bankruptcy case. Although representation comes at a price—which can be considerable—you will have the peace of mind of knowing that someone is watching your back. While we obviously believe that many people can handle their own Chapter 7 bankruptcies, it isn't right for everyone, especially if you have other significant sources of stress in your life or simply don't feel up to handling it all by yourself.

Full-Service Lawyer Representation

There are two types of representation—the type where you hire a lawyer to assume complete responsibility for your bankruptcy and the type where you represent yourself but hire a lawyer to handle one particular aspect of your bankruptcy case. We refer to the first type of representation as "full-service representation" and the second type as unbundled services (discussed below).

When providing full-service representation, a bankruptcy lawyer is responsible for making sure that all of your paperwork is filed on time and that the information in your paperwork is accurate. These duties require the lawyer to review various documents—for instance, your credit report, tax returns, and home value appraisal—both to ensure the accuracy of your paperwork and to make sure that you are filing for bankruptcy under the appropriate chapter. If your paperwork is inaccurate or you filed under Chapter 7 when you should have filed under Chapter 13, the lawyer can be fined a hefty amount and be required to return your fees.

In exchange for their basic fee, full-service bankruptcy lawyers typically are also responsible for appearing on your behalf at the creditors' meeting, representing you if a creditor opposes the discharge of a debt, and eliminating any liens that the bankruptcy laws allow to be stripped from your property.

Sometimes, a case appears to be simple at the beginning but turns out to be complicated later on. In that event, you might start out representing yourself but later decide to hire an attorney to handle a tricky issue that arises. Just keep in mind

that many lawyers aren't comfortable becoming involved with a case midstream.

Before you decide that it's too expensive to get legal representation, see some lawyers and find out. Many offer free consultations. And fees might be negotiable, especially if the lawyer wants your business.

Unbundled Services

Some lawyers are willing to offer their services on a piecemeal basis. In bankruptcy cases, you might find a lawyer willing to step in and handle a particular matter, such as stripping liens from your property or handling a dischargeability action brought by you or a creditor.

When a lawyer does a specific job at a client's request but doesn't contract for full-service representation in the underlying case, that lawyer is said to be providing an unbundled service. For example, you might be able to hire an attorney to handle a specific procedure—such as to defend against a motion for relief from stay—while you handle the main part of the bankruptcy yourself.

Few court cases discuss the boundaries of unbundled services. Some courts have held that attorneys can't "ghostwrite" legal documents for nonlawyers—because that would be a type of fraud on the court—but the issue has not been decided by most courts. Also, nothing prevents a lawyer from appearing for you in a limited capacity and putting their name on associated documents. However, some lawyers aren't willing to do this in courts that consider an attorney who appears for one aspect of the case the attorney for the entire case.

Lawyers providing unbundled services usually charge an hourly fee. As a general rule, you should bring an attorney into the case for an unbundled service only if a dispute involves something valuable enough to justify the attorney's fees. If a creditor objects to the discharge of a $500 debt, and it will cost you $400 to hire an attorney, you might be better off trying to handle the matter yourself, even though this increases the risk that the creditor will win. If the dispute is worth $1,000 and the attorney will cost you $200, hiring the attorney makes better sense.

Unfortunately, many bankruptcy attorneys do not like to appear or do paperwork on a piecemeal basis. Justified or not, these attorneys believe that by doing a little work for you, they might be on the hook if something goes wrong in another part of your case—that is, if they are in for a penny, they are in for a pound. Also, the bar associations of some states frown on unbundled services on ethical grounds. On the other hand, other state bar associations are starting to encourage their attorneys to offer unbundled services simply because so many people—even middle-income people—are unable to afford full representation.

Bankruptcy Consultations

Some lawyers provide bankruptcy consultations for a flat-rate transaction fee based on the service provided or charge according to the amount of time your matter takes. Similar services are available online. You can find a telephonic or online consultation service using Google or another search engine to search for "bankruptcy legal advice telephone or Internet."

You might want an attorney consultation to get advice about whether bankruptcy would be a good option for you. And even if you are planning to file for bankruptcy on your own, you might wish to consult with an attorney about a particular issue or question you have, such as which exemptions you should use or whether you should reaffirm a debt.

As with other debt relief agencies, lawyers offering telephonic services are considered debt relief agencies and must use a contract detailing their services and provide the other notices described above.

How to Find a Bankruptcy Lawyer

Where there's a bankruptcy court, there are bankruptcy lawyers. They're listed by city online and on attorney resource pages, such as on Nolo at www.nolo.com/lawyers/bankruptcy. Bankruptcy can be complicated. You should use an experienced bankruptcy lawyer, not a general practitioner, to handle or advise you on matters associated with bankruptcy. Most attorneys who don't typically practice bankruptcy won't agree to do so.

There are several ways to find the best bankruptcy lawyer for your job:

- **Personal referrals.** This is your best approach. If you know someone who was pleased with the services of a bankruptcy lawyer, call that lawyer first.
- **Legal Aid.** Legal Aid offices are partially funded by the federal Legal Services Corporation and offer legal assistance in many areas. A few offices might do bankruptcies, although most do not. To qualify for Legal Aid, you must have a very low income.
- **Pro bono panels.** Some organizations help link clients to private attorneys who agree to take some cases for free, called pro bono services. Most likely, you'll have to qualify for pro bono services, which usually means having a low income. The American Bankruptcy Institute has a list of pro bono resources on its website. Go to www.bankruptcyresources.org, choose "Find Help," click on your state, then choose "Pro Bono Resources."
- **Legal clinic.** Many law schools sponsor legal clinics and provide free legal advice to consumers. Some legal clinics have the same income

requirements as Legal Aid; others offer free services to low- and moderate-income people.

- **Group legal plans.** If you're a member of a plan that provides free or low-cost legal assistance and the plan covers bankruptcies, make that your first stop in looking for a lawyer.
- **Lawyer-referral panels.** Most county bar associations will give you the names of bankruptcy attorneys who practice in your area. But bar associations might not provide much screening. Take the time to check out the credentials and experience of the person to whom you're referred.
- **Internet directories.** Both bar associations and private companies provide lists of bankruptcy lawyers online, with a lot more information about the lawyer than you're likely to get in a yellow pages ad. A good place to start is Nolo's Lawyer Directory, at www.nolo.com (scroll down to the "Connect With Attorneys" box).

Fees

For a routine Chapter 7 bankruptcy, a full-service lawyer will likely charge you somewhere between $1,200 and $2,000 (plus the $338 filing fee). You will have to pay the attorney in full before your case will be filed because once filed, any money you owe the attorney will be discharged along with your other dischargeable unsecured debts.

On your bankruptcy papers, you must state the amount you are paying your bankruptcy lawyer, and, if you aren't paying, the name of the person who will be footing the bill.

Because every penny you pay to a bankruptcy lawyer is a penny not available to your creditors (at least in theory), the court has the legal authority to make the attorney justify the fee. However, this rarely happens because attorneys know the range of fees generally allowed by local bankruptcy judges and set prices accordingly. So you probably won't find much variation in the amounts charged by lawyers in your area although it never hurts to shop around.

The scope and range of services that the attorney promises you in return for your initial fee will be listed in the Disclosure of Compensation of Attorney For Debtor form. This form is filed as part of your bankruptcy papers. In the typical Chapter 7 case, the attorney's fee will include the routine tasks associated with a bankruptcy filing: counseling, preparing bankruptcy and reaffirmation forms, and attendance at the creditors' meeting. Any task not included in the disclosure form is subject to a separate fee. The costs of litigation aren't included in most flat fees.

A typical bankruptcy attorney charges between $200 and $300 an hour and it would cost approximately $400 to $600 for a court appearance.

Whatever the attorney charges you, you are protected against fee gouging. An attorney must file a supplemental form to obtain the court's permission for any postfiling fees.

Attorneys charge a lot more for Chapter 13 bankruptcies because those cases involve substantially more work. Rates vary significantly depending on case complexity and where you live. Nationwide, most Chapter 13 bankruptcy attorneys charge somewhere between $2,500 and $5,500.

What to Look for in a Lawyer

No matter how you find a lawyer, these three suggestions will help you make sure you have the best possible working relationship.

First, fight any urge you might have to surrender to, or be intimidated by, the lawyer. You should be the one who decides what you feel comfortable doing about your legal and financial affairs; however, be open to the attorney's advice. Keep in mind that you're hiring a lawyer to perform a service for you, so shop around if the price or personality isn't right.

Second, make sure you have good "chemistry" with any lawyer you hire. Ask specific questions. Do you get clear, concise answers? If not, try someone else. Also, pay attention to how the lawyer responds to your knowledge. If you've read this book, you're already better informed than most clients.

TIP

Talk directly to the lawyer. When making an appointment, ask to talk directly to the lawyer. If you can't, this might give you a hint as to how accessible the lawyer will be. Having a paralegal handle the routine aspects of your case under the supervision of a lawyer isn't a problem as long as the attorney will decide the legal strategy and explain the law to you.

Finally, once you find a lawyer you like, make an appointment to discuss your situation fully. The lawyer or a paralegal will tell you what, if anything, to bring to the meeting. If not, be sure to ask ahead of time. Some lawyers will want to see a recent credit report and tax return, while others will send you a questionnaire to complete before your visit. Depending on the circumstances, you might also need to bring bills and documents pertaining to your home and other real estate you own. Other lawyers prefer not to review documents during the first visit.

Your main goal at the initial conference is to find out what the lawyer recommends in your particular case and how much it

will cost. Go home and think about the lawyer's suggestions. If they don't make sense or you have other reservations, call for clarification. If you're still not satisfied, then it might be smart to speak with someone else.

TIP

Look for a state-bar-certified bankruptcy specialist or member of the NACBA. Membership in the National Association of Consumer Bankruptcy Attorneys (NACBA) is a good sign that your lawyer will be tuned in to the nuances of the law and the court interpretations of the law that are sure to come. And a certified bankruptcy specialist is also a good bet due to experience plus other credentials. The credentials vary by state, and not all states have specialists, but might include passing a special bankruptcy exam, handling a certain number of cases, completing a large number of continuing education classes in bankruptcy, and receiving a recommendation from a bankruptcy judge, bankruptcy trustee, and/or other bankruptcy attorneys.

Legal Research

Legal research can vary from the very simple to the hopelessly complex. In this section, we are staying on the simple side. If you would like to learn more about legal research or if you find that our suggestions come up a bit short in your particular case, we recommend that you obtain a copy of *Legal Research: How to Find & Understand the Law*, by the editors of Nolo, which provides a plain-English tutorial on legal research in the law library and online.

Sources of Bankruptcy Law

Bankruptcy law comes from a variety of sources:

- federal bankruptcy statutes passed by Congress
- federal rules about bankruptcy procedure issued by a federal judicial agency
- local rules issued by individual bankruptcy courts
- federal and bankruptcy court cases applying bankruptcy laws to specific disputes
- laws (statutes) passed by state legislatures that define the property, and
- state court cases interpreting state exemption statutes.

Not so long ago, you would have had to visit a law library to find these resources. Now you can find most of them online. However, if you are able to visit a decent-sized law library, your research will be better for it. Using actual books allows you to more easily find and read relevant court interpretations of the underlying statutes and rules—which are crucial to getting a clear picture of what the laws and rules mean.

There is another important reason to visit the law library, if possible. While you can find superficial discussions and overviews of various aspects of bankruptcy online, you'll find in-depth encyclopedias and treatises in the law library that delve into every aspect of bankruptcy. In other words, you can find not only the law itself but also what the experts have to say about all the minor issues that have arisen over the years. Also, most law librarians will point you to helpful resources. They won't interpret the law for you, but they'll help you find what you need.

Finally, books in a law library are almost always subjected to a rigorous quality control process—as is this book—whereas you never know what you're getting online. To avoid getting lost in cyberspace, follow our suggestions below for researching bankruptcy law online and avoid the temptation to settle for the first hit in a Google search.

Below, we show you how to get to the resources you'll most likely be using, whether you are doing your research online or in the law library.

Bankruptcy Background Materials: Overviews, Encyclopedias, and Treatises

Before digging into the primary law sources (statutes, rules, cases, and so on that we discuss below), you might want to do some background reading to get a firm grasp of your issue or question.

The Internet

Some online sites contain large collections of articles written by experts about various aspects of bankruptcy. A good starting place is Nolo's website, Nolo.com, which offers lots of information and resources.

The Law Library

Providing you with a good treatise or encyclopedia discussion of bankruptcy is where the law library shines. This type of resource is not typically available online unless you find a way to access the expensive legal databases—Westlaw and LexisNexis—marketed almost exclusively to lawyers. Call your local law library—you might be able to access them at no cost.

Collier on Bankruptcy

It's a good idea to get an overview of your subject before trying to find a precise answer to a particular question. The best way to do this is to find a general commentary on your subject by a bankruptcy expert. For example, if you want to determine whether a particular debt is nondischargeable, you should start by reading a general discussion about the type of debt you're dealing with. Or, if you don't know whether you're entitled to claim certain property as exempt, a good overview of your state's exemptions would get you started on the right track.

The most complete source of this type of background information is a set of books known as *Collier on Bankruptcy*, by Henry J. Sommer and Richard Levin (Matthew Bender). It's available in virtually all law libraries. *Collier* is both incredibly thorough and meticulously up to date; semiannual supplements, with all the latest developments, are in the front of each volume. In addition to comments on every aspect of bankruptcy law, *Collier* contains the bankruptcy statutes, rules, and exemption lists for every state.

Collier is organized according to the bankruptcy statutes. This means that the quickest way to find information in it is to know what statute you're looking for. (See the Bankruptcy Code sections set out below.) If you still can't figure out the governing statute, start with the *Collier* subject matter index. Be warned, however, that the index can be difficult to use because it contains a lot of bankruptcy jargon you might be unfamiliar with. A legal dictionary will be available in the library.

Foreclosure Resources

If you are facing foreclosure, you'll definitely want to look at *The Foreclosure Survival Guide,* by Amy Loftsgordon (Nolo). This book explains the options available to you, and then walks you through the necessary steps for handling your particular situation. This book is available for purchase online and is carried in many libraries.

Other Background Resources

For general discussions of bankruptcy issues, there are several other good places to start. An excellent all-around resource is called *Consumer Bankruptcy Law and Practice*. This volume, published by the National Consumer Law Center, is updated regularly. It contains a complete discussion of Chapter 7 bankruptcy procedures, the official bankruptcy forms, and an extensive bibliography.

Another good treatise is a legal encyclopedia called *American Jurisprudence*, 2nd Series. Almost all law libraries carry it. The article on bankruptcy has an extensive table of contents, and the entire encyclopedia has an index. Between these two tools, you should be able to zero in on helpful material. Finally, some large and well-stocked law libraries carry a loose-leaf publication known as the Commerce Clearing House (CCH) *Bankruptcy Law Reporter* (BLR). In this publication, you can find all three primary source materials relating to bankruptcy: statutes, rules, and cases.

If you are looking for information on adversary proceedings (such as how to defend against a creditor's challenge to the dischargeability of a debt), turn to *Represent Yourself in Court*, by Paul Bergman and Sara J. Berman (Nolo). It has an entire chapter on representing yourself in adversary proceedings in bankruptcy court. If you need information on court procedures or the local rules of a specific court, consult the *Collier Bankruptcy Manual*.

How to Use Law Libraries

Law libraries that are open to the public are most often found in and around courthouses. Law schools also frequently admit the public at least some of the time (not, typically during exam time, over the summer, or during other breaks in the academic year).

If you're using a library as a member of the public, don't worry if it seems that the library is run mostly to serve members of the legal community. Almost without exception, law libraries come with law librarians. The law librarians will be helpful as long as you ask them the right questions. For example, the law librarians will help you find specific library resources, such as where you can find the federal bankruptcy statutes or rules, but they normally won't teach you the ins and outs of legal research. Nor will they give an opinion about what a law means, how you should deal with the court, or how your particular question should be answered. For instance, if you want to find a state case interpreting a particular exemption, the law librarian will show you where your state code is located on the shelves and might even point out the volumes that contain the exemptions. The librarian won't, however, help you interpret an exemption, apply the exemption to your specific facts, or tell you how to raise the exemption in your bankruptcy case. Nor is the librarian likely to tell you what additional research steps you can or should take. When it comes to legal research in the law library, self-help is the order of the day.

Finding Federal Bankruptcy Statutes

Title 11 of the United States Code contains all the statutes that govern your bankruptcy.

The Internet

If you are using the Internet, go to the Legal Information Institute of Cornell University Law School, www.law.cornell.edu. Cornell lets you browse laws by subject matter and also offers a keyword search. To help you in your browsing, below is a table setting out the various subject matter sections of the U.S. Code that apply to bankruptcy.

The Law Library

Virtually every law library has at least one complete set of the annotated United States Code ("annotated" means that each statute is followed by citations and summaries of cases interpreting that provision). If you already have a citation to the statute you are seeking, you can use the citation to find the statute. However, if you don't have a citation—which is frequently the case—you can use either the index to Title 11 (the part of the Code that applies to bankruptcy) or the table we set out below, which matches various issues that are likely to interest you with specific sections of Title 11.

Once you have found and read the statute, you can browse the one-paragraph summaries of written opinions issued by courts that have interpreted that particular statute. You will be looking to see whether a court has addressed your particular issue. If so, you can find and read the entire case in the law library. Reading what a judge has had to say about the statute regarding facts similar to yours is an invaluable guide to understanding how a judge is likely to handle the issue in your case, although when and where the case was decided might be important.

SEE AN EXPERT

If you're preparing a Chapter 7 bankruptcy case yourself, you should be able to find all of the information you need using a good self-help book such as *How to File for Chapter 7 Bankruptcy* by Cara O'Neill and Albin Renauer. If the question requires a more detailed explanation, you should find the answer in *Collier on Bankruptcy*. Looking for answers in other sources, such as case law, should tip you off to the fact that the issue is complicated and that you probably need legal help. It's likely time to consult with an attorney.

Finding the Federal Rules of Bankruptcy Procedure (FRBP)

The Federal Rules of Bankruptcy Procedure govern what happens if an issue is contested in the bankruptcy court. They also apply to certain routine bankruptcy procedures, such as deadlines for filing paperwork. Because most cases sail through the court without any need for the bankruptcy judge's intervention, you might not need to be familiar with these rules. However, certain types of creditor actions in the bankruptcy court must proceed by way of a regular lawsuit conducted under both these rules and the Federal Rules of Civil Procedure—for example, complaints to determine dischargeability of a debt. If you are representing yourself in such a lawsuit, you'll want to know these rules and look at the cases interpreting them. Any law library will have these rules. Your bankruptcy court's website will also have a link to the rules, as does www.law.cornell.edu.

Keep in mind that litigating a case in federal court is not easy, and retaining a bankruptcy lawyer versed in litigation—not all are—be sure to ask—is recommended.

That said, while federal judges won't try the matter for you, they are required to ensure the law is followed. So if you absolutely can't afford an attorney, do your research, prepare diligently, and nicely— great emphasis being placed on nicely— remind the judge of the duty to apply the appropriate law even if the litigant is confused about what that might be.

Finding Local Court Rules

Every bankruptcy court operates under a set of local rules that govern how it does business and what is expected of the parties who use it. Throughout this book, we have cautioned you to read the rules for your particular court so that your dealings with the court will go smoothly—and so you

won't end up getting tossed out of court if you become involved in litigation, such as an action to determine the dischargeability of a debt or a creditor's motion to lift the automatic stay.

Your bankruptcy court clerk's office will have the local rules available for you. The court will also post the local rules on the court website. To find the website for your court, take these steps:

Step 1: Go to www.uscourts.gov/federal-court-finder/search.

Step 2: Type in the name of your city or town and select the location nearest you. Press enter.

Step 3: Browse the list until you find your court and click on it.

Step 4: Go to the court's website. Click on the local rules link.

Court websites usually contain other helpful information as well, including case information, official and local bankruptcy forms, court guidelines and local rules, information for lawyers and BPPs, information about the court and its judges, and the court calendar.

At the law library, the *Collier Bankruptcy Manual* has the local rules for the nation's bankruptcy courts.

Finding Federal Court Bankruptcy Cases

Court opinions are vital to understanding how a particular law might apply to your

Bankruptcy Code Sections (11 U.S.C.)

§ 101   Definitions

§ 109   Who May File for Which Type of Bankruptcy; Credit Counseling Requirements

§ 110   Rules for Bankruptcy Petition Preparers

§ 111   Budget and Credit Counseling Agencies

§ 302   Who Can File Joint Cases

§ 326   How Trustees Are Compensated

§ 332   Consumer Privacy Ombudsmen

§ 341   Meeting of Creditors

§ 342   Notice of Creditors' Meeting; Informational Notice to Debtors; Requirements for Notice by Debtors

§ 343   Examination of Debtor at Creditors' Meeting

§ 348   Converting From One Type of Bankruptcy to Another

§ 349   Dismissing a Case

§ 350   Closing and Reopening a Case

§ 362   The Automatic Stay

§ 365   How Leases and Executory Contracts Are Treated in Bankruptcy

§ 366   Continuing or Reconnecting Utility Service

§ 501   Filing of Creditors' Claims

§ 506   Allowed Secured Claims and Lien Avoidance

§ 507   Priority Claims

§ 521   Paperwork Requirements and Deadlines

§ 522   Exemptions; Residency Requirements for Homestead Exemption; Stripping Liens From Property

§ 523   Nondischargeable Debts

§ 524   Effect of Discharge and Reaffirmation of Debts

§ 525   Prohibited Postbankruptcy Discrimination

§ 526   Restrictions on Debt Relief Agencies

§ 527   Required Disclosures by Debt Relief Agencies

§ 528   Requirements for Debt Relief Agencies

§ 541   What Property Is Part of the Bankruptcy Estate

§ 547   Preferences

§ 548   Fraudulent Transfers

§ 554   Trustee's Abandonment of Property in the Bankruptcy Estate

§ 707   The Means Test; Dismissal for Abuse; Conversion From Chapter 7 to Chapter 13

§ 722   Redemption of Liens on Personal Property

§ 727   Chapter 7 Discharge; Financial Management Counseling Requirements

§ 1301   Stay of Action Against Codebtor

§ 1302   Duties of the Chapter 13 Trustee

§ 1304   Rights of Chapter 13 Debtor Engaged in Business

§ 1305   Property of the Chapter 13 Bankruptcy Estate

§ 1307   Conversion of Chapter 13 to Another Title and Dismissal

§ 1308   Pre-petition Tax Return Filing Requirement

§ 1322   Required Contents of Chapter 13 Plan

§ 1323   Modification of Plan Before Confirmation

§ 1324   Timing of Confirmation Hearing

§ 1325   Requirements for Confirmation of Plan

§ 1326   Chapter 13 Plan Payments

§ 1327   Effect of Confirmation

§ 1328   Requirements for, and Effect of, Chapter 13 Discharge

§ 1329   Modification of Chapter 13 Plan After Confirmation

individual case. The following levels of federal courts issue bankruptcy-related opinions:

- the U.S. Supreme Court
- the U.S. Courts of Appeals
- the Bankruptcy Appellate Panels
- the U.S. District Courts, and
- the bankruptcy courts.

Most bankruptcy-related opinions are, not surprisingly, issued by the bankruptcy courts. By comparison, very few bankruptcy opinions come out of the U.S. Supreme Court. The other courts are somewhere in the middle.

The Internet

Depending on the date a case was decided, U.S. Supreme Court decisions and U.S. Court of Appeals decisions are available for free online. You can also subscribe to VersusLaw at www.versuslaw.com. VersusLaw provides U.S. Court of Appeals cases for an earlier period than you can get for free— often back to 1950. VersusLaw doesn't require you to sign a long-term contract and you can try it for free. VersusLaw also publishes many U.S. District Court cases on its website. Opinions by the bankruptcy courts are generally not yet available online, unless you subscribe to LexisNexis or Westlaw, both of which are extremely pricey.

U.S. Supreme Court. To find a Supreme Court case, go to www.supremecourt.gov.

U.S. Court of Appeals. Google has federal appeals cases going back to 1925. Go to "Google Scholar." Then simply select "Case Law" and type in a case name.

U.S. District Court and Bankruptcy Court. Cases reported by the bankruptcy courts are generally not available online unless you subscribe to Westlaw or LexisNexis. However, if you know the name of a particular case and the court that decided it, a Google search might lead you to a court's website, where some judges post their decisions. Still, you will probably have to take a trip to a law library if you want to know what the judges are doing in these courts—where the legal rubber meets the judicial road.

The Law Library

U.S. Supreme Court cases are published in three different book series:

- *Supreme Court Reports*
- *Supreme Court Reporter*, and
- *Supreme Court Lawyer's Edition.*

Some law libraries carry all three of these publications; others have only one. The cases are the same, but each series has different editorial enhancements.

U.S. Court of Appeals cases are published in the *Federal Reporter* (abbreviated simply as "F."). Most law libraries, large and small, carry this series.

Many U.S. District Court cases are published in the *Federal Supplement* (F.Supp.), a series available in most law libraries.

The Structure of the Court System for Bankruptcy Cases

Bankruptcy court decisions play a role in the overall bankruptcy law. Every state has at least one bankruptcy court and most states have several. Each of these courts is called on to decide contested issues arising in the bankruptcy cases filed in that court. Many of these decisions are published in *West's Bankruptcy Reporter*, published by Thomson Reuters.

If a party doesn't like the outcome of the bankruptcy court's decision, and can afford it, it can appeal the case (ask a higher court to review the decision) to the U.S District Court in the area where the bankruptcy court is located. In many parts of the country, the party can opt instead to appeal to the Bankruptcy Appellate Panel, or BAP, in the judicial circuit in which the bankruptcy court is located. U.S. District Court decisions do not have to be followed by other courts that decide the same issue, but the opinions by the BAP must be followed by the bankruptcy courts in the same judicial circuit unless

these opinions conflict with a higher circuit court (see below). These decisions are routinely published in volumes covering the U.S. District Court and the U.S. Court of Appeals.

If a party doesn't like a decision issued by a U.S. District Court or BAP, it can appeal the decision again to the U.S. Court of Appeals in the appropriate judicial circuit. A decision by the Court of Appeals supersedes decisions by the U.S. District Court or BAP and becomes law for that circuit. These decisions are also published alongside other Court of Appeal decisions.

Finally, a party to a U.S. Court of Appeals decision can appeal that decision to the U.S. Supreme Court in a process called "petitioning for certiorari." The U.S. Supreme Court can decide to hear the case, or not. Decisions by the U.S. Supreme Court are the last word on any particular issue. These decisions are published along with other U.S. Supreme Court decisions.

Written opinions of bankruptcy judges, and related appeals, are published in the *Bankruptcy Reporter* (B.R.), available in most mid- to large-sized libraries. To accurately understand how your bankruptcy court is likely to interpret the laws in your particular case, sooner or later you will need access to the *Bankruptcy Reporter*.

State Statutes

The secret to understanding what property you can keep frequently lies in the exemptions that your state allows you to claim. These exemptions are found in your state's statutes.

The Internet

Every state has its statutes online, including its exemption statutes. This means that you can read your state's exemption statutes for yourself. Follow these steps:

Step 1: Go to the exemption file on this book's online companion page located at www.nolo.com/back-of-book/FIBA.html. At the top of your state's exemption table, you'll see a general reference to the collection of laws for your state that contains the exemption statutes.

Step 2: Go to www.nolo.com/legal-encyclopedia/bankruptcy-exemptions-state.

Step 3: Under "State Bankruptcy Exemptions," click on your state.

Step 4: Click on the link to your state's code.

Step 5: Use the exemption citation to the far right of your state's exemption table to search for the statute.

The Law Library

Your law library will have your state's statutes in book form, usually referred to as your state's code, annotated statutes, or compiled laws. Use this book's online companion page to find a reference to the exemption statute you want to read, then use that reference to locate the exemption statute in the code. Once you find and read the statute, you can browse the summaries of court opinions interpreting the statute and, if you wish, read the cases in their entirety.

Alternatively, if your library has a copy of *Collier on Bankruptcy* (see above), you can find the exemptions for your state, accompanied by annotations summarizing state court interpretations.

State Court Cases

State courts are sometimes called on to interpret exemption statutes. If a court has interpreted the statute in which you are interested, you'll definitely want to read the relevant case for yourself.

The Internet

All states make their more recent cases available free online—usually back to about 1996. To find these cases for your state:

Step 1: Go to www.law.cornell.edu/states/opinions#state.

Step 2: Click on your state.

Step 3: Locate the link to the court opinions for your state. This might be one link, or there could be separate links for your state's supreme court and your state's courts of appeal (the lower trial courts seldom publish their opinions, so you probably won't be able to find them).

If you want to go back to an earlier case, consider subscribing to VersusLaw at www.versuslaw.com. As mentioned earlier, you don't have to sign a long-term contract.

The Law Library

Your law library will have a collection of books that contains opinions issued by your state's courts. If you have a citation, you can go right to the case. If you don't have a citation, you'll need to use a digest to find relevant bankruptcy cases. Finding cases by subject matter is a little too advanced for this brief summary. See *Legal Research: How to Find & Understand the Law,* by the editors of Nolo, for more help.

Other Helpful Resources

The Office of the United States Trustee's website, at www.justice.gov/ust, provides lists of approved credit and financial management counseling agencies, median income figures for every state, the IRS national, regional, and local expenses you will need to complete the means test. You can download official bankruptcy forms from www.uscourts.gov/forms/

bankruptcy-forms. However, this site doesn't include required local forms; for those, you'll have to visit your court or its website.

As part of the bankruptcy process, you are required to give the replacement or retail value for all of the property you list in Schedule A/B. These figures are also the key to figuring out which of your property is exempt. Here are some tips on finding these values:

- **Cars.** Use the *Kelley Blue Book*, at www.kbb.com, or the website of the National Auto Dealers Association, www.nada.com.
- **Other personal property.** Check prices on eBay, www.ebay.com.
- **Homes.** Check the prices for which comparable homes have sold in the recent past. Information such as purchase price, sales date, and address is available free from sites like www.zillow.com and www.realtor.com.

Alternatives to Bankruptcy

After reading the previous 11 chapters, you should have a pretty good idea about what filing for Chapter 7 or Chapter 13 bankruptcy will involve and the benefits you can hope to get out of it. Before you decide whether it's the right solution, consider the other options described in this chapter. Although bankruptcy is the only sensible remedy for some people with debt problems, an alternative course of action might fit your needs well.

Do Nothing

Surprisingly, the best approach for some deeply in debt is to take no action at all. You can't be thrown in jail for being unable to pay your debts (except in rare cases in which a court finds you in contempt of a court order), and your creditors can't collect money from you that you don't have.

Creditors Must Sue to Collect

Except for taxing agencies and student loan creditors, creditors must first sue you in court and get a money judgment before they can go after your income and property. The big exception to this general rule is that a creditor can take back collateral—foreclose on your home or repossess a car or furniture, for example—when you default on a debt that's secured by that collateral. (If you're worried about home foreclosure, see Ch. 5.)

Under the typical security agreement (a contract involving collateral), the creditor can repossess the property without first going to court. But the creditor will not be able to go after your other property and income for any "deficiency" (the difference between what you owe and what the repossessed property fetches at auction) without first going to court for a money judgment.

Much of Your Property Is Protected

Even if creditors get a money judgment against you, they can't take away such essentials as:

- basic clothing
- ordinary household furnishings
- personal effects
- food
- Social Security or SSI payments
- unemployment benefits
- public assistance
- bank accounts with direct deposits from government benefit programs, and
- 75% of your wages (but child support judgments and taxing authorities can grab a larger share).

The state exemptions described in Ch. 4 (and listed on the online companion page at www.nolo.com/back-of-book/FIBA.html) apply whether or not you file for bankruptcy. Even creditors who get a money judgment against you can't seize these protected items to satisfy the judgment. However, neither the federal bankruptcy exemptions nor the California System 2 exemptions described in Ch. 4 apply if a creditor sues you. Those are bankruptcy-only exemptions. And once in a while, a state might have an exemption that applies in bankruptcy but not to judgment creditors.

What It Means to Be Judgment Proof

If all of the property you own is exempt, you are what is commonly referred to as "judgment proof." Whoever sues you and wins will be holding a useless piece of paper simply because you don't have anything that can legally be taken (at least temporarily). While money judgments last a long time—typically ten years—and can be renewed, this won't make any difference unless your finances change for the better. If that happens, you might reconsider bankruptcy at that time.

If your creditors know that their chances of collecting a judgment from you any time soon are slim, they probably won't sue you in the first place. Instead, they'll simply write off your debt and treat it as a deductible business loss for income tax purposes. After some years have passed—usually between four and ten—the debt will become legally uncollectable, under state laws known as statutes of limitation. You can learn about the statute of limitations in your state in Civil Statutes of Limitations at www.nolo.com/legal-encyclopedia/statute-of-limitations-state-laws-chart-29941.html.

Even if the creditor sues you in time, lawsuits cost money. If a creditor decides not to go to court at the present time, it is unlikely to seek a judgment at a later date, although it could happen. For instance, money judgments become more valuable when the real estate market is in an upswing because of how quickly equity can build in a home or other property. In short, because creditors are reluctant to throw good money after bad, your poor economic circumstances might shield you from trouble. Just keep in mind that if your economic outlook changes for the better. If that's a possibility, it's likely better to file for bankruptcy sooner rather than later.

CAUTION

Watch out for later liens, even if you don't currently own real estate. Even though you might technically be judgment proof because you don't own any real estate, a lien recorded in your county could cause problems later on if you buy a house. In some states (including California), creditors can record liens even if you don't own any property. If you later purchase property, the lien will "pop up" and attach to the property, meaning you'll have to deal with it. If this happens after you've completed a bankruptcy, you might be able to reopen the bankruptcy and file a motion to avoid the lien (See Ch. 10).

CAUTION

Don't restart the clock. The statute of limitations can be renewed if you revive an old debt by, for example, admitting that you owe it or making a payment. As soon as you acknowledge a debt, the clock starts all over again. Savvy creditors are aware of this loophole and might try to trick you into admitting the debt so they can sue to collect it. Sometimes, it might be a good idea to try to repay a debt, particularly one to a local merchant with whom you wish to continue doing business. But unless you are planning to make good on the debt or try to negotiate a new payment schedule, you should avoid any admissions. (You'll find a sample letter that avoids admitting a debt below.)

Stopping Debt Collector Harassment

Many people are moved to file for bankruptcy to stop their creditors from making harassing telephone calls and writing threatening letters. (See Ch. 1 for more on the automatic stay.) Fortunately, there is another way to get annoying creditors off your back if they are collecting consumer debts. (This law doesn't apply to the collection of business debts.) Federal law forbids collection agencies from threatening you, lying about what they can do to you, or invading your privacy. And many state laws prevent original creditors from taking similar actions.

Sample Letter to Collection Agency

November 11, 20xx
Sasnak Collection Service
49 Pirate Place
Topeka, Kansas 69000

Attn: Marc Jacobs

Re: Lee Anne Ito

Account No. 88-90-92

Dear Mr. Jacobs:

For the past three months, I have received several phone calls and letters from you concerning an overdue VisaCard account.

This is my formal notice to you under 15 U.S.C. § 1692c to cease all further communications with me except for the reasons specifically set forth in the federal law.

This letter is not meant in any way to be an acknowledgment that I owe this money.

Very truly yours,

Lee Anne Ito
Lee Anne Ito

Under the federal Fair Debt Collection Practices Act, 15 U.S.C. § 1692, you can legally force collection agencies to stop phoning or writing you by simply demanding that they stop in writing, even if you owe them a bundle and can't pay a cent. For more information, see *Solve Your Money Troubles,* by Amy Loftsgordon and Cara O'Neill (Nolo). Above is a sample letter asking a creditor to stop contacting the debtor.

Negotiate With Your Creditors

If you have some income or have assets you're willing to sell, you might be better off negotiating with your creditors than filing for bankruptcy. Negotiation could buy you some time to get back on your feet, or you and your creditors might agree to settle your debts for less than the amount you owe.

Creditors don't like instituting collection proceedings or turning debt-owing customers into former customers. To avoid the collection process and keep customers, creditors sometimes will reduce the debtor's expected payments, extend the time to pay, drop their demands for late fees, and make similar adjustments. They're most likely to be lenient if they believe you are making an honest effort to deal with your debt problems and if you can't pay the current amount.

As soon as it becomes clear to you that you're going to have trouble paying a bill, call or write to the creditor. Explain the problem—whether it's an accident,

job layoff, divorce, emergency expense for your child, unexpected tax bill, or something else.

Token payments might make a difference to local creditors if you want to keep that credit or business relationship. In that case, paying even a small amount might help. On the other hand, keep in mind that it probably won't make any difference with larger companies. You'll continue to incur late fees each month until you make up all back payments. Also, if it's been a long time since you've made any payments, you might want to hold off on any payment until you've checked on the "statute of limitations" for that debt. The statute of limitations is the state time limit after which the debt goes away if no court action has been filed to collect it.

Your payment might have the unfortunate effect of starting up a new limitations period. Restarting the statute of limitations period gives the creditor more time to sue you.

Your success in getting creditors to give you time to pay will depend on the types of debts you have, how far behind you are, and the creditors' policies toward debts that are in arrears.

If you are not yet behind on your bills, be aware that some creditors have a policy that requires you to default—and in some cases, become at least 90 days past due—before they will negotiate with you for better repayment terms. If any creditor makes this a condition of negotiating, find out from the creditor if it can keep the default out of your credit report.

Other creditors require that you submit financial proof that you can't afford to pay in the form of bank statements, paycheck stubs, and more. Before you agree to turn anything over, remember that you're giving the creditor information that will be useful to garnish your wages or levy against your checking or savings account at a future date.

Some creditors refuse to negotiate with debtors. Even though creditors get at least something when they negotiate settlements, many ignore debtors' pleas for help, continue to make telephone calls demanding payment (unless you assert your right under federal law not to receive the calls—see "Stopping Debt Collector Harassment," above) and leave debtors with few options other than to file for bankruptcy. Many people who file bankruptcy do so because of the unreasonableness of their creditors or the collection agencies hired by their creditors.

To help your creditors see the benefit of settling with you on reasonable terms, it often won't hurt to mention the fact that you're thinking of filing for bankruptcy. Creditors know that they are very likely to get nothing in a bankruptcy case and might settle for a reasonable discount. This being said, don't be surprised if a creditor tells you to "go ahead and file." More than a few creditors know that it is common for a debtor to threaten bankruptcy without intending to file.

Legal Remedies for Unreasonable Creditor Actions

Creditors sometimes violate federal laws preventing unfair collection practices—such as contacting you when you've made it clear you don't intend to repay a debt. These laws allow you to sue a law-breaking creditor in federal court and recover damages—including damages for emotional distress. If you become seriously irked by an overzealous collector and want to know whether a legal line has been crossed, take a look at *Solve Your Money Troubles*, by Amy Loftsgordon and Cara O'Neill (Nolo). You can also consult a consumer bankruptcy attorney. A good place to start your search for such a lawyer is on the National Association of Consumer Bankruptcy Attorneys website, at www.nacba.org or Nolo's website at www.nolo.com/lawyers/bankruptcy.

Get Outside Help to Design a Repayment Plan

Many people have trouble negotiating with creditors, either because they don't have the skills or negotiating experience to do a good job or because they find the whole process exceedingly unpleasant. Because the ability to negotiate is an art, many people benefit from outside help.

If you don't want to negotiate with your creditors, you can turn to a lawyer or a credit counseling agency. These agencies come in two basic varieties: nonprofit and for profit. They all work on the same basic principle: A repayment plan is negotiated with all of your unsecured creditors. You make one monthly payment to the agency, which distributes the payment to your creditors as provided in the plan. As long as you make the payments, the creditors will not take any action against you. And, if you succeed in completing the plan, one or more of your creditors might be willing to offer you new credit on reasonable terms.

The nonprofit agencies tend to be funded primarily by the major creditors in the form of a commission for each repayment plan they negotiate and by moderate fees charged to the users. The for-profit agencies are funded by the same sources but tend to charge much higher fees.

Credit Counseling Agencies
As explained above, bankruptcy filers are required to get credit counseling. You must get this counseling from a nonprofit agency that meets particular requirements and has been approved by the U.S. Trustee. If you decide to get help with a repayment plan, you will do well to choose one of these agencies—the U.S. Trustee's office oversees their operation, which gives you some protection against fraudulent practices. You can find a list of approved agencies at the U.S. Trustee's website, at www.justice.gov/ust.

The big downside to entering into one of the repayment plans is that if you fail to make a payment, the creditors might pull the plug on the deal and come after you, regardless of how faithful you've been in the past—although this is unlikely if you make up the missed payment quickly. It's more likely that you could have a change in the ability to pay at all, such as if you face a job loss or if new expenses arise. When that happens, you might find that you would have been better off filing for bankruptcy in the first place because your payments won't be returned and you'll have paid them unnecessarily.

How Debt Management Typically Works

To use a credit counseling agency to help you pay your debts, you must have a steady income. A counselor will contact your creditors to let them know that you've sought assistance and need more time to pay. Based on your income and debts, the counselor and your creditors will decide how much you must pay and for how long. You must then make one payment each month to the counseling agency, which in turn will pay your creditors. The agency will ask the creditors to return a small percentage of the money received to the agency office to fund its work. This arrangement is generally referred to as a "debt management program."

Some creditors will make overtures to help you when you're participating in a debt management program, such as reducing interest, waiving minimum payments, and forgiving late charges. But many creditors will not make interest concessions, such as waiving a portion of the accumulated interest to help you repay the principal portion of the debt. Even if you successfully complete a debt management program, your credit will still be damaged.

Disadvantages of Debt Management

Participating in a credit counseling agency's debt management program is a little bit like filing for Chapter 13 bankruptcy. But working with a credit or debt counseling agency has one significant advantage: No bankruptcy will appear on your credit record. On the other hand, a debt management program has two disadvantages when compared to Chapter 13 bankruptcy. First, if you miss a plan payment in Chapter 13, you will often be provided a way to make it up and the bankruptcy will continue to protect you from creditors who would otherwise start collection actions. A debt management program has no such protection, so any creditor can pull the plug on your plan. Also, a debt management program plan usually requires you to pay your unsecured debts in full over time. In Chapter 13, you often are only required to pay a small fraction of your nonpriority unsecured debts, such as credit card and medical debts.

Critics of credit counseling agencies point out that the counselors tilt toward signing people up for a repayment plan in circumstances where bankruptcy would be in their best interest—so the agency will get a commission from the creditors that isn't available for cases that end up in bankruptcy. Creditors who would receive nothing in a Chapter 7 case, or little in Chapter 13, benefit greatly, as well. However, credit counseling agencies approved by the Office of the U.S. Trustee have a number of requirements placed on them to protect against undue influence by creditors and are required to make a number of disclosures that should prevent you from being treated unfairly. (See Ch. 2 for more on these rules.)

File for Chapter 11 Bankruptcy

Chapter 11 bankruptcy is ordinarily used by financially struggling businesses to reorganize their affairs. However, it is also available to individuals. Individuals who consider Chapter 11 bankruptcy usually have debts over one or both of the Chapter 13 bankruptcy limits—$419,275 of unsecured debts and $1,257,850 of secured debts—or substantial nonexempt assets, such as several pieces of real estate (these figures could change on April 1, 2022).

The initial filing fee is currently $1,738 compared to $338 for Chapter 7 or $313 for Chapter 13 bankruptcy. In addition, you must pay a quarterly fee, based on a percentage of the disbursements made to pay your debts.

You'll need a lawyer to file for Chapter 11, and most attorneys will require a minimum $15,000 retainer fee or more to handle your case. Add to that the Chapter 11 bankruptcy court fees, which could run from $1,000 to $10,000 per year, and you can see that Chapter 11 isn't for everyone.

Because Chapter 11 bankruptcy is typically long and expensive, many Chapter 11 filings are converted to Chapter 7 once legal fees gobble up the assets.

However, don't shy away from Chapter 11 bankruptcy because of the fees and costs. Be sure to consider all factors when choosing the type of bankruptcy that will work best for your situation.

File for Chapter 12 Bankruptcy

Chapter 12 bankruptcy is like Chapter 13 bankruptcy in many respects. However, only people and entities that meet the definition of a family farmer can use it. To qualify as a family farmer, all of the following must be true:

- Your debts cannot exceed $4,411,400 (amount could change April 1, 2022).
- Fifty percent or more of your debt must have arisen from the farming operation, not including a purchase money mortgage.
- Fifty percent or more of your income must have been earned from the farming operation in the year preceding the filing of the petition.
- Your income must be "sufficiently stable and regular" to enable payments under a Chapter 12 plan.

Like Chapter 13, you must file a schedule of assets and liabilities and a statement of financial affairs. Even though a trustee is appointed to supervise the plan, the farm debtor remains in possession of the farm assets and actions by creditors are automatically stayed upon filing the petition.

As in Chapter 13, you must file a plan that meets Chapter 12 requirements. The plan must provide that all unsecured debts are paid in full or, alternatively, all disposable income is used to pay down the unsecured debt over the ensuing three-year period (which can be extended to five years with court permission). Plan payments must pay unsecured creditors at least what they would have received in a Chapter 7 bankruptcy. After completion of the plan, all debts are discharged except those that wouldn't be dischargeable in Chapter 7.

Chapter 12 has several advantages over Chapter 13 bankruptcy. The court has unrestricted authority to modify (cram down) secured debts, such as mortgages and car notes, so the debt matches the market value of the property. (See Ch. 6 for more on cramdowns.) This is different from Chapter 13, where cram-downs cannot be used for mortgages on your primary residence and recent car loans. Another advantage of Chapter 12: Secured debts that extend beyond the plan period can be modified without having to pay them all off in the plan. That is, payments can extend beyond the plan until the debt is paid off in the normal course of time. And unlike Chapter 13, priority debts do not have to be paid in full so long as all disposable income over a five-year period is devoted to the plan.

If you are interested in Chapter 12 bankruptcy, consult with a lawyer.

Glossary

341 meeting. See "meeting of creditors."

341 notice. A notice sent to the debtor and the debtor's creditors announcing the date, time, and place for the first meeting of creditors. The 341 notice is sent along with the notice of bankruptcy filing and information about important deadlines by which creditors have to take certain actions, such as filing objections.

342 notice. A notice that the court clerk is required to give to debtors pursuant to Section 342 of the Bankruptcy Code, to inform them of their obligations as bankruptcy debtors and the consequences of not being completely honest in their bankruptcy case.

707(b) action. An action taken by the U.S. Trustee, the regular trustee, or any creditor, under authority of Section 707(b) of the Bankruptcy Code, to dismiss a debtor's Chapter 7 filing on the ground of abuse.

Abuse. Misuse of the Chapter 7 bankruptcy remedy. This term is typically applied to Chapter 7 bankruptcy filings that should have been filed under Chapter 13 because the debtor appears to have enough disposable income to fund a Chapter 13 repayment plan.

Accounts receivable. Money or other property that one person or business owes to another for goods or services. Accounts receivable most often refer to the debts owed to a business by its customers.

Administrative expenses. The trustee's fee, the debtor's attorney's fee, and other costs of bringing a bankruptcy case that a debtor must pay in full in a Chapter 13 repayment plan. Administrative costs are typically 10% of the debtor's total payments under the plan.

Administrative Office of the United States Courts. The federal government agency that issues court rules and forms to be used by the federal courts, including bankruptcy courts.

Adversary action. Any lawsuit beginning with the filing of a formal complaint and formal service of process on the parties being sued. In a bankruptcy case, adversary actions are often brought to determine the dischargeability of a debt or to recover property transferred by the debtor shortly before filing for bankruptcy.

Affidavit. A written statement of facts, signed under oath in front of a notary public.

Allowed secured claim. A debt that is secured by collateral or a lien against the debtor's property, for which the creditor has filed a proof of claim with the bankruptcy court. The claim is secured only to the extent of the value of the property—for example, if a debtor owes $5,000 on a note for a car that is worth only $3,000, the remaining $2,000 is an unsecured claim.

Amendment. A document filed by the debtor that changes one or more documents previously filed with the court. A debtor often files an amendment because the trustee requires changes to the debtor's paperwork based on the testimony at the meeting of creditors.

Animals. An exemption category in many states. Some states specifically exempt pets or livestock and poultry. If your state simply allows you to exempt "animals," you may include livestock, poultry, or pets. Some states exempt only domestic animals, which are usually considered to be all animals except pets.

Annuity. A type of insurance policy that pays out during the life of the insured, unlike life insurance, which pays out at the insured's death. The insured receives monthly payments once the age specified in the policy is reached, until death.

Appliance. A household apparatus or machine, usually operated by electricity, gas, or propane. Examples include refrigerators, stoves, washing machines, dishwashers, vacuum cleaners, air conditioners, and toasters.

Arms and accoutrements. Arms are weapons (such as pistols, rifles, and swords); accoutrements are the furnishings of a soldier's outfit, such as a belt or pack, but not clothes or weapons.

Arms-length creditor. A creditor with whom the debtor deals in the normal course of business, as opposed to an insider (a friend, relative, or business partner).

Articles of adornment. See "jewelry."

Assessment benefits. See "stipulated insurance."

Assisted person. Any person contemplating or filing for bankruptcy who receives bankruptcy assistance, whose debts are primarily consumer debts, and whose nonexempt property is valued at less than $192,450 (amount subject to adjustment April 1, 2022). A person or an entity that offers help to an assisted person is called a "debt relief agency."

Automatic stay. An injunction automatically issued by the bankruptcy court when a debtor files for bankruptcy. The automatic stay prohibits most creditor collection activities, such as filing or continuing lawsuits, making written requests for payment, or notifying credit reporting bureaus of an unpaid debt.

Avails. Any amount available to the owner of an insurance policy other than the actual proceeds of the policy. Avails include dividend payments, interest, cash or surrender value (the money you'd get if you sold your policy back to the insurance company), and loan value (the amount of cash you can borrow against the policy).

Bankruptcy Abuse Prevention and Reform Act of 2005. The formal name of the bankruptcy law that took effect on October 17, 2005.

Bankruptcy administrator. The official responsible for supervising the administration of bankruptcy cases, estates, and trustees in Alabama and North Carolina, where there is no U.S. Trustee.

Bankruptcy Appellate Panel. A specialized court that hears appeals of bankruptcy court decisions.

Bankruptcy assistance. Goods or services provided to an "assisted person" for the purpose of providing information, advice, counsel, document preparation or filing, or attendance at a creditors' meeting; appearing in a case or proceeding on behalf of another person; or providing legal representation.

Bankruptcy Code. The federal law that governs the creation and operation of the bankruptcy courts and establishes bankruptcy procedures. (You can find the Bankruptcy Code in Title 11 of the United States Code.)

Bankruptcy estate. All of the property you own when you file for bankruptcy, except for most pensions and educational trusts. The trustee technically takes control of your bankruptcy estate for the duration of your case.

Bankruptcy lawyer. A lawyer who specializes in bankruptcy and is licensed to practice law in the federal courts.

Bankruptcy petition preparer. Any nonlawyer who helps someone with his or her bankruptcy. Bankruptcy petition preparers (BPPs) are a special type of debt relief agency, regulated by the U.S. Trustee. Because they are not lawyers, BPPs can't represent anyone in bankruptcy court or provide legal advice.

Bankruptcy Petition Preparer Fee Declaration. An official form bankruptcy petition preparers must file with the bankruptcy court to disclose their fees.

Bankruptcy Petition Preparer Notice to Debtor. A written notice that bankruptcy petition preparers must provide to debtors who use their services. The notice explains that bankruptcy petition preparers aren't attorneys and that they are permitted to perform only certain acts, such as entering information in the bankruptcy petition and schedules under the direction of their clients.

Benefit or benevolent society benefits. See "fraternal benefit society benefits."

Building materials. Items, such as lumber, brick, stone, iron, paint, and varnish, that are used to build or improve a structure.

Burial plot. A cemetery plot.

Business bankruptcy. A bankruptcy in which the debts arise primarily from the operation of a business, including bankruptcies filed by corporations, limited liability companies, and partnerships.

Certification. The act of signing a document under penalty of perjury. (The document that is signed is also called a certification.)

Chapter 7 bankruptcy. A liquidation bankruptcy, in which the trustee sells the debtor's nonexempt property and distributes the proceeds to the debtor's creditors. At the end of the case, the debtor receives a discharge of all remaining debts, except those that cannot legally be discharged.

Chapter 7 Means Test Calculation. The means test used to determine whether a Chapter 7 bankruptcy would constitute abuse.

Chapter 7 Statement of Your Current Monthly Income. The official bankruptcy form a debtor must file in a Chapter 7 filing that shows the debtor's current monthly income, calculates whether the debtor's income is higher than the state's median family income.

Chapter 9 bankruptcy. A type of bankruptcy restricted to governmental units.

Chapter 11 bankruptcy. A type of bankruptcy intended to help businesses reorganize their debt load in order to remain in business. A Chapter 11 bankruptcy is typically much more expensive than a Chapter 7 or 13 bankruptcy because all of the lawyers must be paid out of the bankruptcy estate.

Chapter 12 bankruptcy. A type of bankruptcy designed to help small farmers reorganize their debts.

Chapter 13 bankruptcy. A type of consumer bankruptcy designed to help individuals reorganize their debts and pay all or a portion of them over three to five years.

Chapter 13 Calculation of Your Disposable Income. The official bankruptcy form used to calculate the amount of the debtor's projected disposable income that will be available to pay the debtor's unsecured creditors.

Chapter 13 plan. A document filed in a Chapter 13 bankruptcy in which the debtor shows how all of his or her projected disposable income will be used over a three- to five-year period to pay all mandatory debts—for example, back child support, taxes, and mortgage arrearages—as well as some or all unsecured, nonpriority debts, such as medical and credit card bills.

Chapter 13 Statement of Your Current Monthly Income and Calculation of Commitment Period. The official bankruptcy form a debtor must file in a Chapter 13 case, setting out the debtor's current monthly income and required repayment plan length.

Claim. A creditor's assertion that the bankruptcy filer owes it a debt or obligation.

Clothing. As an exemption category, the everyday clothes you and your family need for work, school, household use, and protection from the elements. In many states, luxury items and furs are not included in the clothing exemption category.

Codebtor. A person who assumes an equal responsibility, along with the debtor, to repay a debt or loan.

Collateral. Property pledged by a borrower as security for a loan.

Common law property states. States that don't use a community property system to classify marital property.

Community property. Certain property owned by married couples in Arizona, California, Idaho, Louisiana, New Mexico, Nevada, Texas, Washington, Wisconsin, and, if both spouses agree, Alaska. Very generally, all property acquired during the marriage is considered community property, belonging equally to both spouses, except for gifts and inheritances to one spouse. Similarly, all debts incurred during the marriage are considered community debts, owed equally by both spouses, with limited exceptions.

Complaint. A formal document that initiates a lawsuit.

Complaint to determine dischargeablity. A complaint initiating an adversary action in bankruptcy court that asks the court to decide whether a particular debt should be discharged at the end of the debtor's bankruptcy case.

Condominium. A building or complex in which separate units, such as townhouses or apartments, are owned by individuals, and the common areas (lobby, hallways, stairways, and so on) are jointly owned by the unit owners.

Confirmation. The bankruptcy judge's ruling approving a Chapter 13 plan.

Confirmation hearing. A court hearing conducted by a bankruptcy judge in which the judge decides whether a debtor's proposed Chapter 13 plan appears to be feasible and meets all applicable legal requirements.

Consumer bankruptcy. A bankruptcy in which a preponderance of the debt was incurred for personal, family, or household purposes.

Consumer debt. A debt incurred by an individual for personal, family, or household purposes.

Contingent debts. Debts that may be owed if certain events happen or conditions are satisfied.

Contingent interests in the estate of a decedent. The right to inherit property if one or more conditions to the inheritance are satisfied. For example, a debtor who will inherit property only if he survives his brother has a contingent interest.

Conversion. When a debtor who has filed one type of bankruptcy switches to another type—as when a Chapter 7 debtor converts to a Chapter 13 bankruptcy, or vice versa.

Cooperative housing. A building or another residential structure that is owned by a corporation formed by the residents. In exchange for purchasing stock in the corporation, the residents have the right to live in particular units.

Cooperative insurance. Compulsory employment benefits provided by a state or federal government, such as old age, survivors, disability, and health insurance, to ensure a minimum standard of living for lower- and middle-income people. Also called social insurance.

Court clerk. The court employee who is responsible for accepting filings and other documents, and generally maintaining an accurate and efficient flow of paper and information in the court.

Cramdown. In a Chapter 13 bankruptcy, the act of reducing a secured debt to the replacement value of the collateral securing the debt.

Credit counseling. Counseling that explores the possibility of repaying debts outside of bankruptcy and educates the debtor about credit, budgeting, and financial management. Under the new bankruptcy law, a debtor must undergo credit counseling with an approved provider before filing for bankruptcy.

Credit insurance. An insurance policy that covers a borrower for an outstanding loan. If the borrower dies or becomes disabled before paying off the loan, the policy will pay off the balance due.

Creditor. A person or an institution to whom money is owed.

Creditor committee. In Chapter 11 bankruptcy, a committee that represents the unsecured debtors in reorganization proceedings.

Creditor matrix. A specially formatted list of creditors that a debtor must file with the bankruptcy petition. The matrix helps the court notify creditors of the bankruptcy filing and the date and time set for the first meeting of creditors.

Creditors' meeting. See "meeting of creditors."

Crops. Products of the soil or earth grown and raised annually and gathered in a single season. Oranges on the tree or harvested are crops; an orange tree isn't.

Current market value. What property could be sold for. This is how a debtor's property was previously valued for purposes of determining whether the property is protected by an applicable exemption. Under the new bankruptcy law, property must be valued at its "replacement cost."

Current monthly income. A bankruptcy filer's total gross income (whether taxable or not) averaged over the six-month period immediately preceding the month in which the bankruptcy is filed. The current monthly income is used to determine whether the debtor can file for Chapter 7 bankruptcy, among other things.

Debt. An obligation of any type, including a loan, credit, or promise to perform a contract or lease.

Debt relief agency. An umbrella term for any person or agency—including lawyers and bankruptcy petition preparers, but excluding banks, nonprofit and government agencies, and employees of debt relief agencies—that provides "bankruptcy assistance" to an "assisted person."

Debtor. Someone who owes money to another person or business. Also, the generic term used to refer to anyone who files for bankruptcy.

Declaration. A written statement that is made under oath but not witnessed by a notary public.

Declaration of homestead. A form filed with the county recorder's office to put on record your right to a homestead exemption. In most states, the homestead exemption is automatic—that is, you are not required to record a homestead declaration in order to claim the homestead exemption. A few states do require such a recording, however.

Disability benefits. Payments made under a disability insurance or retirement plan when the insured is unable to work because of disability, accident, or sickness.

Discharge. A court order, issued at the conclusion of a Chapter 7 or Chapter 13 bankruptcy case, which legally relieves the debtor of personal liability for debts that can be discharged in that type of bankruptcy.

Discharge exceptions. Debts that are not discharged in a bankruptcy case. The debtor continues to owe these debts even after the bankruptcy is concluded.

Discharge hearing. A hearing conducted by a bankruptcy court to explain the discharge, urge the debtor to stay out of debt, and review reaffirmation agreements to make sure they are feasible and fair.

Dischargeability action. An adversary action brought by a party who asks the court to determine whether a particular debt qualifies for discharge.

Dischargeable debt. A debt that is wiped out at the conclusion of a bankruptcy case, unless the judge decides that it should not be.

Dismissal. When the court orders a case to be closed without providing the relief available under the bankruptcy laws. For example, a Chapter 13 case might be dismissed because the debtor fails to propose a feasible plan; a Chapter 7 case might be dismissed for abuse.

Disposable income. The difference between a debtor's "current monthly income" and allowable expenses. This is the amount that the bankruptcy law deems available to pay into a Chapter 13 plan.

Domestic animals. See "animals."

Domestic support obligation. An obligation to pay alimony or child support to a spouse, child, or government entity pursuant to an order by a court or another governmental unit.

Doubling. The ability of married couples to double the amount of certain property exemptions when filing for bankruptcy together. The federal bankruptcy exemptions allow doubling. State laws vary—some permit doubling and some do not.

Education Individual Retirement Account. A type of account to which a person can contribute a certain amount of tax-deferred funds every year for the educational benefit of the debtor or certain relatives. Such an account is not part of the debtor's bankruptcy estate.

Emergency bankruptcy filing. An initial bankruptcy filing that includes only the petition and the creditor matrix, filed right away because the debtor needs the protection of the automatic stay to prevent a creditor from taking certain action, such as a foreclosure. An emergency filing case will be dismissed if the other required documents and forms are not filed in a timely manner.

Endowment insurance. An insurance policy that gives an insured who lives for a specified time (the endowment period) the right to receive the face value of the policy (the amount paid at death). If the insured dies sooner, the beneficiary named in the policy receives the proceeds.

Equity. The amount you get to keep if you sell property—typically the property's market value, less the costs of sale and the value of any liens on the property.

ERISA-qualified benefits. Pensions that meet the requirements of the Employee Retirement Income Security Act (ERISA), a federal law that sets minimum standards for such plans and requires beneficiaries to receive certain notices.

Executory contract. A contract in which one or both parties still have a duty to carry out one or more of the contract's terms.

Exempt property. Property described by state and federal laws (exemptions) that a debtor is entitled to keep in a Chapter 7 bankruptcy. Exempt property cannot be taken and sold by the trustee for the benefit of the debtor's unsecured creditors.

Exemptions. State and federal laws specifying the types of property creditors are not entitled to take to satisfy a debt, and the bankruptcy trustee is not entitled to take

and sell for the benefit of the debtor's unsecured creditors.

Farm tools. Tools used by a person whose primary occupation is farming. Some states limit farm tools of the trade to handheld items, such as hoes, axes, pitchforks, shovels, scythes, and the like. In other states, farm tools also include plows, harnesses, mowers, reapers, and so on.

Federal exemptions. A list of exemptions contained in the federal Bankruptcy Code. Some states give debtors the option of using the federal exemptions rather than the state exemptions.

Federal Rules of Bankruptcy Procedure. A set of rules issued by the Administrative Office of the United States Courts, which govern bankruptcy court procedures.

Filing date. The date a bankruptcy petition in a particular case is filed. With few exceptions, debts incurred after the filing date are not discharged. Similarly, property owned before the filing date is part of the bankruptcy estate, while property acquired after the filing date is not.

Fines, penalties, and restitution. Debts owed to a court or a victim as a result of a sentence in a criminal matter. These debts are generally not dischargeable in bankruptcy.

Foreclosure. The process by which a creditor with a lien on real estate forces a sale of the property to collect on the lien. Foreclosure typically occurs when a homeowner defaults on a mortgage.

Fraternal benefit society benefits. Benefits, often group life insurance, paid for by fraternal societies, such as the Elks, Masons, Knights of Columbus, or the Knights of Maccabees, for their members. Also called benefit society, benevolent society, or mutual aid association benefits.

Fraud. Generally, an act that is intended to mislead another for financial gain. In a bankruptcy case, fraud is any writing or representation intended to mislead creditors to obtain a loan or credit, or any act intended to mislead the bankruptcy court or the trustee.

Fraudulent transfer. In a bankruptcy case, a transfer of property to another for less than the property's value regardless of intent. Fraudulently transferred property can be recovered and sold by the trustee for the benefit of the creditors to recover the difference between the real value of the property and the amount received by the debtor.

Fraudulently concealed assets. Property that a bankruptcy debtor deliberately fails to disclose as required by the bankruptcy rules.

Furnishings. An exemption category recognized in many states, which includes furniture, fixtures in your home (such as a heating unit, furnace, or built-in lighting), and other items with which a home is furnished, such as carpets and drapes.

Good faith. In a Chapter 13 case, when a debtor files for bankruptcy with the sincere purpose of paying off debts over the period required by law rather than for manipulative purposes—such as to prevent foreclosure that by all rights should be allowed to proceed.

Goods and chattels. See "personal property."

Group life or group health insurance. A single insurance policy covering individuals in a group (for example, employees) and their dependents.

Head of household. A person who supports and maintains, in one household, one or more people who are closely related to the person by blood, marriage, or adoption. Also referred to as "head of family."

Health aids. Items needed to maintain their owner's health, such as a wheelchair, crutches, prosthesis, or a hearing aid. Many states require that health aids be prescribed by a physician.

Health benefits. Benefits paid under health insurance plans, such as Blue Cross/Blue Shield, to cover the costs of health care.

Heirloom. An item with special monetary or sentimental value, which is passed down from generation to generation.

Home equity loan. A loan made to a homeowner based on the equity in the home —and secured by the home in the same manner as a mortgage.

Homestead. A state or federal exemption applicable to property where the debtor lives when filing for bankruptcy— the homestead exemption sometimes includes boats and mobile homes.

Homestead declaration. See "declaration of homestead."

Household good. As an exemption category, an item of permanent nature (as opposed to items consumed, like food or cosmetics) used in or about the house. This includes linens, dinnerware, utensils, pots and pans, and small electronic equipment like radios. Many state laws specifically list the types of household goods that fall within this exemption, as do the federal bankruptcy laws.

Householder. A person who supports and maintains a household, with or without other people. Also called a "housekeeper."

Impairs an exemption. When a lien, in combination with any other liens on the property and the amount the debtor is entitled to claim as exempt, exceeds the value of the property the debtor could claim in the absence of any liens. For example, if property is worth $15,000, there are $5,000 worth of liens on the property, and the debtor is entitled to a $5,000 exemption in the property, a lien that exceeded $5,000 would impair the debtor's exemption. Certain types of liens that impair an exemption may be removed (avoided) by the debtor if the court so orders.

Implement. As an exemption category, an instrument, tool, or utensil used by a person to accomplish his or her job.

In lieu of homestead (or burial) exemption. Designates an exemption that is available only if you don't claim the homestead (or burial) exemption.

Injunction. A court order prohibiting a person or an entity from taking specified actions—for example, the automatic stay that prevents most creditors from trying to collect their debts is a type of injunction.

Insider creditor. A creditor with whom the debtor has a personal relationship, such as a relative, friend, or business partner.

Intangible property. Property that cannot be physically touched, such as an ownership share in a corporation or a copyright. Documents—such as a stock certificate—may provide evidence of intangible property.

Involuntary dismissal. When a bankruptcy judge dismisses a case because the debtor fails to carry out his or her duties—such as filing papers in a timely manner and cooperating with the trustee—or because the debtor files the bankruptcy in bad faith or engages in abuse by wrongfully filing for Chapter 7 instead of Chapter 13.

Involuntary lien. A lien placed on the debtor's property without the debtor's consent—for instance, when the IRS places a lien on property for back taxes.

IRS expenses. A table of national and regional expense estimates published by the IRS. Debtors whose "current monthly income" is more than their state's "median family income" must use the IRS expenses to calculate their average net income in a Chapter 7 case, or their disposable income in a Chapter 13 case.

Jewelry. Items created for personal adornment; usually includes watches. Also called "articles of adornment."

Joint debtors. Married people who file for bankruptcy together and pay a single filing fee.

Judgment proof. A description of a person whose income and property are such that a creditor can't (or won't) seize them to enforce a money judgment—for example, a dwelling protected by a homestead exemption or a bank account containing only a few dollars.

Judicial lien. A lien created by the recording of a court money judgment against the debtor's property—usually real estate.

Lease. A contract that governs the relationship between an owner of property and a person who wishes to use the property for a specific period— as in car and real estate leases.

Lien. A legal claim against property that must be paid before title to the property can be transferred. Liens can also often be collected through repossession (personal property) or foreclosure (real estate), depending on the type of lien.

Lien avoidance. A bankruptcy procedure in which certain types of liens can be removed from certain types of property. Liens that are not avoided survive the bankruptcy even though the underlying debt may be canceled—for instance, a lien remains on a car even if the debt evidenced by the car note is discharged in the bankruptcy.

Life estate. The right to live in, but not own, a specific home until your death.

Life insurance. A policy that provides for the payment of money to an individual (called the beneficiary) in the event of the death of another (called the insured). The policy matures (becomes payable) only when the insured dies.

Lifting the stay. When a bankruptcy court allows a creditor to continue with debt collection or other activities that are otherwise banned by the automatic stay. For instance, the court might allow a landlord to proceed with an eviction or a lender to repossess a car because the debtor has defaulted on the note.

Liquid assets. Cash or items that are easily convertible into cash, such as a money market account, stock, U.S. Treasury bill, or bank deposit.

Liquidated debt. An existing debt for a specified amount arising out of a contract or court judgment. In contrast, an unliquidated debt is a claim for an as-yet uncertain amount, such as for injuries suffered in a car accident before the case goes to court.

Lost future earnings. The portion of a lawsuit judgment intended to compensate an injured person for the money he or she won't be able to earn in the future because of the injury. Also called lost earnings payments or recoveries.

Luxuries. In bankruptcy, goods or services purchased by the debtor that a court decides were not appropriate in light of the debtor's insolvency. This might include vacations, jewelry, costly cars, or frequent meals at expensive restaurants.

Mailing matrix. See "creditor matrix."

Marital debts. Debts owed jointly by a married couple.

Marital property. Property owned jointly by a married couple.

Marital settlement agreement. An agreement between a divorcing couple that sets out who gets what percentage (or what specific items) of the marital property, who pays what marital debts, and who gets custody and pays child support if there are children of the marriage.

Materialmen's and mechanics' liens. Liens imposed by statute on real estate when suppliers of materials, labor, and contracting services used to improve the real estate are not properly compensated.

Matured life insurance benefits. Insurance benefits currently payable because the insured person has died.

Means test. A formula that uses predefined income and expense categories to determine whether a debtor whose income is more than the median family income for his or her state should be allowed to file a Chapter 7 bankruptcy.

Median family income. An annual income figure for which there are as many families with incomes below that level as there are above that level. The U.S. Census Bureau publishes median family income figures for each state and for different family sizes. In bankruptcy, the median family income is used as a basis for determining whether a debtor must pass the means test to file Chapter 7 bankruptcy, and whether a debtor filing a Chapter 13 bankruptcy must commit all his or her projected disposable income to a five-year repayment plan.

Meeting of creditors. A meeting that the debtor is required to attend in a bankruptcy case, at which the trustee and creditors may ask the debtor questions about his or her property, information in the documents and forms filed, and his or her debts.

Mortgage. A contract in which a loan is made with real estate as collateral. If the borrower defaults on loan payments, the lender can foreclose on the property.

Motion. A formal legal procedure in which the bankruptcy judge is asked to rule on a dispute in the bankruptcy case. To bring a motion, a party must file a document explaining what relief is requested, the facts of the dispute, and the legal reasons why the court should grant the relief. The party bringing the motion must mail these documents to all affected parties and let them know when the court will hear argument on the motion.

Motion to avoid judicial lien on real estate. A motion brought by a bankruptcy debtor that asks the bankruptcy court to remove a judicial lien on real estate because the lien impairs the debtor's homestead exemption.

Motion to lift stay. A motion in which a creditor asks the court for permission to continue a court action or collection activities in spite of the automatic stay.

Motor vehicle. A self-propelled vehicle suitable for use on a street or road. This includes a car, truck, motorcycle, van, and moped. See also "tools of the trade."

Musical instrument. An instrument having the capacity, when properly operated, to produce a musical sound. Pianos, guitars, drums, drum machines, synthesizers, and harmonicas are all musical instruments.

Mutual aid association benefits. See "fraternal benefit society benefits."

Mutual assessment or mutual life. See "stipulated insurance."

Necessities. Articles needed to sustain life, such as food, clothing, medical care, and shelter.

Newly discovered creditors. Creditors who the debtor discovers after the bankruptcy is filed. If the case is still open, the debtor can amend the list to include the creditors; if the case is closed, it usually can be reopened to accommodate the amendment.

Nonbankruptcy federal exemptions. Federal laws that allow a debtor who has not filed for bankruptcy to keep creditors away from certain property. The debtor can also use these exemptions in bankruptcy if the debtor is using a state exemption system.

Nondischargeable debt. Debt that survives bankruptcy, such as back child support and most student loans.

Nonexempt property. Property in the bankruptcy estate that is unprotected by the exemption system available to the debtor (this is typically—but not always—the exemption system in the state where the debtor files bankruptcy). In a Chapter 7 bankruptcy, the trustee may sell it for the benefit of the debtor's unsecured creditors. In a Chapter 13 bankruptcy, debtors must propose a plan that pays their unsecured creditors at least the value of their unsecured property.

Nonpossessory, nonpurchase money lien. A lien placed on property that is already owned by the debtor and is used as collateral for the loan without being possessed by the lender. In contrast, a nonpurchase money, possessory lien exists on collateral that is held by a pawnshop.

Nonpriority debt. A type of debt that is not entitled to be paid first in bankruptcy, as priority debts are. Nonpriority debts do not have to be paid in full in a Chapter 13 case.

Nonpriority, unsecured claim. A claim that is not for a priority debt (such as child support) and is not secured by collateral or other property. Typical examples include credit card debt, medical bills, and student loans. In a Chapter 13 repayment plan, nonpriority, unsecured claims are paid only after all other debts are paid.

Notice of appeal. A form that must be filed with a court when a party wishes to appeal a judgment or an order issued by the court. Often, the notice of appeal must be filed within ten days of the date the order or judgment is entered in the court's records.

Objection. A document one party files to oppose a proposed action by another party—for instance, when a creditor or trustee files an objection to a bankruptcy debtor's claim of exemption.

Order for relief. The court's automatic injunction against certain collection and other activities that might negatively affect the bankruptcy estate. Another name for the "automatic stay."

Oversecured debt. A debt secured by collateral that is more valuable than the balance owed.

PACER. An online, fee-based database containing bankruptcy court dockets (records of proceedings in bankruptcy cases) and federal court documents, such as court rules and recent appellate court decisions.

Pain and suffering damages. The portion of a court judgment intended to compensate for past, present, and future mental and physical pain, suffering, impairment of ability to work, and mental distress caused by an injury.

Partially secured debt. A debt secured by collateral that is worth less than the debt itself—for instance, when a person owes $15,000 on a car that is worth only $10,000.

Party in interest. Any person or entity that has a financial interest in the outcome of a bankruptcy case, including the trustee, the debtor, and all creditors.

Pension. A fund into which payments are made to provide an employee income after retirement. Typically, the beneficiary can't access the account without incurring a significant penalty, usually a tax. There are many types of pensions, including defined benefit pensions provided by many large corporations and individual pensions (such as 401(k)s and IRAs). In bankruptcy, most pensions are not considered part of a bankruptcy estate and are therefore not affected by a bankruptcy filing.

Personal financial responsibility counseling. Under the new bankruptcy law, a two-hour class intended to teach good budget management. Every consumer bankruptcy filer must attend such a class in order to obtain a discharge in Chapter 7, Chapter 12, or Chapter 13 bankruptcy.

Personal injury cause of action. The right to seek compensation for physical and mental suffering, including injury to body, reputation, or both. For example, someone who is hit and injured by a car might have a personal injury cause of action against the driver.

Personal injury recovery. The portion of a lawsuit judgment or insurance settlement that is intended to compensate someone for physical and mental suffering, including physical injury, injury to reputation, or both. Bankruptcy exemptions usually do not apply to compensation for pain or suffering or punitive damages—in other words, that part of the recovery can be taken by the trustee in a Chapter 7 case.

Personal property. All property not classified as real property, including tangible items such as cars and jewelry, and intangible property such as stocks, pensions, royalties, and residuals.

Petition. The document a debtor files to officially begin a bankruptcy case and ask for relief. Other documents and schedules must be filed to support the petition at the time it is filed, or shortly afterward.

Pets. See "animals."

Preference. A payment made by a debtor to a creditor within a defined period prior to filing for bankruptcy—within three months for arms-length creditors (regular commercial creditors) and one year for insider creditors (close family and business associates). Because a preference gives that debtor an edge over other debtors in the bankruptcy case, the trustee can recover the preference and distribute it among all of the creditors.

Prepetition. Any time prior to the moment the bankruptcy petition is filed.

Prepetition counseling. Debt or credit counseling that occurs before the bankruptcy petition is filed—as opposed to personal financial management counseling, which occurs after the petition is filed.

Presumed abuse. In a Chapter 7 bankruptcy, when the debtor has a current monthly income in excess of the family median income for the state where the debtor lives, and has sufficient income to propose a Chapter 13 plan under the "means test." If abuse is presumed, the debtor has to prove that his or her Chapter 7 filing is not abusive in order to proceed further.

Primarily business debts. When the majority of debt owed by a bankruptcy debtor—in dollar terms—arises from debts incurred to operate a business.

Primarily consumer debts. When the majority of debt owed by a bankruptcy debtor—in dollar terms—arises from debts incurred for personal or family purposes.

Priority claim. See "priority debt."

Priority creditor. A creditor who has filed a Proof of Claim showing that the debtor owes it a priority debt.

Priority debt. A type of debt that is paid first if there are distributions to be made from the bankruptcy estate. Priority debts include alimony and child support, fees owed to the trustee and attorneys in the case, and wages owed to employees. With one exception (back child support obligations assigned to government entities), priority claims must be paid in full in a Chapter 13 bankruptcy.

Proceeds for damaged exempt property. Money received through insurance coverage, arbitration, mediation, settlement, or a lawsuit to pay for exempt property that has been damaged or destroyed. For example, if a debtor had the right to use a $30,000 homestead exemption, but his or her home was destroyed by fire, the debtor can instead exempt $30,000 of the insurance proceeds.

Projected disposable income. The amount of income remaining each month after deducting allowable expenses, payments on mandatory debts, and administrative expenses from his or her current monthly income. This is the amount the debtor must pay toward his or her unsecured nonpriority debts in a Chapter 13 plan.

Proof of Claim. A formal document filed by bankruptcy creditors in a bankruptcy case to assert their right to payments from the bankruptcy estate, if any payments are made.

Proof of service. A document signed under penalty of perjury by the person serving a document showing how the service was made, who made it, and when.

Property of the estate. See "bankruptcy estate."

Purchase money loans. Loans that are made to purchase specific property items, and that use the property as collateral to assure repayment, such as car loans and mortgages.

Purchase money security interest. A claim on property owned by the holder of a loan that was used to purchase the property and that is secured by the property (as collateral).

Reaffirmation. An agreement entered into after a bankruptcy filing (postpetition) between the debtor and a creditor in which the debtor agrees to repay all or part of a prepetition debt after the bankruptcy is over. For instance, a debtor makes an agreement with the holder of a car note that the debtor can keep the car and must continue to pay the debt after bankruptcy. A reaffirmation agreement restores the original contract to what it was prior to the bankruptcy case.

Real property. Real estate (land and buildings on the land, usually including mobile homes attached to a foundation).

Reasonable investigation. A bankruptcy attorney's obligation to look into the information provided to him or her by a client.

Redemption. In a Chapter 7 bankruptcy, when the debtor obtains legal title to collateral for a secured debt by paying the secured creditor the replacement value of the collateral in a lump sum. For example, a debtor may redeem a car note by paying the lender the replacement value of the car (what a retail vendor would charge for the car, considering its age and condition).

Reopen a case. To open a closed bankruptcy case—usually for the purpose of adding an overlooked creditor or filing a motion to avoid an overlooked lien. A debtor must request that the court reopen the case.

Repayment plan. An informal plan to repay creditors most or all of what they are owed outside of bankruptcy. Also refers to the plan proposed by a debtor in a Chapter 13 case.

Replacement cost. What it would cost to replace a particular item by buying it from a retail vendor, considering its age and condition—for instance, when buying a car from a used car dealer, furniture from a used furniture shop, or electronic equipment on eBay.

Repossession. When a secured creditor takes property used as collateral because the debtor has defaulted on the loan secured by the collateral.

Request to lift the stay. A written request filed in bankruptcy court by a creditor, which seeks permission to engage in debt collection activity otherwise prohibited by the automatic stay.

Schedule A/B. The official bankruptcy form a debtor must file to describe all of his or her property, including real estate and personal property owned by the debtor, such as jewelry and vehicles, and tangible property, such as investments and accounts receivable.

Schedule C. The official bankruptcy form a debtor must file to describe the property the debtor is claiming as exempt, and the legal basis for the claims of exemption.

Schedule D. The official bankruptcy form a debtor must file to describe all secured debts owed by the debtor, such as car notes and mortgages.

Schedule E/F. The official bankruptcy form a debtor must file to describe all unsecured debts, including priority debts, such as back child support and taxes, and nonpriority debts, such as most credit card balances, medical bills, and student loans.

Schedule G. The official bankruptcy form a debtor must file to describe any leases and executory contracts (contracts under which one or both parties still have obligations) to which the debtor is a party.

Schedule H. The official bankruptcy form a debtor must file to describe all codebtors that might be affected by the bankruptcy.

Schedule I. The official bankruptcy form a debtor must file to describe the debtor's income.

Schedule J. The official bankruptcy form a debtor must file to describe the debtor's actual monthly expenses.

Schedules. Official bankruptcy forms a debtor must file, detailing the debtor's property, debts, income, and expenses.

Second deed of trust. A loan against real estate made after the original mortgage (or first deed of trust). Most home equity loans are second deeds of trust.

Secured claim. A debt secured by collateral under a written agreement (for instance, a mortgage or car note) or by operation of law—such as a tax lien.

Secured creditor. The owner of a secured claim.

Secured debt. A debt secured by collateral.

Secured interest. A claim to property used as collateral. For instance, a lender on a car note retains legal title to the car until the loan is paid off.

Secured property. Property that is collateral for a secured debt.

Serial bankruptcy filing. A practice used by some debtors to file and dismiss one bankruptcy after another to obtain the protection of the automatic stay, even though the bankruptcies themselves offer no debt relief—for instance, when a debtor files successive Chapter 13 cases to prevent foreclosure of his or her home even though there are no debts to repay.

Sickness benefits. See "disability benefits."

State exemptions. State laws that specify the types of property creditors are not entitled to take to satisfy a debt, and the bankruptcy trustee is not entitled to take and sell for the benefit of the debtor's unsecured creditors.

Statement About Your Social Security Numbers. The official bankruptcy form a debtor must file to disclose the debtor's complete Social Security number.

Statement of Financial Affairs for Individuals Filing for Bankruptcy. The official bankruptcy form a debtor must file to describe the debtor's legal, economic, and business transactions for the several years prior to filing, including gifts, preferences, income, closing of deposit accounts, lawsuits, and other information that the trustee needs to assess the legitimacy of the bankruptcy and the true extent of the bankruptcy estate.

Statement of Intention for Individuals Filing Under Chapter 7. The official bankruptcy form a debtor must file in a Chapter 7 case to tell the court and secured creditors how the debtor plans to treat his or her secured debts—that is, reaffirm the debt, redeem the debt, or surrender the property and discharge the debt.

Statutory lien. A lien imposed on property by law, such as tax liens and mechanics' liens, as opposed to voluntary liens (such as mortgages) and liens arising from court judgments (judicial liens).

Stay. See "automatic stay."

Stipulated insurance. An insurance policy that allows the insurance company to assess an amount on the insured, above the standard premium payments, if the company experiences losses worse than had been calculated into the standard premium. Also called assessment, mutual assessment, or mutual life insurance.

Stock options. A contract between a corporation and an employee that gives the employee the right to purchase corporate stock at a specific price mentioned in the contract (the strike price).

Stripdown of lien. In Chapter 13 bankruptcy, when the amount of a lien on collateral is reduced to the collateral's replacement value. See "cramdown."

Student loan. A type of loan made for educational purposes by nonprofit or commercial lenders with repayment and interest terms dictated by federal law. Student loans are not dischargeable in bankruptcy unless the debtor can show that repaying the loan would impose an "undue hardship."

Substantial abuse. Under the old bankruptcy law, filing a Chapter 7 bankruptcy when a Chapter 13 bankruptcy was feasible.

Suits, executions, garnishments, and attachments. Activities engaged in by creditors to enforce money judgments, typically involving the seizure of wages and bank accounts.

Summary of Your Assets and Liabilities and Certain Statistical Information. The official bankruptcy form a debtor must file to summarize the property and debt information contained in a debtor's schedules.

Surrender value. See "avails."

Surrendering collateral. In Chapter 7 bankruptcy, the act of returning collateral to a secured lender in order to discharge the underlying debt—for example, returning a car to discharge the car note.

Tangible personal property. See "tangible property" and "personal property."

Tangible property. Property that can be physically touched. Examples include money, furniture, cars, jewelry, artwork, and houses. Compare "intangible property."

Tax lien. A statutory lien imposed on property to secure payment of back taxes —typically income and property taxes.

Tenancy by the entirety. A way that married couples can hold title to property in about half of the states. When one spouse dies, the surviving spouse automatically owns 100% of the property. In most cases, this type of property is not part of the bankruptcy estate if only one spouse files.

To ___ acres. A limitation on the size of a homestead that may be exempted.

Tools of the trade. Items needed to perform a line of work that you are currently doing and relying on for support. For a mechanic, plumber, or carpenter, for example, tools of trade are the implements used to repair, build, and install. Traditionally, tools of the trade were limited to handheld items. Most states, however, now embrace a broader definition, and a debtor may be able to fit many items under a tool of trade exemption.

Transcript of tax return. A summary of a debtor's tax return provided by the IRS upon the debtor's request, usually acceptable as a substitute for the return in the instances when a return must be filed under the new bankruptcy law.

Trustee. An official appointed by the bankruptcy court to carry out the administrative tasks associated with bankruptcy, such as selling nonexempt property in Chapter 7 or dispersing plan payments in Chapter 13.

U.S. Trustee. An official employed by the Office of the U.S. Trustee (a division of the U.S. Department of Justice) who is responsible for overseeing bankruptcy trustees, regulating credit and personal financial management counselors, regulating bankruptcy petition preparers, auditing bankruptcy cases, ferreting out fraud, and generally making sure that the bankruptcy laws are obeyed.

Undersecured debt. A debt secured by collateral that is worth less than the debt.

Undue hardship. The conditions under which a debtor may discharge a student loan—for example, when the debtor has no income and little chance of earning enough to repay the loan in the future.

Unexpired lease. A lease that is still in effect as of the filing of the bankruptcy.

Unmatured life insurance. A policy that is not yet payable because the insured is still alive.

Unscheduled debt. A debt that is not included in the schedules accompanying a bankruptcy filing, perhaps because it was overlooked or intentionally left out.

Unsecured priority claims. Priority claims that aren't secured by collateral, such as back child support or taxes for which no lien has been placed on the debtor's property.

Valuation of property. The act of determining the replacement value of property for the purpose of describing it in the bankruptcy schedules, determining whether it is protected by an applicable exemption, redeeming secured property, or cramming down a lien in Chapter 13 bankruptcy.

Voluntary dismissal. When a Chapter 13 debtor dismisses a case without court involvement; by contrast, a Chapter 7 filer cannot voluntarily dismiss a case and must receive court approval.

Voluntary lien. A lien agreed to by the debtor, as when the debtor signs a mortgage, car note, or second deed of trust.

Weekly net earnings. The earnings a debtor has left after mandatory deductions, such as income tax, mandatory union dues, and Social Security contributions, have been subtracted from his or her gross income.

Wildcard exemption. A dollar value that the debtor can apply to any type of property to make it—or more of it—exempt. In some states, filers may use the unused portion of a homestead exemption as a wildcard exemption.

Willful and malicious act. An act done with the intent to cause harm. In a Chapter 7 bankruptcy, a debt arising from the debtor's willful and malicious act is not discharged if the victim proves to the bankruptcy court's satisfaction that the act occurred.

Willful or malicious act resulting in a civil judgment. A bad act that was careless or reckless, but was not necessarily intended to cause harm. In a Chapter 13 case, a debt arising from the debtor's act that was either willful or malicious is not discharged if it is part of a civil judgment.

Wrongful death cause of action. The right to seek compensation for having to live without a deceased person. Usually only the spouse and children of the deceased have a wrongful death cause of action.

Wrongful death recoveries. The portion of a lawsuit judgment intended to compensate a plaintiff for having to live without a deceased person. The compensation is intended to cover the earnings and the emotional comfort and support the deceased would have provided. ●

How to Use the Downloadable Forms on the Nolo Website

This book comes with downloadable files that you can access online at: **www.nolo.com/back-of-book/FIBA.html** To use the files, your computer must have specific software programs installed. The files provided by this book are in PDF form. You can view these files with Adobe Reader, free software from www.adobe.com.Government PDFs are sometimes fillable using your computer, but most PDFs are designed to be printed out and completed by hand.

CAUTION

In accordance with U.S. copyright laws, the forms provided by this book are for your personal use only.

List of Forms Available on the Nolo Website

To download any of the files listed on the following pages go to:

www.nolo.com/back-of-book/FIBA.html

Form Title	File Name
Worksheet A: Current Monthly and Yearly Income	WorksheetA.pdf
Worksheet B: Allowable Monthly Expenses	WorksheetB.pdf
Worksheet C: Monthly Disposable Income	WorksheetC.pdf
Worksheet D: The Means Test	WorksheetD.pdf
Worksheet E: Personal Property Checklist	WorksheetE.pdf
Worksheet F: Property Value Schedule	WorksheetF.pdf
State and Federal Exemption Charts	StateFederalExemption.pdf
Median Family Income Chart	MedianFamilyIncome.pdf
Form 101—Voluntary Petition for Individuals Filing for Bankruptcy	Form101.pdf
Form 106A/B—Schedule A/B: Property	Form106AB.pdf
Form 106C—Schedule C: The Property You Claim as Exempt	Form106C.pdf
Form 106D—Schedule D: Creditors Who Have Claims Secured By Property	Form106D.pdf
Form 106E/F—Schedule E/F: Creditors Who Have Unsecured Claims	Form106EF.pdf

Form Title	File Name
Form 106G—Schedule G: Executory Contracts and Unexpired Leases	Form106G.pdf
Form 106H—Schedule H: Your Codebtors	Form106H.pdf
Form 106I—Schedule I: Your Income	Form106I.pdf
Form 106J—Schedule J: Your Expenses	Form106J.pdf
Form 106Dec—Declaration About an Individual Debtor's Schedules	Form106Dec.pdf
Form 106Sum—Summary of Your Assets and Liabilities and Certain Statistical Information	Form106Sum.pdf
Form 107—Statement of Financial Affairs for Individuals Filing for Bankruptcy	Form107.pdf
Form 108—Statement of Intention for Individuals Filing Under Chapter 7	Form108.pdf
Creditor Matrix Cover Sheet	CreditorMatrixCover.pdf
Creditor Mailing Matrix	CreditorMailingMatrix.pdf
Verification of Master Address List	VerificationAddressList.pdf
Form 119—Bankruptcy Petition Preparer's Notice, Declaration, and Signature	Form119.pdf
Form 121—Statement About Your Social Security Numbers	Form121.pdf
Form 122A-1—Chapter 7 Statement of Your Current Monthly Income	Form122A1.pdf
Form 122A-1 Supp—Statement of Exemption from Presumption of Abuse Under § 707(b)(2)	Form122A1Sup.pdf
Form 122A-2—Chapter 7 Means Test Calculation	Form122A2.pdf
Form 423—Certification About a Financial Management Course	Form423.pdf
Form 427—Cover Sheet for Reaffirmation Agreement	Form427.pdf
Form 2010—Notice Required by 11 U.S.C. § 342(b) for Individuals Filing for Bankruptcy	Form2010.pdf
Form 2030—Disclosure of Compensation of Attorney For Debtor	Form2030.pdf
Form 2400A—Reaffirmation Documents	Form2400A.pdf
Form 2400B—Motion For Approval of Reaffirmation Agreement	Form2400B.pdf
Form 2400C—Order on Reaffirmation Agreement	Form2400C.pdf

Index